THE JOHN D. AND CATHERINE T. MACARTHUR FOUNDATION SERIES ON DIGITAL MEDIA AND LEARNING

Engineering Play: A Cultural History of Children's Software, by Mizuko Ito

Hanging Out, Messing Around, and Geeking Out: Kids Living and Learning with New Media, by Mizuko Ito, Sonja Baumer, Matteo Bittanti, danah boyd, Rachel Cody, Becky Herr-Stephenson, Heather A. Horst, Patricia G. Lange, Dilan Mahendran, Katynka Martínez, C. J. Pascoe, Dan Perkel, Laura Robinson, Christo Sims, Lisa Tripp, with contributions by Judd Antin, Megan Finn, Arthur Law, Annie Manion, Sarai Mitnick, David Schlossberg, and Sarita Yardi

The Civic Web: Young People, the Internet, and Civic Participation, by Shakuntala Banaji and David Buckingham

Connected Play: Tweens in a Virtual World, by Yasmin B. Kafai and Deborah A. Fields

The Digital Youth Network: Cultivating New Media Citizenship in Urban Communities, edited by Brigid Barron, Kimberley Gomez, Nichole Pinkard, and Caitlin K. Martin

Connected Code: Children as the Programmers, Designers, and Makers for the 21st Century, by Yasmin B. Kafai and Quinn Burke

The Interconnections Collection: Understanding Systems through Digital Design, developed by Kylie Peppler, Melissa Gresalfi, Katie Salen Tekinbaş, and Rafi Santo

   Gaming the System: Designing with Gamestar Mechanic, by Katie Salen Tekinbaş, Melissa Gresalfi, Kylie Peppler, and Rafi Santo

   Script Changers: Digital Storytelling with Scratch, by Kylie Peppler, Rafi Santo, Melissa Gresalfi, and Katie Salen Tekinbaş

   Short Circuits: Crafting E-Puppets with DIY Electronics, by Kylie Peppler, Katie Salen Tekinbaş, Melissa Gresalfi, and Rafi Santo

   Soft Circuits: Crafting E-Fashion with DIY Electronics, by Kylie Peppler, Melissa Gresalfi, Katie Salen Tekinbaş, and Rafi Santo

Inaugural Series Volumes

Six edited volumes were created through an interactive community review process and published online and in print in December 2007. They are the precursors to the peer-reviewed monographs in the series. For more information on these volumes, visit http://mitpress.mit.edu/books/series/john-d-and-catherine-t-macarthur-foundation-series-digital-media-and-learning.

Script Changers
Digital Storytelling with Scratch

by Kylie Peppler, Rafi Santo, Melissa Gresalfi,
and Katie Salen Tekinbaş

The MIT Press
Cambridge, Massachusetts
London, England

MIT Press books may be purchased at special quantity discounts for business or sales promotional use. For information, please email special_sales@mitpress.mit.edu.

This book was set in Melior LT Std 9.5/13 by Toppan Best-set Premedia Limited, Hong Kong. Printed and bound in the United States of America.

Library of Congress Cataloging-in-Publication Data

Peppler, Kylie A.
Script changers : digital storytelling with Scratch / Kylie Peppler,
Rafi Santo, Melissa Gresalfi, and Katie Salen Tekinbaş.
    pages cm — (The John D. and Catherine T. Macarthur Foundation series on digital media and learning)
Includes bibliographical references and index.
ISBN 978-0-262-02782-3 (hardcover : alk. paper)   1. Interactive
multimedia.   2. Digital storytelling.   3. Education—Data processing.   4. Scratch
(Electronic resource)   I. Santo, Rafi, 1982–   II. Gresalfi, Melissa,
1977–   III. Tekinbaş, Katie Salen.   IV. Scratch (Electronic resource)   V. Title.
QA76.76.I59P46 2014
371.33'4—dc23
                                2014003792

10   9   8   7   6   5   4   3   2   1

CONTENTS

SERIES FOREWORD

In recent years, digital media and networks have become embedded in our everyday lives and are part of broad-based changes to how we engage in knowledge production, communication, and creative expression. Unlike the early years in the development of computers and computer-based media, digital media are now *commonplace* and *pervasive*, having been taken up by a wide range of individuals and institutions in all walks of life. Digital media have escaped the boundaries of professional and formal practice, and of the academic, governmental, and industry homes that initially fostered their development. Now they have been taken up by diverse populations and noninstitutionalized practices, including the peer activities of youth. Although specific forms of technology uptake are highly diverse, a generation is growing up in an era when digital media are part of the taken-for-granted social and cultural fabric of learning, play, and social communication.

This book series is founded upon the working hypothesis that those immersed in new digital tools and networks are engaged in an unprecedented exploration of language, games, social interaction, problem solving, and self-directed activity that leads to diverse forms of learning. These diverse forms of learning are reflected in expressions of identity, in how individuals express independence and creativity, and in their ability to learn, exercise judgment, and think systematically.

The defining frame for this series is not a particular theoretical or disciplinary approach, nor is it a fixed set of topics. Rather, the series revolves around a constellation of topics investigated from multiple disciplinary and practical frames. The series as a whole looks at the relation between youth, learning, and digital media, but each contribution to the series might deal with only a subset of this constellation. Erecting strict topical boundaries would exclude some of the most important work in the field. For example, restricting the content of the series only to people of a certain age would mean artificially reifying an age boundary when the phenomenon demands otherwise. This would become particularly problematic with new forms of online participation where one important outcome is the mixing of participants of different ages. The same goes for digital media, which are increasingly inseparable from analog and earlier media forms.

The series responds to certain changes in our media ecology that have important implications for learning. Specifically, these changes involve new forms of media *literacy* and developments in the modes of media *participation*. Digital media are part of a convergence between interactive media (most notably gaming), online networks, and existing media forms. Navigating this media ecology involves a palette of literacies that are being defined through practice but require more scholarly scrutiny before they can be fully incorporated pervasively into educational initiatives. Media literacy involves not only ways of understanding, interpreting, and critiquing media, but also the means for creative and social expression, online search and navigation, and a host of new technical skills. The potential gap in literacies and participation skills creates new challenges for educators who struggle to bridge media engagement inside and outside the classroom.

The John D. and Catherine T. MacArthur Foundation Series on Digital Media and Learning, published by the MIT Press, aims to close these gaps and provide innovative ways of thinking about and using new forms of knowledge production, communication, and creative expression.

FOREWORD

Over forty years ago, Buckminster Fuller—architect, designer, engineer, scientist, cartographer, inventor, educator, and poet—popularized the term *synergy*. "Bucky" reminded packed audiences around the world that synergy was "… the only word in our language that means *behavior of whole systems unpredicted by the separately observed behaviors of any of the system's separate parts or any subassembly of the system's parts.* There is nothing in the chemistry of a toenail that predicts the existence of a human being" (Fuller, *Operating Manual for Spaceship Earth*, 1969, p. 78).

Looking back at myself as a student forty years ago, my curriculum was for the most part compartmentalized: science was taught in one class, math in another, English in yet another, and never the twain shall meet. Such a fragmented approach reinforced the notion that knowledge was made up of many unrelated parts, leaving me with little opportunity to see recurring patterns of behavior across subjects and disciplines, to look for synergies, or for that matter, to think or talk about "whole systems."

My teachers were preparing me for a world in which "new technologies" like the computer were just beginning to play a role, and though I didn't know it at the time, the middle-aged gentleman teaching "computer science" was desperately trying to stay one step ahead of his eager students. With the shock of the gas crisis in the 1970s came a nascent awareness of the relationship between nonrenewable resources and population growth (what we call *carrying capacity* today).

It was a world that author and *New York Times* columnist Thomas Friedman describes as being "characterized by one overarching feature—and that was *division*. That world was a divided-up, chopped-up place, and whether you were a country or a company, your threats and opportunities in the cold war system tended to grow out of who you were divided from. Appropriately, this cold war system was symbolized by a single word— *wall*, the Berlin Wall." (Friedman, *Longitudes and Attitudes: Exploring the World After September 11*, 2002, p. 3)

Today, our international system is different. We've gone from an international system built around *division and walls* to a system increasingly built around *integration and webs*, a shift Friedman aptly describes here:

> The globalization system is different. It also has one overarching feature and that is *integration*. The world has become an increasingly interwoven place, and today whether you are a company or a country, your threats and opportunities increasingly derive from who you are connected to. This globalization system is also characterized by a single word—*web*, the World Wide Web. (Friedman, *Longitudes and Attitudes*, pp. 3–4)

Today's children are growing up in a world of webs and networks, of increasing interdependence and multiculturalism, of shrinking global borders, and of even more limited natural resources. For students of today, nothing exists in isolation. More and more of the pressing challenges children see in the headlines—global warming, economic breakdowns, food insecurity, institutional malfeasance, biodiversity loss, and escalating conflict—are generated by complex human systems.

Indeed our lives are embedded in systems. However, this presents a dilemma: Many of us were not explicitly taught skills related to understanding the behaviors and dynamics of complex systems. Indeed, in my research, I've found that deep misconceptions about the dynamics of complex systems persist, even among highly educated adults. Research in dynamic decision making shows that when adults are faced with dynamically complex systems—containing multiple feedback processes, time delays, nonlinearities, and accumulations—performance is systematically biased and suboptimal.

What to do? Facing a similar question, Buckminster Fuller once said: "If you want to teach people a new way of thinking, don't bother trying to teach them. Instead, give them a tool, the use of which will lead to new ways of thinking."

Enter the *The Interconnections Collection: Understanding Systems through Digital Design*. The four modular curricula represent a new tool, and as such, they are both a revelation *and* a revolution in education and design. Rooted in a design-based research approach, the four scalable toolkits each use the power of new media and design to develop a hands-on approach to understanding complex systems, while promoting design and systems thinking dispositions in young people through widely accessible activities.

As a systems educator and children's book author, I am particularly excited about the inclusion of the *Script Changers* toolkit. Using the medium of digital storytelling, this toolkit encourages children to use everyday situations—from playground fights in grade school to "homework burnout" in high school, from virus outbreaks to the boom-and-bust markets they hear about on the news—to develop new systems-based storytelling muscles. This is an essential twenty-first-century skill particularly in the face of the predominantly linear nature of much of the information they receive both in school and through the media. Simply, *Script Changers* gives children the tools, language, and visuals to more closely mirror and represent the complex interrelationships and dynamics of their world.

> Linda Booth Sweeney, systems educator and award-winning author of *The Systems Thinking Playbook*, *Connected Wisdom*, and *When a Butterfly Sneezes: A Guide for Helping Kids Explore Interconnections in Our World Through Favorite Stories*

ACKNOWLEDGMENTS AND PROJECT HISTORY

ACKNOWLEDGMENTS

This book collection would not have been possible without the involvement of so many people, who were as inspired as we were by the idea of having youths develop powerful new ways for seeing and acting in the world. It's the result of years of collaboration with research and design partners across the United States, cycles of testing and feedback from teachers, and helpful insights from advisors and friends. In particular, we'd like to thank the following:

- Connie Yowell (Director of Education for U.S. Programs at the John D. and Catherine T. MacArthur Foundation), for the ongoing support provided to this project through the MacArthur Foundation's Digital Media and Learning (DML) initiative. The project would have been impossible without not only the funding provided, but also the incredible networks of colleagues within the DML field that she has done so much to foster.

- This material also is based in part upon work supported by the National Science Foundation under Grant No. 0855852, awarded to Kylie A. Peppler.

- Nichole Pinkard (Associate Professor of Interactive Media, Human Computer Interaction, and Education, DePaul University), for seeing the need for the project from the beginning and catalyzing this incredible group of partners to come together to work on it.

- The hard-working team of graduate research assistants at Indiana University who have contributed to this project over the years, including Sinem Siyyahan, Diane Glosson, Charlene Volk, Mike Downton, Leon Gordon, Jackie Barnes, Sophia Bender, and Kate Shively, not to mention the broader Learning Sciences student body, who have all engaged in conversations with us around this work one way or another.

- Our colleagues and teacher leaders at the National Writing Project (NWP), who worked with us to pilot the activities in this book and helped us integrate their valuable insights into the final manuscript: Christina Cantrill, Paul Oh, Steve Moore, Lori Sue Garner, Janie Brown, Deidra Floyd, Laura Beth Fay, Carol Jehlen, Travis Powell, Laura Lee Stroud, Eric Tuck, Kevin Hodgson, Janelle Bence, Laura Fay Beth, Cliff Lee, Chad Sansing, and Trina Williams.

- The many institutions in Bloomington, Indiana, that have worked with us to pilot the activities in these books, including the Boys and Girls Club, under the leadership of Matthew Searle; and the Bloomington Project School, under the leadership of Daniel Baron.

- Our advisory board, which has provided valuable feedback both on the treatment of the ideas in these books and how they fit into the broader field: Linda Booth Sweeney, Natalie Rusk, Amon Millner, and Cindy Hmelo-Silver.

HISTORY OF THE GRINDING NEW LENSES PROJECT

One of the important lessons to be learned from working on systems thinking is that nothing is created in a vacuum; the same is true of all the work shared in this book. In this section, we briefly share the background on the Grinding New Lenses (GNL) project, which has led to this book collection and shaped its focus.

Taking a systems perspective, it's somewhat challenging to tell a linear story about what led to this work. But a good place to start might be a school called Quest to Learn (Q2L; q2l.org), which was opened by Katie Salen and Institute of Play in New York City in 2009 (www.instituteofplay.org) with support from the MacArthur Foundation's Digital Media and Learning initiative (Salen et al., 2010). The school was designed as a proof of concept to answer a unique question: How can school-based learning be designed based on powerful learning principles found in the best games—ones that inspire engagement, collaboration, critical thinking, and, of course, systems thinking?

In answering this question, Q2L did a number of things differently from traditional schools. To begin with, it reorganized the curriculum so that disciplines with natural intersections that were usually kept separate were joined together. Mathematics and

English language arts became "Codeworlds," a class that focused on symbolic and representational systems. Another class called "The Way Things Work," taught science and math combined, and still another class called "Being, Space, and Place" was put together to teach history and English literature. Assessment and testing also was done differently—instead of finals at the end of each semester, each class broke up into teams that needed to work collaboratively on a week-long "boss level," which challenged the youths to integrate insights from the rest of the course. More broadly, the school made the idea of youths as designers and makers of systems central to the overall setup of Q2L's learning environment an idea that was reflected in the after-school activities, the course design, the boss levels, and the school's integration of design thinking throughout the curriculum. All the different parts of the school aimed to have kids use what they were learning to make or design something concrete.

While the Q2L school represented great innovations in learning and was lucky to have the freedom to do a lot of things differently, it was just one school. How could what was being learned there be shared, tested, and added to by the wealth of innovative educators and schools in the world already doing great work? In many ways, the GNL project, titled from the idea that systems thinking offers a powerful new "lens" to see the world, came from a desire to do just this. In the initiative, Kylie Peppler and Melissa Gresalfi, researchers and educational designers from Indiana University's Learning Sciences program (**education.indiana.edu/learnsci**), began to work with Katie Salen from Institute of Play (**instituteofplay.org**), Nichole Pinkard from DePaul University, and the Digital Youth Network (DYN; **digitalyouthnetwork.org**) to develop a series of modular toolkits that used the design of digital media as a means to develop systems thinking skills, all based on the existing approaches taken in the Q2L school. With the financial support of the MacArthur Foundation and the help of additional partners like the NWP (**www.nwp.org**) (a network of educators and local writing project sites that serve up to 100,000 teachers annually), the initiative worked for three years to make this idea a reality.

The main goal of the initiative was twofold: to create a series of scalable modular toolkits that used the power of designing with new media to promote engagement in design and systems thinking dispositions in young people; and to conduct research on what kind of curricular supports lead to the development of systems thinking dispositions through design activities.

Ultimately, four sets of modular curricula were developed in close coordination with teachers in the NWP network at every step of the process. Each of these uses a different technology and provides unique ways to engage in design with various approaches to understanding systems. The *Gaming the System* curricula involves game design with the Gamestar Mechanic (G*M) platform (Salen, 2007) and focuses on understanding games as systems and young people as designers of those systems. A second set of curricula, *Script Changers*, focuses on the idea of using narrative and stories to understand systems, and uses the Scratch programming environment (Resnick et al., 2009) as a way to tell digital stories about systems by way of a computational system. The final two sets of curricula, *Short Circuits* and *Soft Circuits,* use physical computing technology like light-emitting diodes (LEDs), sensors, and the wearable technology controlled by the LilyPad Arduino (Buechley, 2006) to show how youths can create electronics embedded in paper, clothing, and other everyday objects and understand how these creations operate as systems.

Using an approach called Design-Based Research (DBR) (Brown, 1992), which employs approaches found in the world of engineering to engage in an iterative and cyclical design process around learning activities in which each implementation yields lessons that are incorporated into final designs, we piloted and tested the modules in many contexts. A particularly positive benefit of DBR is that it acknowledges that you're not necessarily going to get things right the first time (we certainly didn't!) but trusts a process of embracing failures and missteps as learning opportunities that are really gifts in disguise. For us, the process of being active learners about what worked and where was a central part of the work that we did in developing the activities being shared here.

Many of the activities were, as mentioned, initially developed and tested in New York City at Q2L; others were developed and piloted at local schools like the Bloomington Project School in Indiana, as well as at a local Boys and Girls Club that serves a wide range of youths from varied ethnic and socioeconomic backgrounds. A significant amount of testing was done in close coordination with our NWP partners in sites across the United States and through extended, project-specific summer workshops hosted at DePaul University in Chicago and elsewhere. Testing and refinement also was done in Chicago in schools affiliated with partners at the DYN. Additionally, DYN's parent institution, DePaul University, hosted a summer camp that served as a major testing ground for the curricula. Over the course of four weeks in the summer of 2011, expert teachers from across the United States affiliated with the NWP worked with researchers from Indiana University and designers from Institute of Play to refine the modules based on lessons born of implementing them with almost 100 youths native to Chicago, again with a mix of kids from different backgrounds. These educators are too numerous to list here, but their voices and contributions to this volume are recognized both in our list of contributors and in the "Voices from the Field" sections that you will see throughout all three of these volumes. The exercises, ideas, and guiding pedagogical ideas throughout these books are infused with their perspectives.

In developing the volumes, we wanted to ensure that the work was grounded both in insights from the academic literature on systems thinking and the learning sciences, and also in the lived experiences of educators. The research team contained a number of members who had worked as educators for many years in both formal learning contexts like public schools and informal ones like after-school programs, libraries, and museums. Most importantly, though, the initiative's partnership with the NWP meant that the kind of educators interested in the sort of innovative approaches that we were developing were kept at the center of our designs. They played important roles in testing and refining the modules as previously described, as well as serving on an editorial advisory board (including, most prominently, the assistance of Christina Cantrill, Paul Oh, and Steve Moore) that offered insights, made substantial edits, gave productive feedback, and helped to create many of the activities and materials found in these volumes. They were indispensable to the core design team throughout the project. Through this partnership, we hope that the current volumes are useful to educators in a wide variety of settings to engage youths in design activities that will help them to become systems thinkers, with the ultimate goal of transforming the world that we live in today.

As you might have already noticed, this project brought together many different participants with divergent backgrounds, including game designers from Institute of Play; researchers with backgrounds in the arts, mathematics, and civic education at Indiana University; out-of-school educators at DYN; and professional teachers from the NWP. So, what common threads brought all of these partners together? While there was certainly a common interest in systems thinking as a critical skill for an increasingly complex world, the group also shared a common belief that kids in the twenty-first century had new opportunities for learning as a result of the changing technological landscape. Like many forward-thinking educators, we all saw that the ways that we've been educating young people as a society, through focusing on skill and drill rather than innovation and exploration, and through teaching to the test rather than teaching to youths' interests, were doing a major disservice to young people.

Each of these partners was involved in a broader movement started by the MacArthur Foundation in 2006 to investigate the ways that digital media was changing how kids learned and how these technologies might be leveraged to create new opportunities for learning that might have been previously unimaginable. The Digital Media and Learning (DML) initiative has supported over $80 million in grants to research and develop innovations in digital learning at the time of this writing. It has focused on youth-interest-driven activity in digital spaces as a source of inspiration for creating new learning environments that incorporated the kinds of engagement and higher-order skill development found in places like massively multiplayer online games or do-it-yourself online creative communities like those centered around fan fiction, video blogging, and many other forms of making, tinkering, and designing. The Q2L school and the G*M platform used in the game design module were two examples of learning environments that came out of the DML initiative. Both aimed to build off of interests that youths already brought to school with them, as well as focus on the kinds of twenty-first-century skills they'll need to thrive in the world.

We share this background to enable the reader to think about the activities and resources in this collection not as an isolated approach to teaching, but rather as part of a larger movement to rethink learning in a digital age. There is an incredible amount of innovation happening at the edges of education, and in places that people tend not to think of as learning spaces. We see youths learning in new ways connected to pursuing their interests, engaging deeply, and solving problems through engagement with technology. We want to bring that kind of learning into more formal learning spaces, and we know that we're not alone in this desire. If you're reading this, it's probably because you agree with us that education can be done differently, that youths can engage in problems that are meaningful for them, are connected to their lives, and prepare them for lifelong learning in a changing and complex world.

A TEACHER'S REFLECTION

In concluding this section on the history of the project, we wanted to share the voice and experience of one of the many talented educators that worked on this project. Laura Lee Stroud—a secondary teacher and English language arts instructional coach in the Round Rock Independent School District, as well as a member of the Central Texas Writing Project—reflected on her experience as a maker and learner while engaging with the GNL curriculum during the GNL summer camp in 2011. As part of a playtesting moment, Stroud joined a number of other teachers to construct her own understanding of tools like G*M, Scratch, and e-textiles, as well as facilitate understanding for youths at the camp:

> The Grinding New Lenses camp experience was unlike any experience I'd ever had the opportunity to engage in. NWP teachers from all over the nation gathered for one month in Chicago, away from our homes and families, hoping to learn about systems thinking concepts and internalize them into our existing teaching repertoires. The only thing that we all knew about each other and the work was that we believed in the lifelong learning process and that we had the NWP in common.

The group of educators, in partnership with researchers from Indiana University, Institute of Play, and the DYN, participated in conversations and activities that would evolve into the challenges described in these volumes. As the teachers explored platforms and tools in the service of systems thinking by doing what they soon would be asking youths to do, they also provided feedback, suggestions, and their own mods, contributing to the overall development of the modules as they exist today. As Stroud says, "As a professional, I was viewed as a professional and asked to help edit and revise the curriculum." This feedback and response process with the educators continued throughout the camp experience:

> After we were comfortable with the first layers of the curriculum we were to learn, we split into the modules we were to teach. We were partnered with another teacher and reviewed the materials, learned new vocabulary, and tried to familiarize ourselves with this newfound systems thinking perspective. Every day, in preparation for the summer camp youths, we processed the modules as learners and created the products—be it games, digital narratives with sprites as characters, or e-textile clothing and accessories.

Stroud was a facilitator of the *Soft Circuits* curriculum with youths, but also saw herself as a learner. By entering this brand new world of e-textiles (though it easily could have been a "brand new world of game development" or "brand new world of the programming of a digital story"), she discovered the gaps that existed in her own knowledge—about circuits and circuitry, for instance. This made her that much more sympathetic to the needs of her youths, which in turn allowed her to support them in relating the e-textiles work to their life experiences:

> As the youth entered the camps, for the most part not one teacher assumed the comfortable position of "expert" with our novice youths learning under us. Instead, we were positioned as learners alongside our campers. In some cases, our campers knew more about the content than did we the teachers. We had to remember our new value of supporter, encourager, observer, and researcher. We provided scaffolds for the new concepts, such as an immersion into the new vocabulary, and created a space in the modules for explicit vocabulary instruction. For example, the youths needed to know how to sew a "running stitch" before they could complete a circuit with conductive thread. In fact, in creating the e-cuff, we realized that many of the youths had never made a hem, which is created with a running stitch. As we tried to explain to them how we teachers learned to sew a running stitch, a previously disinterested camper had a light bulb moment as she realized she in fact knew how to sew. She'd worked with her mother in a beauty shop in which they sewed in extra hair for clients. She not only knew how to create a running stitch, she was able to teach the other children how to do it, too! This experience reinforced for me the iterative process of discovering the

strengths available within our classrooms that in turn make our instructional systems most productive.

Stroud concluded by saying:

When we teachers had group time to reflect on our experience, we found that we all struggled in one way or another and as a result we had a newfound level of respect for our youths' learning processes and struggles, as well as a wonderful glimpse into our own learning process.

LIST OF CONTRIBUTORS

Jackie Barnes, Indiana University
David Burton, Bloomington Project School
Christina Cantrill, National Writing Project
Avri Coleman, Digital Youth Network
Michael Downton, Indiana University
Deidra Floyd, Central Texas Writing Project
Leon Gordon, Indiana University
Katya Hott, E-Line Media
Steve Moore, Greater Kansas City Writing Project
Paul Oh, National Writing Project
Nichole Pinkard, DePaul University
Travis Powell, Oregon Writing Project
Scott Price, E-Line Media
Sinem Siyyahan, Arizona State University, Play2Connect Research Group
Charlene Volk, Indiana University
Scott Wallace, Bloomington Project School
Janis Watson, Indiana University
Malcolm Williams, Digital Youth Network

SYSTEMS THINKING CONCEPTS IN THIS BOOK COLLECTION

The goal of the *Interconnections: Understanding Systems through Digital Design* book collection is to make available an accessible set of activities that can help youths develop a "systems lens" for seeing the world—a lens they can use to make sense of problems around them. Our hope is that youths will be able to see, anticipate, and understand patterns in the systems that make up that world, and use those understandings to eventually design better systems.

In these modules, we share a range of practices and concepts related to systems thinking. These concepts by no means represent a comprehensive list of every major idea in systems thinking—instead, we have chosen to focus on a subset of key ideas that focus centrally on *understanding systems,* and, in some of the volumes, on more complex ideas related to *system dynamics.* Understanding systems involves recognizing the elements that structure a system, and, more important, the ways that those elements interconnect to impact each other and the overall function of a system. These understandings are mostly oriented toward analyzing a system at a particular point in time, which is a common focus in these modules. In contrast, the study of system dynamics is fundamentally concerned with understanding the behavior of systems *over time.* Examining how a system changes and the kinds of patterns that emerge over time is crucial to understanding how to intervene effectively in systems. As is detailed next, not all the modules deal with these ideas in the same way—the *Gaming the System* module focuses almost exclusively on supporting youths' understanding of systems, while the *Script Changers* module is more fundamentally concerned with understanding (and orchestrating) system changes over time.

The choices made about which concepts and practices to include were driven by the kinds of design activities that we envisioned for youths, and those ideas that are particularly easy to see via the tinkering and iteration processes associated with design. For example, all modules spend a significant amount of time helping youths to see the kinds of *interconnections* that take place among elements of a system and the kinds of system dynamics that emerge through these interconnections. This focus is easily revealed through design work because youths can define interconnections, observe the functioning of the system, and then, through iterations on their designs, change the nature of these interconnections and immediately observe the resulting changes in system function. For example, when youths are designing a videogame (in *Gaming the System),* they can see immediately how changing the behavior of a single element (such as the health of an avatar, or the damage that an enemy can do) can immediately change how challenging the game is (the overall *function* of the game—the way it works). Likewise, in *Short Circuits* and *Soft Circuits,* youths can observe how changing the structure of light-emitting-device (LED) connections (i.e., the ways that they're linked to each other) can immediately affect the number of LEDs that can light up.

Although there is a lot of overlap among the concepts covered in the four books, each one tackles these ideas uniquely, and there are some particular systems thinking concepts that are covered only in some modules. In the following sections, we describe and define the "big ideas" that are addressed in the modules. In the table that follows, the specifics of those big ideas and where they are addressed in each book and module are portrayed.

1. IDENTIFY SYSTEMS.

A *system* is a collection of two or more elements and processes that interconnect to function as a whole. For example, speed and comfort in a car are created by the interactions of the car's parts, so they are "greater than the sum" of all the separate parts of the car. The way that a system works is not the result of a single part; rather, it is produced by the *interactions* among the elements and/or individual agents within it. A key way to differentiate whether something is a system or not is to consider whether the overall way that it works in the world will change if you remove one part of it.

2. USE LANGUAGE THAT REVEALS A SYSTEM'S CHARACTERISTICS AND FUNCTION.

A key indicator of youths' understanding of systems involves listening for the ways that they describe and make sense of a system. When using a systems thinking approach effectively, youths will be able to identify a system's *elements*, the *behaviors* of those elements, how those behaviors are shaped by the *system's structure*, and how these behaviors *interconnect* to form broader *system dynamics* that move the system toward a particular *function*. At times, a system is designed to meet a particular *goal*, which can be (but is not always) aligned with the actual function of the system.

3. MAKE SYSTEMS VISIBLE.

When we learn to "make the system visible"—whether through a system model drawn on the back of a napkin, a computer simulation, a game, a picture, a diagram, a set of mathematical computations, or a story—we can use these representations to communicate about how things work. At their best, good pictures of systems help both the creator and the "reader" or "audience" to understand not only the parts of the system (the elements), but also, how those elements work together to produce the whole.

4. SEEK OUT COMMON SYSTEM PATTERNS.

Beyond the core aspects of a system (i.e., elements, behaviors, interconnections, dynamics, and function), there are a number of common patterns that are important for young people to look for when engaging with systems. Specifically, systems often have *reinforcing feedback loops* that cause growth or decline, as well as *balancing feedback loops* that create stability in a system. These loops are directly related to the *stocks and flows* of a system—what is coming into a system and what is going out. In particular, when more is flowing out of a system than is coming in, there begins to be a concern about *limited resources* within a system. Sometimes patterns in systems can be seen best by examining the ways that systems are *nested* within each other.

5. DESIGN AND INTERVENE IN SYSTEMS.

A key practice of a systems thinker involves both designing new systems and fixing systems that are out of balance. These interventions allow youths to go beyond simply interrogating existing systems in the world to use their understanding of how systems work to actually change the world around them, while doing so in a conscious way that respects the complexity of systems. The process of *designing* a system involves thinking deeply about the state of the system that you have envisioned, and how the particular elements you have to work with might interconnect with other elements for that state to be realized. This process of design involves more than understanding inter-connections, however; it is also about considering what to do when things go wrong—the most productive *leverage point* to intervene or change a system, why a proposed solution might *fail*, and what *unintended consequences* might occur based on your design.

6. SHIFT PERSPECTIVES TO UNDERSTAND SYSTEMS.

Systems thinkers regularly shift perspectives as they look at systems to get the full picture of what's happening. They think about the actors in a system and what *mental models* they bring to the system that affect the way that they participate. They shift among different *levels of perspective*—from events, to patterns, to structures, and finally to the mental models that give rise to a system—to better understand that system. And finally, they change the *time horizon* associated with looking at a system in order to find *time delays* from prior actions in a system.

	Gaming the System: Designing with Gamestar Mechanic						Script Changers: Digital Storytelling with Scratch						Short Circuits: Crafting e-Puppets with DIY Electronics				Soft Circuits: Crafting e-Fashion with DIY Electronics			
	CH 1	CH 2	CH 3	CH 4	CH 5	CH 6	CH 1	CH 2	CH 3	CH 4	CH 5	CH 6	CH 1	CH 2	CH 3	CH 4	CH 1	CH 2	CH 3	CH 4
1. Identify systems	x	x	x	x	x	x	x	x	x	x	x	x	x	x	x	x	x	x	x	x
2. Use language that reveals a system's characteristics and function — Identifying the way that a system is functioning	x	x	x	x	x	x	x	x	x	x	x	x	x	x	x	x	x	x	x	x
Distinguishing the goal of a system	x	x	x	x		x		x					x	x	x	x		x	x	
Identifying elements	x	x	x	x	x	x	x	x	x	x	x	x	x	x	x	x	x	x	x	x
Identifying behaviors	x	x	x	x	x	x	x	x	x	x	x	x	x	x	x	x	x	x	x	x
Identifying interconnections	x	x	x	x	x	x	x	x	x	x	x	x	x	x	x	x	x	x	x	x
Perceiving dynamics								x	x	x	x		x	x			x		x	
Considering the role of system structure			x						x						x	x		x	x	x
3. Make systems visible		x	x			x	x	x	x	x	x	x	x	x	x	x	x	x	x	x
4. Seek out common system patterns — Reinforcing feedback loops										x										
Vicious cycles											x									
Virtuous cycles										x										
Balancing feedback loops						x					x		x	x			x			
Stocks and flows																				
Limited resources in systems													x	x			x			x
Nested systems								x											x	
Dynamic equilibrium																				x
5. Design and intervene in systems — Designing a system		x	x	x	x	x	x	x	x	x	x	x	x	x	x	x	x	x	x	x
Fixes that fail											x									
Leverage points																x		x		
Unintended consequences												x								
6. Shift perspectives to understand systems — Mental models									x											
Levels of perspective									x						x					
Time horizons and delays								x												

ALIGNMENT TO COMMON CORE STATE STANDARDS

The following tables represent an at-a-glance view of the alignment of Design Challenges from all four books in the *Interconnections: Understanding Systems through Digital Design* collection to relevant Common Core State Standards (CCSS) for English Language Arts and Literacy in History/Social Studies, Science and Technical Subjects. Only relevant standards are included in these tables. (For the complete list of standards, go to www.corestandards.org/ELA-Literacy.)

The Common Core State Standards for English Language Arts and Literacy in History/Social Studies, Science, and Technical Subjects are the result of an initiative to provide a shared national framework for literacy development to prepare youths for college and the workforce. The CCSS span kindergarten through twelfth grade, divided into three bands: K–5, 6–8, and 9–12. The CCSS may be thought of as a "staircase" of increasing complexity that details what youths should be expected to read and write, both in English and in targeted content areas. The CCSS are built upon a set of guiding "anchor standards" that evolve through grade-level progression and emphasize informational text and argumentative writing, particularly at the middle and high school levels. In addition, the CCSS include a strand that emphasizes literacy skills associated with production and distribution via technology.

For newcomers, a useful way to enter into the English Language Arts standards is to read the online About the Standards page at the CCSS website (www.corestandards.org/about-the-standards), and then read the anchor standards for each grade band, as well as for the content areas.

Through the Design Challenges, youths are introduced to a range of core skills and information that stretch their learning potential and build on prior knowledge. Expect them to encounter material described in the English Language Arts standards for reading informational text for key ideas and detail, as well as the integration of knowledge and ideas; for producing and distributing writing with technology; and for speaking and listening tasks that prepare youths for college and careers through comprehension and collaboration, as well as the presentation of knowledge and ideas.

Because the *Interconnections* collection presents curricula that engage youths in literacy practices that fall in the English Language Arts domain, as well as the domains of History/Social Studies and Science and Technical Subjects, the letter-number designation that accompanies each standard in the table aligns with the CCSS letter-number designation as follows:

- R—Reading Literature
- RI—Reading Informational Text
- W—Writing
- SL—Speaking & Listening
- RST—Reading in Science and Technical Subjects
- WHST—Writing in History/Social Studies, Science and Technical Subjects

The standards included in these tables serve as a guide through which the Design Challenges can be understood in conjunction with the CCSS. They do not represent an exhaustive list of all possible alignments, but rather those most prevalent and immediate to the central tasks.

Common Core English Language Arts Standards	Gaming the System: Designing with Gamestar Mechanic					
	CH 1	CH 2	CH 3	CH 4	CH 5	CH 6
R.6-12.7 (anchor standard) Integrate and evaluate content presented in diverse formats and media, including visually and quantitatively, as well as in words.	x					x
RI.7.3 Analyze the interactions between individuals, events, and ideas in a text (e.g., how ideas influence individuals or events, or how individuals influence ideas or events).						x
RI.7.7 Compare and contrast a text to an audio, video, or multimedia version of the text, analyzing each medium's portrayal of the subject (e.g. how the delivery of a speech affects the impact of the words).						x
RI.7.9 Analyze how two or more authors writing about the same topic shape their presentations of key information by emphasizing different evidence or advancing different interpretations of facts.	x		x	x	x	
W.6-8.3 Write narratives to develop real or imagined experiences or events using effective technique, relevant descriptive details, and well-structured event sequences.	x	x	x	x	x	
W.7.6 Use technology, including the Internet, to produce and publish writing and link to and cite sources as well as to interact and collaborate with others, including linking to and citing sources.						x
RST.6-8.3 Follow precisely a multistep procedure when carrying out experiments, taking measurements, or performing technical tasks.	x	x	x	x	x	
RST.6-8.4 Determine the meaning of symbols, key terms, and other domain-specific words and phrases as they are used in a specific scientific or technical context relevant to grades 6–8 texts and topics.						
RST.6-8.7 Integrate quantitative or technical information expressed in words in a text with a version of that information expressed visually (e.g., in a flowchart, diagram, model, graph or table).	x	x	x	x	x	x
RST.6-8.9 Compare and contrast the information gained from experiments, simulations, video, or multimedia sources with that gained from reading a text on the same topic.	x	x	x	x	x	x
RST.11-12.9 Synthesize information from a range of sources (e.g., texts, experiments, simulations) into a coherent understanding of a process, phenomenon, or concept, resolving conflicting information when possible.						x
SL.6-12.4 (anchor standard) Present information, findings, and supporting evidence such that listeners can follow the line of reasoning and the organization, development, and style are appropriate to task, purpose, and audience.	x	x	x	x	x	x
SL.7.5 Include multimedia components and visual displays in presentations to clarify claims and findings and emphasize salient points.	x	x	x	x	x	

Common Core English Language Arts Standards	Script Changers: Digital Storytelling with Scratch					
	CH 1	CH 2	CH 3	CH 4	CH5	CH 6
R.6-12.3 (anchor standard) Analyze how and why individuals, events and ideas develop and interact over the course of a text.			x	x	x	x
R.6-12.7 (anchor standard) Integrate and evaluate content presented in diverse formats and media, including visually and quantitatively, as well as in words.	x	x	x	x	x	x
RI.7.3 Analyze the interactions between individuals, events, and ideas in a text (e.g., how ideas influence individuals or events, or how individuals influence ideas or events).		x	x	x	x	x
W.6-12.2 (anchor standard) Write informative/explanatory texts to examine and convey complex ideas and information clearly and accurately through the effective selection, organization, and analysis of content.		x	x	x	x	x
W.6-8.3 Write narratives to develop real or imagined experiences or events using effective technique, relevant descriptive details, and well-structured event sequences.	x					
W.8.6 Use technology, including the Internet, to produce and publish writing and present the relationships between information and ideas efficiently as well as to interact and collaborate with others.	x	x	x	x		x
W.8.7 Conduct short research projects to answer a question (including a self-generated question), drawing on several sources and generating additional related, focused questions that allow for multiple avenues of exploration.					x	
W.6-12.7 (anchor standard) Conduct short as well as more sustained research projects based on focused questions, demonstrating understanding of the subject under investigation.		x	x	x	x	x
W.6-12.9 (anchor standard) Draw evidence from literary or informational texts to support analysis, reflection and research.			x	x	x	x
RST.6-8.3 Follow precisely a multistep procedure when carrying out experiments, taking measurements, or performing technical tasks.	x	x	x	x	x	x
RST.6-8.4 Determine the meaning of symbols, key terms, and other domain-specific words and phrases as they are used in a specific scientific or technical context relevant to grades 6–8 texts and topics.						

Common Core English Language Arts Standards	Script Changers: Digital Storytelling with Scratch					
	CH 1	CH 2	CH 3	CH 4	CH 5	CH 6
RST.6-8.7 Integrate quantitative or technical information expressed in words in a text with a version of that information expressed visually (e.g., in a flowchart, diagram, model, graph or table).		x		x		x
RST.11-12.9 Synthesize information from a range of sources (e.g., texts, experiments, simulations) into a coherent understanding of a process, phenomenon, or concept, resolving conflicting information when possible.						x
SL.7.2 Analyze the main ideas and supporting details presented in diverse media and formats (e.g., visually, quantitatively, orally) and explain how the ideas clarify a topic, text or issue under study.		x		x	x	x
SL.7.4 Present claims and findings, emphasizing salient points in a focused, coherent manner with pertinent descriptions, facts, details, and examples; use appropriate eye contact, adequate volume, and clear pronunciation.						
SL.6-12.4 (anchor standard) Present information, findings, and supporting evidence such that listeners can follow the line of reasoning and the organization, development, and style are appropriate to task, purpose, and audience.		x	x	x	x	x
SL.7.5 Include multimedia components and visual displays in presentations to clarify claims and findings and emphasize salient points.			x	x		x
WHST.6-8.4 Produce clear and coherent writing in which the development, organization, and style are appropriate to task, purpose, and audience.						x
WHST.6-8.5 With some guidance and support from peers and adults, develop and strengthen writing as needed by planning, revising, editing, rewriting, or trying a new approach, focusing on how well purpose and audience have been addressed.						x
WHST.6-8.6 Use technology, including the Internet, to produce and publish writing and present the relationships between information and ideas clearly and efficiently.						x
WHST.6-8.7 Conduct short research projects to answer a question (including a self-generated question), drawing on several sources and generating additional related, focused questions that allow for multiple avenues of exploration.			x			x

Common Core English Language Arts Standards	Short Circuits: Crafting e-Puppets with DIY Electronics				Soft Circuits: Crafting e-Fashion with DIY Electronics			
	CH 1	CH 2	CH 3	CH 4	CH 1	CH 2	CH 3	CH 4
R.6-12.7 (anchor standard) Integrate and evaluate content presented in diverse formats and media, including visually and quantitatively, as well as in words.								x
RI.7.3 Analyze the interactions between individuals, events, and ideas in a text (e.g., how ideas influence individuals or events, or how individuals influence ideas or events).			x	x		x		
RI.7.4 Determine the meaning of words and phrases as they are used in a text, including figurative, connotative, and technical meanings; analyze the impact of a specific word choice on meaning and tone.					x			x
RI.7.5 Include multimedia components and visual displays in presentations to clarify claims and findings and emphasize salient points.			x	x			x	
RI.8.5 Analyze in detail the structure of a specific paragraph in a text, including the role of particular sentences in developing and refining a key concept.							x	
RI.8.7 Evaluate the advantages and disadvantages of using different mediums (e.g., print or digital text, video, multimedia) to present a particular topic or idea.							x	
W.6-12.2 (anchor standard) Write informative/explanatory texts to examine and convey complex ideas and information clearly and accurately through the effective selection, organization, and analysis of content.	x				x			x
W.6-8.3 Write narratives to develop real or imagined experiences or events using effective technique, relevant descriptive details, and well-structured event sequences.	x	x			x			
W.7.6 Use technology, including the Internet, to produce and publish writing and link to and cite sources as well as to interact and collaborate with others, including linking to and citing sources.								x
W.8.6 Use technology, including the Internet, to produce and publish writing and present the relationships between information and ideas efficiently as well as to interact and collaborate with others.			x					x
W.8.7 Conduct short research projects to answer a question (including a self-generated question), drawing on several sources and generating additional related, focused questions that allow for multiple avenues of exploration.			x					

Common Core English Language Arts Standards	Short Circuits: Crafting e-Puppets with DIY Electronics				Soft Circuits: Crafting e-Fashion with DIY Electronics			
	CH 1	CH 2	CH 3	CH 4	CH 1	CH 2	CH 3	CH 4
RST.6-8.3 Follow precisely a multistep procedure when carrying out experiments, taking measurements, or performing technical tasks.		x		x		x	x	x
RST.6-8.4 Determine the meaning of symbols, key terms, and other domain-specific words and phrases as they are used in a specific scientific or technical context relevant to grades 6–8 texts and topics.	x	x			x			x
RST.6-8.7 Integrate quantitative or technical information expressed in words in a text with a version of that information expressed visually (e.g., in a flowchart, diagram, model, graph or table).	x				x			x
RST.6-8.9 Compare and contrast the information gained from experiments, simulations, video, or multimedia sources with that gained from reading a text on the same topic.						x		x
RST.11-12.9 Synthesize information from a range of sources (e.g., texts, experiments, simulations) into a coherent understanding of a process, phenomenon, or concept, resolving conflicting information when possible.	x		x		x			
SL.6-12.4 (anchor standard) Present information, findings, and supporting evidence such that listeners can follow the line of reasoning and the organization, development, and style are appropriate to task, purpose, and audience.	x		x		x			
SL.7.2 Analyze the main ideas and supporting details presented in diverse media and formats (e.g., visually, quantitatively, orally) and explain how the ideas clarify a topic, text, or issue under study.						x		
SL.7.4 Present claims and findings, emphasizing salient points in a focused, coherent manner with pertinent descriptions, facts, details, and examples; use appropriate eye contact, adequate volume, and clear pronunciation.				x				
SL.7.5 Include multimedia components and visual displays in presentations to clarify claims and findings and emphasize salient points.			x			x		
WHST.6-8.4 Produce clear and coherent writing in which the development, organization, and style are appropriate to task, purpose, and audience.			x					x
WHST.6-8.6 Use technology, including the Internet, to produce and publish writing and present the relationships between information and ideas clearly and efficiently.							x	

NEXT GENERATION SCIENCE STANDARDS

Because the *Interconnections* book collection presents curricula that engage youths in design activities that embrace the sciences, the standards included in this table serve as a guide through which the challenges can be understood in conjunction with the Next Generation Science Standards (NGSS; found at **www.nextgenscience.org/ next-generation-science-standards**). They do not represent an exhaustive list of all possible alignments, but rather those most prevalent and immediate to the central tasks.

As the NGSS are explicit in assigning specific scientific topics and learning to specific grade levels, the correlations in these tables range from third grade to high school. The following tables were created to help identify which national science standards align to our Design Challenges, to what grade, and in which challenge each is addressed. Please note, however, that all the Design Challenges have been tested in a wide range of ability, grade, and age groups.

NGSS CODE DESIGNATIONS

- 3–5: Upper elementary grades
- MS: Middle school grades 6–8
- HS: High school grades 9–12
- ESS = Earth and Space Science
- ETS = Engineering, Technology, and Applications of Science
- PS = Physical Sciences

Next Generation Science Standards	Gaming the System: Designing with Gamestar Mechanic					
	CH 1	CH 2	CH 3	CH 4	CH 5	CH 6
ETS1 Engineering Design						
3-5-ETS1-1. Define a simple design problem reflecting a need or a want that includes specified criteria for success and constraints on materials, time, or cost.	x	x		x	x	x
3-5-ETS1-2. Generate and compare multiple possible solutions to a problem based on how well each is likely to meet the criteria and constraints of the problem.	x	x		x	x	x
3-5-ETS1-3. Plan and carry out fair tests in which variables are controlled and failure points are considered to identify aspects of a model or prototype that can be improved.	x	x		x	x	x
MS-ETS1-1. Define the criteria and constraints of a design problem with sufficient precision to ensure a successful solution, taking into account relevant scientific principles and potential impacts on people and the natural environment that may limit possible solutions.			x	x	x	x
MS-ETS1-2. Evaluate competing design solutions using a systematic process to determine how well they meet the criteria and constraints of the problem.	x	x	x	x	x	x
MS-ETS1-3. Analyze data from tests to determine similarities and differences among several design solutions to identify the best characteristics of each that can be combined into a new solution to better meet the criteria for success.				x	x	x
MS-ETS1-4. Develop a model to generate data for iterative testing and modification of a proposed object, tool, or process such that an optimal design can be achieved.	x	x	x	x	x	x

Next Generation Science Standards	Script Changers: Digital Storytelling with Scratch					
	CH 1	CH 2	CH 3	CH 4	CH 5	CH 6
ETS1 Engineering Design						
3-5-ETS1-1. Define a simple design problem reflecting a need or a want that includes specified criteria for success and constraints on materials, time, or cost.	x			x	x	x
3-5-ETS1-2. Generate and compare multiple possible solutions to a problem based on how well each is likely to meet the criteria and constraints of the problem.			x	x	x	x
3-5-ETS1-3. Plan and carry out fair tests in which variables are controlled and failure points are considered to identify aspects of a model or prototype that can be improved.				x	x	x
MS-ETS1-1. Define the criteria and constraints of a design problem with sufficient precision to ensure a successful solution, taking into account relevant scientific principles and potential impacts on people and the natural environment that may limit possible solutions.	x	x	x	x	x	x
MS-ETS1-2. Evaluate competing design solutions using a systematic process to determine how well they meet the criteria and constraints of the problem.			x	x	x	x
MS-ETS1-3. Analyze data from tests to determine similarities and differences among several design solutions to identify the best characteristics of each that can be combined into a new solution to better meet the criteria for success.					x	x
MS-ETS1-4. Develop a model to generate data for iterative testing and modification of a proposed object, tool, or process such that an optimal design can be achieved.		x	x	x	x	x
ESS3 Human Impacts						
MS-ESS3-3. Apply scientific principles to design a method for monitoring and minimizing a human impact on the environment.		x	x	x	x	x

Next Generation Science Standards	Short Circuits: Crafting e-Puppets with DIY Electronics				Soft Circuits: Crafting e-Fashion with DIY Electronics			
	CH 1	CH 2	CH 3	CH 4	CH 1	CH 2	CH 3	CH 4
PS2 Motion and Stability: Forces and Interactions								
3-PS2-3. Ask questions to determine cause and effect relationships of electric or magnetic interactions between two objects not in contact with each other.	x	x	x	x	x	x	x	x
MS-PS2-3. Ask questions about data to determine the factors that affect the strength of electric and magnetic forces.	x	x	x	x	x	x	x	x
PS3 Energy								
4-PS3-2. Make observations to provide evidence that energy can be transferred from place to place by sound, light, heat, and electric currents.	x	x	x	x	x	x	x	x
4-PS3-4. Apply scientific ideas to design, test, and refine a device that converts energy from one form to another.		x	x	x		x	x	x
MS-PS3-2. Develop a model to describe that when the arrangement of objects interacting at a distance changes, different amounts of potential energy are stored in the system.		x				x	x	
HS-PS3-3. Design, build, and refine a device that works within given constraints to convert one form of energy into another form of energy.								x
ETS1 Engineering Design								
3-5-ETS1-1. Define a simple design problem reflecting a need or a want that includes specified criteria for success and constraints on materials, time, or cost.	x	x	x	x	x	x	x	x
3-5-ETS1-2. Generate and compare multiple possible solutions to a problem based on how well each is likely to meet the criteria and constraints of the problem.	x	x	x	x	x	x	x	x
3-5-ETS1-3. Plan and carry out fair tests in which variables are controlled and failure points are considered to identify aspects of a model or prototype that can be improved.		x	x	x		x	x	x
MS-ETS1-1. Define the criteria and constraints of a design problem with sufficient precision to ensure a successful solution, taking into account relevant scientific principles and potential impacts on people and the natural environment that may limit possible solutions.								x
MS-ETS1-2. Evaluate competing design solutions using a systematic process to determine how well they meet the criteria and constraints of the problem.	x	x	x	x	x	x	x	x
MS-ETS1-4. Develop a model to generate data for iterative testing and modification of a proposed object, tool, or process such that an optimal design can be achieved.		x	x	x		x	x	x

INTRODUCTION

You think that because you understand "one" that you must therefore understand "two" because one and one make two. But you forget that you must also understand "and."

—*Sufi teaching*

Few would argue with the idea that the world is growing more complex as the twenty-first century unfolds. We live in a time that not only requires us to work across disciplines to solve problems, but also one in which these problems are of unprecedented scale, coming from a world that is more interconnected than ever. In such a context, power rests in the hands of those who understand the nature of the interdependent systems that organize the world, and, more important, can identify where to act or how to intervene in order to change those systems. Effective intervention requires considering not just simple causal relations, but also the complex interconnections that work together in often-unexpected ways to produce an outcome. Taking action in our complex world requires a set of twenty-first century skills and competencies called "systems thinking."

Systems thinking is best characterized by the old dictum that the whole is always greater than the sum of its parts. It's an approach that involves considering not just the behavior of individual elements of a system, but also the complex interconnections between multiple parts that work together to form a whole. Systems are ubiquitous in our world—which includes natural systems that deal with climate and biodiversity, economic systems that drive production and labor trends, and political systems that enact governance of communities and nations. And, of course, these systems are themselves connected to one another in important ways, so understanding the nature of these interconnections, not just within but also across systems, is becoming ever more vital. The promise of learning to reason about how systems work is that of creating a new and effective lens for seeing, engaging with, and changing the world.

Systems thinking allows one not just to understand better how systems function, but also to decide the best way to intervene to *change* systems. Systems thinkers have the potential to have a significant impact on the world around them—an impact that is often denied to those who think in simple cause-and-effect terms. As a consequence, we believe that to effectively and ethically educate children to thrive in the twenty-first century, we must create contexts in which young people are supported in learning to be creative and courageous about making changes to systems in the world and to understand that those changes will always have an impact on other parts of the system—everything is interconnected. It's not enough to instill this competency in current leaders—we must prepare the next generation to be effective and thoughtful stewards of the world that they will inherit soon. Helping young people to understand how systems work, how they are represented, and how they change—via direct or indirect means—is critically important to this larger project. Furthermore, it's important that young people learn about systems not in a distant and unfamiliar context, but in contexts that have meaning to today's youth—those rooted in popular culture, design, and new technologies. This approach is the basis of this collection.

Digital media are central in almost every aspect of daily life, most notably in how we communicate, understand political issues, reflect, produce, consume, and share knowledge. We are living in an era in which digital media is rapidly becoming a driving force in globalization, scientific advances, and the intersection of cultures. The growing accessibility of digital tools and networks, the prevalence of many-to-many distribution models, and the large-scale online aggregation of information and culture are leading to profound changes in how we create and access knowledge. Perhaps nowhere is this digital influence contested more than in education, where questions arise about the ability of traditional systems to prepare young people for the social, economic, and political demands of a complex and connected new century.

This collection, *Interconnections: Understanding Systems through Digital Design,* builds on the existing work of educators, management theorists, designers, and learning scientists who are aiming to promote systems thinking in young people. The project uses a design-based approach to learning and offers up a toolkit for supporting systems thinking in ways that are aligned to current Common Core State Standards (CCCS) and relevant to youth interests in digital culture. Through a collaborative effort across a leading group of designers and educators from Institute of Play, Indiana University's Creativity Labs, the Digital Youth Network (DYN), and the National Writing Project (NWP), we've developed an innovative approach to supporting the development of systems thinking in young people; one that allows them to see how systems are at play in the digital contexts that they regularly engage with and one that puts them in the position of designers of those systems. Most prior work on teaching systems thinking has focused on the biological, physical, and social sciences. By contrast, this collection aligns itself with a growing body of work emerging from the fields of game design, digital storytelling, and do-it-yourself (DIY) electronics as contexts for engaging in systems thinking. Creating animated digital stories about aspects of their community they would like to see changed, for example, provides young people with rich opportunities for observation, analysis, and problem solving.

Each of the four books in the collection is rooted in *constructionist* learning theory, which positions young people as active creators of their own understanding by engaging in the design, iteration, and sharing of media artifacts within communities of interest (Papert, 1980; Kafai, 2006). Each book teaches systems thinking concepts and skills in the context of a specific digital media platform and includes an average of six design "challenges" totaling between 25 and 40+ hours of project time.

The first book in the collection, *Gaming the System: Designing with Gamestar Mechanic*, orients readers to the nature of games as systems, how game designers need to think in terms of complex interactions between game elements and rules, and how to involve systems concepts in the design process. The core curriculum uses Gamestar Mechanic (G*M), an online game design environment with a strong systems thinking focus. *Script Changers: Digital Storytelling with Scratch*, focuses on how stories offer an important lens for seeing the world as a series of systems and provides opportunities for young people to create interactive and animated stories about the systems around them. The projects in this book use the Scratch visual programming environment as a means to tell stories about how to affect change in youths' local communities. The two final books, *Short Circuits: Crafting e-Puppets with DIY Electronics* and *Soft Circuits: Crafting e-Fashion with DIY Electronics,* both explore the fields of electronics and "e-textiles," which involves physical computing projects making fabrics and other everyday materials, including incorporating microprocessors into these materials and programming them with an accessible tool called Modkit.

WHAT IDEAS ABOUT SYSTEMS WILL YOUTH LEARN IN THE *SCRIPT CHANGERS?*

Although typically systems thinking curricula are concerned with encouraging youths to describe the behavior of systems, the goal of the *Script Changers* module is for them to experience the internal structure and interconnections within systems. This is accomplished by creating design experiences that allow youths to conceptualize and design systems and examine the impact of those design decisions on the overall functioning of the system. Specifically, our goal is that, by the end of the module, youths will have had opportunities to consider practices such as the following:

- **Identifying a system:** Understanding that a system is a collection of parts, or elements, which interconnect to function as a whole.

- **Identify the way a system is functioning:** Understanding what a system is actually doing—the "state" it is moving toward.

- **Distinguishing the goal of a system:** Identifying the ideal state or function of a system from the particular perspective of the designer.

- **Identifying elements:** Considering what a system is composed of—the parts that work together to make a system function as it does.

- **Identifying behaviors:** Identifying the different ways that each element can act.

- **Identifying interconnections:** Identifying the different ways that a system's parts, or elements, interact with each other through their behaviors, and through those interactions, change the behaviors of other elements.

- **Considering the role of system structure:** Understanding that the way the system works (i.e., what it actually does) is the product of a set of complex interconnections between elements that cannot simply be reduced to an account of the elements themselves—these sorts of system dynamics emerge from the way the elements interconnect, and these interconnections largely are determined by the way that the system's structure sets them up in relation to one another.

- **Identifying balancing feedback loops:** Identifying relationships in which two or more elements of a system keep each other in balance, with one (or more) elements leading to increase, and one (or more) elements leading to decrease.

- **Identifying reinforcing feedback loops:** Identifying relationships in which two or more elements of a system cause each other to increase, such as in escalation cycles, or decrease, such as in resource drain cycles, in a way that's "out of control" or creates a "snowball effect."

- **Locating nested systems:** Almost all systems are nested within larger systems. In nested systems, a larger system affects the way that a subsystem behaves, and the subsystem affects the way that the larger system behaves.

- **Locating leverage points:** Finding the particular places within a system where a small shift in one thing can produce big changes in everything.

- **Designing systems:** Students are consistently engaging in an iterative design process (i.e., designing systems, tweaking elements of those designs, and creating new iterations), and then reflecting on how changes they made fundamentally shape the ways those systems function and whether these changes meet with their own goal for the system.

- **Modeling systems:** Students create versions of existing systems as designed games; that creation involves the act of translating what they understand about the target system to a new domain with new representations.

These are just a subset of the ideas relevant to systems thinking that are covered in the *Script Changers* module. Each challenge details the ideas about systems thinking that are specifically covered. In addition, these ideas are explored in more depth in the "Delving Deeper into Systems Thinking" chapter that appears at the end of the Design Challenges.

WHAT IS DESIGN THINKING?

To know the world one must construct it.
—*Cesare Pavese*

When a young person creates a video, a poster, an animation, a customized T-shirt, or a digital app, she is operating within the space of design. Design is a particularly important activity for learning because it positions the learner as an active agent in the creation process. As learners construct a public artifact, they externalize their mental models and iterate on them throughout the design process (Papert, 1980; Kafai, 2006). In contrast to prescriptive approaches to design, where youths all construct the same artifact in parallel or arrive at an idealized solution through design, the challenges in this book strike a balance between structure and free exploration (Colella, Klopfer, & Resnick, 2001). The activities presented here engage youths in design activities to encourage them to learn key systems thinking concepts. We also acknowledge that learning happens best when it's done in a collaborative setting and there are purposeful moments for reflection. As such, the challenges in each volume share a common structure of activities, based on the creative design spiral proposed by Rusk, Resnick, and Cooke (2009).

Resnick (2007) describes the creative process of design as an idea that is realized by iteratively imagining, creating, playing, sharing, and reflecting on the work. *Imagining* begins with youths' open exploration of the materials to ignite their creativity and imagination to take the work in unexpected and personally meaningful directions. *Creating* places an emphasis on building, designing, and making artifacts that can be shared with a broader community. The act of construction not only provides opportunities to develop and enrich creative thinking, but also presents youths with the chance to experience disciplinary content through hands-on reconstruction of their prior knowledge. *Play*, the next step in the design cycle, is where playful experimentation with ideas is done in a low-risk environment to explore and test the boundaries of the materials. The public presentation or *sharing* of work in progress or completed work is also critical to the learning and motivation in the design process, where youths become more engaged and find new inspiration and an audience for their ideas. Resnick also argues for systematic *reflection* on both the design and learning process, where youths discuss and reflect on their thinking. Making the thinking process visible through easy access to the design artifacts from various parts of the creative process is crucial to learning. Finally, Resnick describes this pathway through the design process as a spiral that is then iteratively repeated.

To this work, we add two more steps to the design cycle: Research and Publish. *Research* encapsulates the information gathering that is critical to high-quality teaching and learning. This includes the introduction and definition of key terms and vocabulary, the introduction of key concepts that are important to systems thinking and disciplinary content, and the activities used to gather this information (including the use of videos, diagrams, and other information sources). We also disentangle the sharing of the final product, which we call *Publish*, from more informal moments where sharing is done within the local community to assist in iteration. Current research has demonstrated

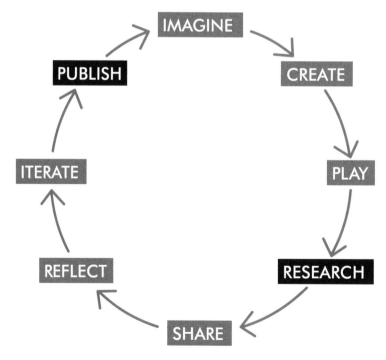

Design-based approach to learning.

that this is an important moment for learning and community building, and that there are some crucial differences in who is likely to post in the informal, interest-driven hours (Lenhart and Madden, 2007).

As a methodology for learning about systems, design is all about providing constructive contexts in which to explore ideas, interactions, and expressions. Linking design to digital media tools expands this context further: digital tools often make it easier, faster, and less risky to test ideas. There is no need to worry about wasting expensive materials, and erasing a mistake is as easy as clicking a mouse. The act of designing incorporates complex technical, linguistic, and symbolic elements from a variety of domains, at a variety of different levels, and for a variety of different purposes. Designers explicate and defend design ideas, describe design issues and user interactions at a meta-level, imagine new possibilities, create and test hypotheses, and reflect on the impact of each of their creations as a distinctive medium in relation to other media. And each of these involves a melding of technological, social, communicational, and artistic concerns in the framework of a form of scientific thinking in the broad sense of the term. Designers make and think about complex interactive systems, a characteristic activity today, both in the media and in science.

The challenges included within this book emphasize a process of prototyping and iteration based on a design methodology: youths envision new solutions to open-ended problems, work through multiple versions of any idea, integrate ongoing feedback into the learning process, and identify the strengths and weaknesses of both their processes and solutions. In some cases, youths may choose to build on previous solutions or approaches of their peers, seeing themselves as contributors to a larger body of collaboratively generated knowledge.

DESIGNING A SUPPORTIVE LEARNING ENVIRONMENT

Before sharing the Design Challenges that we've developed, it's important to provide a set of guiding design principles for creating a supportive learning environment that are never stated explicitly, but form the base assumptions about what kind of pedagogy they're aiming to promote. As you adapt (and appropriate, of course), the activities in this book, we hope that the principles here might help guide you.

A design-oriented experience, particularly one created to support systems understandings has to be ... well, designed. The curriculum modules shared in this book focus on activity structures and learning outcomes—what learners might be doing, with what tools, and in what kinds of configurations. Young people must experience the activities robustly when they take into account a set of larger principles defining the qualities of the learning context itself. The principles outlined next help to structure a learning setting that is itself understood as a dynamic system—one where the interactions among learners and mentors, peers, resources, and social contexts has been considered and where specific attention has been paid to the ways in which these different relationships reinforce or amplify each other.

The principles are intended to offer suggestions for how the experience of learning might be designed to support the learning resources offered later in the book. Please note that the principles should be understood as working together within a system—that is, no single principle does much on its own. It is in the relationships between principles that the robustness of the system resides. For example, creating learning experiences where a challenge is ongoing likely will fail miserably if it doesn't also include feedback that is immediate and ongoing. Organizing a classroom environment where authority is shared, expertise is distributed, and a broad range of ways to participate is allowed matters only if there are also visible ways for learners to share and exchange expertise and discover resources. The whole is far greater than the sum of its parts. The fact that the principles are listed separately should be understood as a limitation of the page, not as a feature of the principles.

1. Everyone is a participant.

Create a shared culture and practice where everyone contributes. Design learning experiences that invite participation and provide many different ways for individuals and groups to contribute. Build in roles and supports for teachers, mentors, and instructors to act as translators and bridge-builders for learners across domains and contexts. Make sure that there are opportunities for participants (especially new participants) to lurk and leech (i.e., observe and borrow), and that peer-based exchange, like communication and sharing, is easy and reciprocal. Provide a diverse set of resources to support teaching and peer-to-peer mentorship activities, allowing youths with various forms of expertise to take on leadership roles.

2. Feedback is everywhere; iteration is assumed.

Encourage youths to assume that their first draft is never the final version—they should make something and then gather feedback, rather than waiting to share their creation until they "get it right." Feedback should include structures for guidance and mentorship, which may take place via the online communities associated with the modules, or in classroom, after-school, or home settings. Make sure that there are plenty of ways for participants to share their work in progress with their peers, solicit feedback, teach others how to do things, and reflect on their own learning. Provide opportunities for participants to incorporate feedback in iterative design cycles. One key aspect of this latter element is allowing every participant's contribution to be visible to everyone else in the group through frequent posting, sharing, group discussion, or a combination of the three. Utilize the tools associated with the module platform to enable communication and exchange between peers who may or may not be part of the same program or setting to broaden the kind of feedback that youths receive.

3. Create a need to know.

One of the more powerful features of challenge-based experiences is that they create a *need to know* by challenging youths to solve a problem whose resources are accessible but require work to find. They must develop expertise in order to access the resources, and they are motivated to do so either because they find the problem context itself engaging or because it connects to an existing interest or passion. Make sure that challenges are implemented within learning environments that support situated inquiry and discovery so that youths have rich contexts within which they can practice using concepts and content. As participants advance through a challenge, provide a diverse array of opportunities for them to build social and cultural capital around their progress. Allow youths to collaborate in many different ways as they explore different roles or identities related to the design project at hand.

4. Learning happens by doing.

Modules emphasize performance-based activities that give rise to authentic learning tasks. These experiences provide opportunities for participants to develop knowledge and understanding through direct discovery and engagement with a complex but well-ordered problem space. These spaces often require participants to figure out the nature of the problem space itself, rather than proposing a specific problem to be solved.

Make sure that learners have access to robust mechanisms for discoverability; a number of resources to support this type of inquiry are included in this volume (on Systems Thinking Concept cards and Gaming the System Challenge cards), while additional resources—peer-produced tutorials and other materials—should be easy to find, use, and share. Think of ways to situate challenges within a context that has meaning or relevance for participants, whether in peer, interest-driven, or academic contexts. Provide participants with multiple, overlapping opportunities to interact with experts and mentors who model expert identities associated with the problem space. Explore teaming and competing structures like competitions and collaborations that mix collaborative and competitive elements in the service of problem discovery and solving.

5. Create meaningful public contexts for sharing.

In addition to sharing and receiving feedback during the design and iteration cycles, encourage the sharing of final products and projects with both local and global audiences. Knowing that there will be an audience, especially one that youths care about, is motivating, but also promotes a sense of creating something with a particular audience in mind. This contrasts with creating things in a vacuum, which is too often the case in educational contexts.

Create infrastructures for youths to share their work, skills, and knowledge with others across networks. These channels might take the form of online public portfolios, streamed video or podcasts, student-led parent conferences, or public events where work is critiqued and displayed, to name only a few options. Allow participants to develop identities in contexts of their own choosing; create opportunities for acquiring status via achievements that are visible in a range of home, school, workplace, and peer group settings. Provide diverse forms of recognition and assessment, which might take varied forms, including prizes, badges, ranking, ratings, and reviews.

6. Encourage play and tinkering.

Youths often learn best by experimentation, tinkering, and doing things that might look like they're "wasting time." As much as possible, build in open-ended spaces for playing and tinkering with the tools, materials, and platforms in addition to more structured challenges. Invite interaction and inquiry into the limits and possibilities of the platform, media, or form in which youths are working. Support learners in defining goals that structure the nature of their interaction and inquiry from moment to moment, as well as over a longer term.

7. Position youths as change agents.

The whole process of design implies agency—that people are able to create innovative solutions in the face of problems, be they large or small. And a big idea behind a pedagogy of systems thinking is that young people who bring this lens to complex problems can envision better solutions than those who don't. Help youths reflect on the choices that they are making in the design or transformation of a system—empower them to see themselves as agents of change.

WHO IS THIS BOOK COLLECTION FOR?

These materials were designed for both in- and out-of-school spaces. Educators and mentors using the materials and tools in this book, such as Scratch, do not need to be experts in computer programming. The activities in this book are designed to spur a range of interactions between young people and the digital platform or tool, as well as between peers. Educators should serve as facilitators for youth discussion, reflection, and ideation. The principles of systems thinking encourage young people to figure things out, put puzzle pieces together, look for similar patterns, and work together to ask questions and find answers across disciplines. The activities have been designed to invite young people to teach one another, because the act of playing and making products for each other (be they games, stories, or physical objects) places learning into a collaborative context. Youths can show others what they've discovered as they work on their projects, which provides an opportunity for them to act as experts. We recommend that educators try and support youths taking on these roles in the classroom, serving as teachers and mentors to their peers.

APPROACH TO CONVERSATION AND CRITIQUE IN THIS VOLUME

With the aim of creating a participatory environment where feedback is welcomed and iteration is assumed, several processes and protocols have been included that support productive conversation and critique within groups. For example, there are many points where youths share their work with each other, with the goal of getting feedback to refine and improve their designs. This can be a tricky endeavor, as they might be reluctant to let others see their work, and not all youths are practiced at offering feedback that goes beyond being simply laudatory or critical, to hit a point of being *constructively critical.* Although there are many ways to help them learn to find this "sweet spot" of feedback, in these Design Challenges, we encourage them to give a balance of "warm" and "cool" feedback to each other, taking turns as presenter and responder. In any community that does not have much experience providing constructive feedback and critique, the warm and cool feedback protocol can be a really effective tool. Next, we give details about this process, as well as a few related suggestions. All of these could be modeled and discussed beforehand with youths to support familiarity and ease of use.

Warm/cool feedback: This type of feedback begins with a few minutes of warm feedback from the responder, which should include comments about how the work presented seems to meet the desired goals. Next, the responder provides a few minutes of cool feedback, sometimes phrased in the form of reflective questions. Cool feedback may include perceived disconnects, gaps or problems in attaining the goal. This is an opportunity to include suggestions for making changes as well. You might note that people feel encouraged to improve something that they have worked on when they feel *good* about it. A young designer especially can become discouraged without some positive feelings and compliments about the design.

Consider role-playing this, with you—the teacher or mentor—taking on the part of the partner receiving feedback. Ask for a volunteer to give you examples of feedback, starting with warm feedback and then moving to cool. When processing the results

WARM FEEDBACK

elements that work well
goals that were met
things to build on

COOL FEEDBACK

areas of wondering
gaps or disconnects
suggestions for improvement

afterward, focus first on what felt like helpful feedback. Then explore with the group what types of feedback seemed unhelpful. Provide examples of several feedback sentence starters that might lead to more constructive conversation. (e.g., "Have you thought about ...?," "What were you thinking when you ...?" "I was confused when ... Can you help me understand?")

"Yes, and ..." feedback: Another way to support youths in developing ideas together is to have them generate "Yes, and ..." feedback as opposed to "Yes, but ..." or negative feedback. This type of feedback reserves judgment, challenge, or dismissal, and instead focuses on refining the original idea that the youths generated. It is a technique often used in supporting iteration in a design process.

One way to demonstrate the difference between these two types of feedback is to create a silly or neutral situation in which one person presents an idea (such as "I think we should get rid of all money. We don't need it."), and then a larger group answers only with "Yes, but ..." feedback (e.g., "Yes, but how can we buy things online without money?"). Then ask the presenter to present the same idea again and have the larger group answer only with "Yes, and ... feedback (e.g., "Yes, and then maybe we could then use [suggestion] when we want to buy something online."). Ask the presenter, and then the group, to describe the differences between the two experiences.

Response starters: At any given moment, not everyone in any community will agree completely about what's working or not working in a creative project. Sometimes this means that debate is necessary to clarify ideas, and healthy debate can support the development of critical thinking skills around systems at play in their communities. To help youths respond to each other civilly while still disagreeing—during both formal response times and informal collaborative work periods—you may want to post in the room a range of possible response starters that introduce disagreement respectfully, such as the following:

- "I see your point, and ..."
- "I am wondering about ..."
- "I understand that you see this as a way to ..., and from my perspective ..."
- "What if ...?"
- "Yes, and ..."

APPROACH TO ASSESSMENT IN THIS VOLUME

Assessment is designed to happen in three ways in these modules: informally, through *embedded discussions* within challenges; and formally, as *structured reflections* and design feedback in the challenges, and as *written assessments,* which can be administered as pre- and post-tests. Of course, all assessments can and should be used at the discretion of the educator. All of the assessment opportunities that we included here were designed to be formative, serving not just as an important opportunity for the educator to get information on how youths are learning, but for the youths themselves to gain insight into their own understanding of the key ideas being explored and the areas that they might want to work to improve.

With the goal of helping to prepare you to listen for and evaluate youths' understanding, we also include rubrics that offer an overview of what "novice" versus "expert" understanding of the concepts in each section would look like. These rubrics are intended to be used for instructional decision making, so that the educator can determine whether students are ready to move on, must talk more about a particular idea, or need more chances to show what they know.

Informal assessments are marked with this "Let's talk" icon. These assessments are designed to be formative and informal, in that they take place within the context of the Design Challenge as small-group or whole-group conversations. These conversations should serve both to help youths formalize some of the ideas that they've been working on and to create an opportunity for the educator to gauge what they understand about a particular idea.

Structured assessments indicated by the "hands on" icon, are times when youth write down and document what they understand about a particular idea. Structured assessments come in a variety of forms. For example, this might a piece of peer feedback about another person's design, a sketch or diagram about their own design, or perhaps a paragraph in which they reflect on a particular idea. These assessments are intended to help youth formalize their understanding of a particular idea, but are also designed to provide educators with a formal representation (i.e., a hard copy!) of what youth understand about a particular idea at a particular time. If desired, these assessments can be graded and returned to youth as a means of tracking performance toward a grade in the context of classroom use.

Written assessments are given only at the end of the module (and perhaps at the beginning, if the educator is interested in pre- and post-change information). The written assessment is designed to measure what youths have learned across the entire module, and it targets both youths' understanding of key systems-thinking content and what they've learned about a particular technology platform.

Information about ways that students might reason about the content can be found in the *What to Expect* sections of each Design Challenge. We share the end points of student reasoning (novice and expert) but, of course, rarely are youth novices or experts at everything at the same time. The goal of these rubrics is for the educator to be able to determine how students are thinking about the content to inform decisions about how to proceed, review, or intervene.

COMMON CORE STATE STANDARDS (CCSS) AND TIPS FOR INTEGRATION

You might be asking yourself: Why focus on the Common Core State Standards (CCSS) for English Language Arts in a book designed to support understanding of systems thinking concepts through the use of a computer program like Scratch? What do computer programming and literacy have in common? You will find that the art of game design in these challenges involves a number of key literacy arenas.

The CCSS for English Language Arts and Literacy in History/Social Studies, Science, and Technical Subjects are the result of an initiative to provide a shared national framework for literacy development. The CCSS span kindergarten through twelfth grade and may be thought of as a "staircase" of increasing complexity for what youths should be expected to read and write, both in English and in targeted content areas. The CCSS are built upon a set of guiding "anchor standards" that evolve through grade-level progression and emphasize (particularly at the middle and high school levels) informational text and argumentative writing. The CCSS also include a strand that emphasizes literacy skills associated with production and distribution via technology.

The challenges in this book rely on youths' ability to *prototype*—that is, draft and revise in an iterative manner until they come up with a final product (a key skill in game design). During the prototyping process, youths chart ideas, devise plans, and then communicate those plans to their peers in small and large groups to receive and incorporate feedback. In addition, youths are asked to analyze "texts," such as explanatory videos, as they relate to particular systems thinking concepts that are manifested in real-world contexts, and then apply what they've understood to their own game design process. Youths are asked to write as part of the reflective process and as a way to demonstrate understanding. As mentioned previously, in these Design Challenges, youths will be involved in a number of key literacy arenas, such as speaking and listening, analyzing texts, and visual literacy, as outlined in the CCSS through anchor standards such as the following:

Speaking and Listening (Presentation of Knowledge and Ideas)

4. Present information, findings, and supporting evidence such that listeners can follow the line of reasoning and the organization, development, and style are appropriate to task, purpose, and audience.

5. Make strategic use of digital media and visual displays of data to express information and enhance understanding of presentations.

Reading (Integration of Knowledge and Ideas)

9. Analyze how two or more texts address similar themes or topics in order to build knowledge or to compare the approaches the authors take.

In addition, technology is woven throughout the standards as a way to gain knowledge, as something to be understood through critical media analysis, and as a means to produce and disseminate work. Once again, the challenges in this book take up the mantle. Throughout, youths employ technology tools to research and then write digitally. They build rich narratives that leverage their understanding of visual composition. And they even move beyond the Common Core State Standards by developing a facility with the *language of code*—a literacy, one might argue, unto itself.

As your youths engage in the task of understanding how to effect change in the complex system that is their community, they will be doing so via challenges in this book that offer a rich toolset of social studies and language arts literacy practices infused with digital media.

TOOLKIT

In this chapter, we offer an explanation of why designing using Scratch is a useful way to help youths learn about systems. We then present an introduction to the platform, Scratch (**scratch.mit.edu/**), upon which the systems thinking and digital storytelling Design Challenges in this curriculum are based.

Throughout, we encourage instructors to follow the *spirit* rather than the letter of what we include in these Design Challenges. Every learning environment is different: a classroom is not a library space, nor an after-school program. Every group of youths is different: tweens are not teens, kids who grew up in a city are different than kids that grew up in rural areas, immigrant youths are different than those youths born in their country of residence. And every educator is different in terms of their style, history, and relationships to youths. So we don't assume that the activities we share will ever (or should ever) be implemented in the exact same way in every context. We assume that these materials will be adapted, reinvented, and even improved in your own environments. This is part of why we spent a good deal of time talking about the "big ideas"—the concepts and principles that drove this work—in the first section of this book. We didn't just see this sort of background as something interesting and informative (though we hope it was); we offered it up so that it might represent tools that you could use as this work is brought to life. We hope that when you inevitably adapt the activities that we share to fit your context, you have a sense of what the spirit behind the activities is, and you have the opportunity to adapt the lessons (and even create new activities) with these key principles in mind. Thus, it is important to note that our suggestions about the timing of the activities, the assessment of youth thinking, and

MENTOR TEXT

SYSTEM ANALYSIS

APPLY TO COMMUNITY CONTEXT

DIGITAL STORY CREATION IN SCRATCH

PUBLISH & REFLECT

Curricular progression of *Script Changers* Design Challenges.

ideas for whole-class discussions can and should be modified to adapt to your unique context.

This book contains a sequence of six design challenges that build upon core systems thinking concepts. Each of the Design Challenges builds off of the last, deepening and extending understandings of systems thinking. The bulk of the Design Challenges, except for the introductory one that serves to familiarize participants with the Scratch platform, follow a similar curricular trajectory (see the figure above). Youths engage mentor texts, in the form or books and/or short videos, which are then subject to analysis through a systems thinking lens, pulling out big ideas around systems. These ideas are then used to examine the local community to see how these systemic patterns are at play in kids' own lives. The final part of most challenges involves using Scratch to tell stories about local communities that touch on the systems concepts that were central to the challenge.

WHAT IS SCRATCH?

In this book, we use Scratch (freely available at **scratch.mit.edu**), a media-rich visual programming environment developed by the MIT Media Lab's Lifelong Kindergarten Group (Resnick et al., 2009). A versatile platform for creating and animating your own games, music videos, and interactive art, Scratch enables youths in this curriculum to easily turn their systems ideas into mixed-media digital stories. Inspired by Seymour Papert's LOGO programming environment, Scratch is a tool that allows youths to mix multiple forms of media and, in the process, learn programming, create projects that are personally meaningful, and share and receive feedback on their creations within a larger online community.

Script Changers
Design Challenges at a Glance

	Targeted Systems Thinking Concepts	General Activities
Design Challenge 1: Getting Oriented: Scratch, Systems Thinking, and Community-Based Digital Storytelling (Time: 135 minutes)	• Identifying a system • Identifying elements • Identifying interconnections • Identifying behaviors	• Embodying Systems: The Paper Airplane Supply Chain • Community Issues from a Systems Perspective • Scratch Introduction and Orientation • Scratch Programming Challenge
Design Challenge 2: Systems, Systems Everywhere! Diving into Systems (Time: 185 minutes)	• Identifying a system • Distinguishing the goal of a system • Identify the way a system is functioning • Identifying elements • Identifying behaviors • Identifying interconnections • Nested systems • Time horizons and delays • Making systems visible	• Diving into Systems: *The Story of Electronics* • Communities as Systems • Scratch Design Challenge: Systems in My Community
Design Challenge 3: It's All about Perspective: Thinking below the Waterline … and across the Table (Time: 365 minutes)	• Perceiving system dynamics • Consider how mental models shape action in a system • Looking at a system from multiple perspectives • Considering multiple levels of perspective • Making systems visible	• Thinking Across the Table • Our Community, from Multiple Perspectives • Scratch Design Challenge: All About Perspective • Thinking below the Waterline • Scratch Design Challenge: All About Perspective (continued)
Design Challenge 4: Out of Control: Reinforcing Feedback (Time: 405 minutes)	• Reinforcing feedback loops • Vicious cycles • Virtuous cycles • Perceiving dynamics • Making systems visible	• Why Is It So Difficult to Stop Being Homeless? • Of Yooks and Zooks and Reinforcing Loops • Scratch Design Challenge: Reinforcing Feedback Loops
Design Challenge 5: Out of Balance: Balancing Feedback and Leverage Points (Time: 120 minutes)	• Balancing feedback loops • Fixes that fail • Leverage points • Perceiving dynamics • Making systems visible	• Looking for Stability • Balancing Feedback in "The Sneetches" • Where to Direct Change: Exploring Leverage
Design Challenge 6: Make a Change! Leverage Points and Unintended Consequences (Time: ~500 minutes)	• Leverage points • Unintended consequences • Making systems visible	• Introduction to Leverage Points • Leverage Points Design Challenge: Preliminary Research and Design • Final Project: Final Design Period

It's easy for both novices in computer programming and emergent readers and writers to get started using Scratch (Peppler and Warschauer 2010; Maloney, Peppeler, Kafai, Resnick, and Rusk 2008). Most people can create a simple working program—for instance, a cat that moves forward each time it's clicked with a mouse—with little or no guidance within minutes of opening the program for the first time. And yet once people start diving into Scratch, they can go quite deep, creating projects of increasing complexity that result in the development of valuable expertise that can be transferred to other areas, such as learning the fundamentals of computer programming (Maloney et al 2008), digital arts (Peppler 2010), and even connecting to language learning (Peppler and Warschauer 2008).

Also important for settings with a large number of English language learners, Scratch accommodates more than 50 world languages. To change the language of the program, youths can select their preferred language within the program's Language menu.

WHY USE SCRATCH IN A SYSTEMS THINKING CURRICULUM?

The curricular challenges in this book use children's stories and issues from youths' local communities as the contexts for *thinking* about systemic concepts, and use Scratch primarily as a tool for *talking* about those systems. However, in creating challenges around systems thinking, we chose to use Scratch for a number of reasons that go beyond the ways that it allows for ease of digital storytelling.

First, each Scratch project in and of itself can be *understood as a system*. Every story youths create in Scratch is made up of interdependent elements—such as computer code, imagery, and sounds—that each take on specific roles as they work together to accomplish a goal: communicating a story. If any of these parts is removed, there is an impact on the whole of the system. Using Scratch allows an educator to provide youths with opportunities to transfer systemic ideas explored in the books and discussions about communities into a new context. This kind of transfer of systemic knowledge and practices is key in developing systems thinking dispositions.

Second, Scratch allows youths to easily incorporate *media that's personally meaningful* within their projects. As a media-rich programming environment, Scratch enables users to import sound and image files with just a couple of clicks. Youths can also draw characters for their own stories, download and edit images linked to their interests, and even import bits of their favorite music and incorporate the music into their creations. Being able to make things with personal relevance deepens engagement and learning outcomes, and the Scratch environment is built to make this as easy as possible for young people.

Scratch is also designed to promote collaboration and peer-to-peer learning through its *online global community*, where youths share, learn from one another, and give feedback on projects. When provided with a community context in which to share their own creations, the likelihood that young people will persist and iterate on a project increases. This sense of community also gives them an audience to keep in mind when they're authoring and lets their voices be heard on a global scale. Importantly, it's also a place where youths can be inspired by each other and even teach one another techniques and practices to improve their ability to be producers of media.

Finally, Scratch has been linked to a host of *twenty-first century skills* beyond systems thinking and design thinking, including computational thinking and "remix" skills. The Lifelong Kindergarten Group at MIT designed Scratch to support youth in exploring a range of computational thinking concepts (e.g., sequence, loops, conditionals), practices (e.g., working iteratively and incrementally, testing and debugging, reusing and remixing), and perspectives (e.g., expressing, connecting, questioning). In a world where interactions between digital and physical spaces become ever more fluid, these competencies are increasingly important. Additionally, Scratch was designed so that youth can easily *remix* existing content. This might mean borrowing code or images developed in one project and using it in a new way in another; downloading and modifying the code from another project; or even incorporating an existing image downloaded off the web. Remix is understood by many as an important new literacy associated with being able to recontextualize and modify existing ideas, technologies, and approaches to spark innovative thinking—long understood as being central to most intellectual endeavors; after all, everyone builds on the shoulders of giants.

For all these reasons, we believe that digital storytelling through Scratch provides a strong avenue for developing systems thinking and twenty-first century skills in youth. That doesn't mean that other kinds of storytelling platforms can't be used, but each will have trade-offs that are important to figure into a curriculum planning process. We'll discuss some of those tools and considerations around them in later sections of this toolkit.

TECHNICAL INFORMATION

GETTING STARTED WITH SCRATCH

Scratch is accessible for free online. One of the most powerful things about Scratch is not just what it allows people to create, but also with whom it allows them to share those creations. With more than 1 million registered users and over 3 million projects shared at the time of this writing, the Scratch website (scratch.mit.edu) boasts one of the most robust online creative communities for young people.

There are two main areas in Scratch: 1) the *project editor* where you create projects, and 2) the *online community* where you can share projects and learn from others.

The project editor in Scratch version 2.0 allows you to create, save, and share online, and does not require any software installation. If you want to work offline without a web connection, you can use the standalone version of the project editor (available for download at **scratch.mit.edu/download**). The examples in this book are illustrated using the online version of Scratch 2.0, but can be adapted for other versions. **Note:** If you have the older Scratch 1.4 software installed on your computer, you can still use that to create projects and share them to the 2.0 website.

While the project editor itself is a powerful tool for learning and creating, the Scratch online community extends and enhances the learning experience. With a clear audience and community that they're speaking to, youths are not creating in a vacuum. By becoming immersed in the community, youths begin to have a sense of what kind of work is valued in the space, what they can draw on, what's considered innovative, and what it means to push new forms of expression. In many ways, this is more like the real world than what most classrooms can offer; in the real world, we're always producing for a specific context, with a specific audience in mind, and these meaningful contexts for production keep us thoughtfully engaged with what we're creating.

At the same time, the community doesn't just provide a platform and audience for broadcasting projects that youths have created; it's also a place of inspiration, innovation, feedback, and learning of new techniques and practices. All projects on the Scratch website let users "look under the hood" and even tinker with a project without making permanent changes to it; in addition, all the projects are available for download. This kind of functionality allows participants to see how any project works, and also allows them to appropriate sprites, sounds, backdrops, and combinations of code to use them in new ways in their own projects. Additionally, the site is full of tutorials, walkthroughs, and support forums where youths can seek and share help with others and find collaborators.

THE SCRATCH HOMEPAGE

Scratch is designed to promote creativity and collaboration among its growing international community of users. The Scratch 2.0 homepage—which showcases the latest projects that the community finds the most interesting or are remixing at the moment—is the first introduction newcomers have to Scratch before starting on their first project. Scratch users, expert or novice, all have the opportunity to explore the latest trends and innovations in the community by running any Scratch project directly from their web browser, as well as adding metadata with social media staples like adding tags to a project (e.g., "Favorite," "Love"), linking to the project from another website (e.g., Facebook or a personal blog) and leaving comments or questions for the designer. Crucially, Scratch 2.0 allows viewers to see the how a particular project is constructed by pressing the "See inside" button in the upper right corner of the screen. Once inside, you can also experiment with the blocks for easy remixing and to create entirely new projects.

TRACKING YOUR YOUTHS' WORK IN THE SCRATCH COMMUNITY

There are a few features that will help you track youths' projects in the larger Scratch community, follow their interests, and connect to other groups using the *Script Changers* curriculum. One feature that will help you keep track of what your youths are doing is to have an individual account for each youth (which either you or the child can set up). Then you can "follow" your youths by simply going to their profile page and clicking the Follow button in the upper right-hand portion of the screen. Once you do, you will

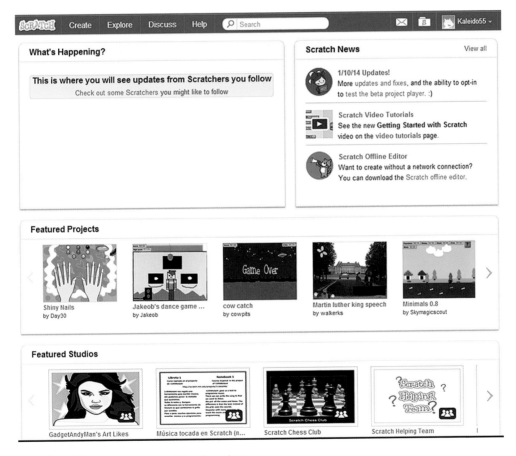

Screenshot of the Scratch homepage (when logged in).

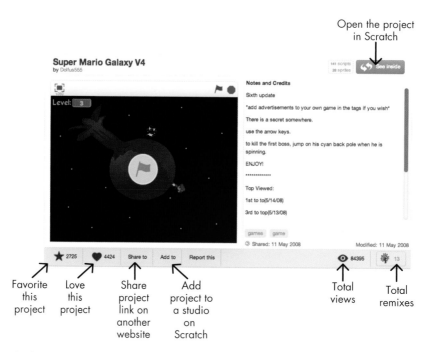

Social media functions on the Scratch website.

have their projects streaming to your homepage and your profile page will list who you're following. You can encourage your youths to follow one another as well as to follow you.

A second Scratch 2.0 feature that supports you and your youths in staying connected in the online community is to create studios, which are collections of projects. You can create your own studio and choose which projects to include (perhaps of work created by your youth or of inspirational projects that you would like to see) *or* follow existing studios that are curated by others. We have set up a studio specifically for this project. We currently have the "Systems Thinking Projects" studio (**scratch.mit.edu/ studios/130810**) that you may wish to follow. This studio contains sample projects from this book as well as projects created by other youths using *Script Changers*.

A BRIEF TOUR OF THE SCRATCH PROJECT EDITOR

Programming a Scratch project is like scripting a play. You choose characters (referred to as *sprites*) and then create *scripts* that tell each sprite what to do. When you first

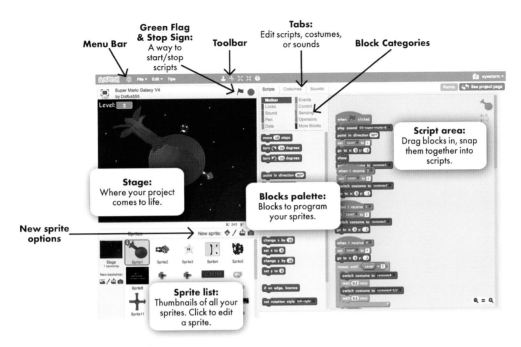

Screenshot of the Scratch project editor.

open Scratch, you see that the project editor is partitioned into six key areas (see the figure above).

The area on the upper left side of the screen is the *Stage*. This is where you see your stories come to life. When viewing a Scratch project in Presentation Mode, the stage— expanded into full-screen view—is all the user sees.

A new Scratch project begins with a single cat *sprite* on the stage. A sprite is an object that performs actions in a Scratch project. For every sprite in your project, a thumbnail appears in the *Sprite List*. To see and edit a sprite's actions, costumes, and sounds, click on its thumbnail in the sprite list or double-click on the sprite itself on the Stage.

From here, you can give instructions to each sprite by pulling graphic blocks from the *Blocks Palette* into the *Scripts Area*, where they can snap into stacks, called *scripts*. When you drag a block from the blocks palette into the scripts area, a white highlight indicates where you can drop the block and form a valid connection with another block. When you click on a script, the corresponding sprite performs the actions indicated in the blocks from top to bottom.

The *Backpack* feature at the bottom of the screen allows you to pull any costume, sprite, sounds, or script from any project on the Scratch 2.0 website and drag it into one of your own for easy remixing and leveraging of best practices. Simply open a new project and pull things from your backpack into the project.

The *Tips Window* provides a step-by-step guide and examples to help you learn to create projects in Scratch. It can be opened by clicking on the Tips menu.

In addition to these six key areas, there are a number of tools in the Scratch project editor to help you get up and running quickly on your first project.

TABS

Above the blocks palette are three tabs: Scripts, Costumes, and Sounds. Clicking on each tab pulls up a new set of controls:

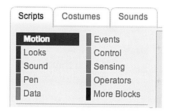

Scripts   The Scripts tab contains the complete set of Scratch programming blocks, organized by color-coded categories. Click on each category to bring up a unique set of blocks to pull into the scripts area.

Costumes   Each sprite can rotate through a series of *costumes*—the term also designates a series of poses or motion captures used to "animate" a sprite. Clicking on the costumes tab replaces the scripts area with a paint editor window and replaces the blocks palette with all of the costumes assigned to a particular sprite. When you click on a thumbnail of the stage's backdrop in the sprite list, this tab changes to Backdrops, but the editing functions stay the same.

Sounds   You can assign audio files to actions by snapping appropriate sound programming blocks into a script. All audio files you use in a project—imported from a file or recorded from within Scratch using the computer's built-in microphone—are stored in the sounds tab, where you can edit the length of the file and apply effects in the sound editor window.

MENUS

The menus in the upper left part of the screen allow you to quickly navigate, open, and save projects.

SCRATCH

Scratch Logo   Jump back to the Scratch homepage.

Languages   Select your preferred language from more than 50 world languages.

File Menu   Use to create a new project, save a copy to your online account, and load and save projects to your computer or other local drive.

> **New**   Create a new project
>
> **Save Now**   Save your project in your online account (you must be logged in to **scratch.mit.edu** with your username and password). The Scratch website automatically saves every couple of minutes to your account. You can use "Save Now" to make sure your project is saved before closing a window.
>
> **Save as a Copy**   Makes a copy of the current project and let you start working on that version.
>
> **Go to My Stuff**   You can manage all your projects and your account on the "My Stuff" page.
>
> **Import from Local Drive**   Opens a project from your computer or other local drive.
>
> **Export to Local Drive**   Save a project to your computer or other local drive.
>
> **Revert**   Discard all changes made since opening the project.

Edit   Undelete objects or scripts that were just deleted, change to small screen layout, and other options.

Tips Opens the tips window to access a step-by-step tutorial, example scripts, and an explanation of each of the blocks.

TOOLBAR

The *Toolbar* is where you can adjust the size and number of sprites in your project, as well as get help if you don't know what something in the interface does. First, click on a button in the Toolbar to select a tool, then click on another object to perform an action, such as:

Duplicate Duplicate sprites, costumes, sounds, blocks, or scripts.

Delete Delete sprites, costumes, sounds, blocks, and scripts.

Grow Make sprites bigger.

Shrink Make sprites smaller. To return to the arrow cursor, click on any blank area of the screen.

Question Mark   Click on the question mark and then on any part of the screen or an object that confuses you, in order to learn more.

VIEW OPTIONS

Scratch lets you move easily between views for working and those for presenting your project.

Presentation Mode   Click this button when you want to present your project, which expands the Stage to full-screen view and hides the other areas of the Scratch screen. To exit Presentation Mode, press the Esc key.

View Mode   Switch between small and large stage view. You can use small stage view to display Scratch on small screens or to expand the Scripts Area.

CREATING SPRITES AND BACKDROPS

You can easily create sprites and scenes within Scratch by clicking on one of the "New sprite" buttons in the Sprites navigation bar:

Import a Sprite from the Scratch Sprite Library   Click on this button to bring up a pop-up window containing more than 144 sprites, organized by category, theme, file type, and more. Click on any sprite in the library to preview its costumes. Import the sprite by clicking the OK button. The new sprite appears on the stage and the sprites area, and its corresponding costumes automatically appear in the costumes tabs.

Paint Your Own Costume for a New Sprite Using the Paint Editor   Click on this button to open the in-program Paint Editor. It creates a new sprite with a blank costume for you to start drawing. Click on "New Costume" to paint or import a second costume for your sprite, or click the paintbrush button again to create another sprite. Click on the sprites or sounds tabs to exit the paint editor. *(See page 31 for more information about the Paint Editor toolbox.)*

Import a Sprite from a Folder on Your Computer   Click on this button to open a pop-up window where you can select a file from your computer as a new sprite. Scratch can import most image file types. Click "Open" to import the file into Scratch.

Take a Picture Using Your Webcam   Click on this button to bring up a pop-up window with a feed from your computer's webcam. Clicking "Save" snaps a picture of you, imports the image onto the stage and sprites list, and closes the pop-up window. If you click on the costumes tab, you can edit the image using the paint editor.

You can delete any sprite by selecting the Delete tool from the Toolbar and clicking on the sprite, or you can right-click (Control+click on a Mac) the sprite and selecting "delete" from the pop-up menu. Deleting a sprite also removes any scripts, costumes, and sounds attached to it.

You can also use the duplicate tool to create an identical copy of your costume and then make small edits to the new costume. This is especially important when you want to "animate" a sprite by programming it to rapidly rotate through a series of costumes.

Just as a sprite can change its appearance by switching costumes, the stage can change its appearance by switching *backdrops*. The process for creating a new backdrop using the paint editor in Scratch is very similar to that of creating a new costume for a sprite.

Click on the Stage thumbnail (on the bottom left of the screen), then find the Backdrop tab and select one of the buttons below the "New Backdrop."

PAINT EDITOR

The Scratch Paint Editor (below) has familiar drawing tools found in many basic paint programs.

The Paint Editor Toolbar has a number of tools, of which the following are important to youth as they import images from the Web, especially the tools listed below.

Fill   Fill connected areas with a solid color or gradient.

Scratch 2.0 Paint Editor.

Eyedropper   Use the tip of the eyedropper to choose a color.

Transparent "Color"   Use the transparent "color" as a solid fill or paintbrush color to render portions of an image, such as the background, invisible. (Transparent areas appear in the paint editor as a gray and white checkerboard pattern.)

When you draw in Scratch your images are stored as *vector* graphics. Vector graphics allow each shape to be changed and resized without degrading the quality of the image. If you import a photo or other image from the web, it will typically be in *bitmap* rather than vector format. You may notice that different tools become available in the editor, depending on whether you are editing a vector graphic or bitmap image.

On your computer, you can usually tell the format of an image from the filename: vector graphics typically end with .svg, while bitmap images end with .png, .jpg, .gif, or .bmp. **Note:** Vector graphics are new in Scratch version 2.0; Scratch 1.4 only has bitmap images.

SOUND EDITOR

Clicking on the sounds tab brings up the Sound Editor. In the sound editor, you can choose a new sound from the library, import a file from your computer, or record a sound with your computer's microphone (see image on next page). Once imported, the file's waveform appears in the editor window, which can then be edited using the Edit and Effects drop-down menus. Back in the scripts area, you can play any imported audio file in a script using the play sound block.

The drop-down menu with that block lists all sounds currently listed in the sound editor tab. (New sprites start with the sound "pop," which can be deleted or replaced.

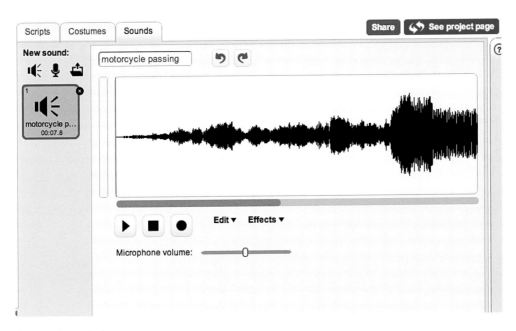

The Scratch sound editor.

GREEN FLAG AND STOP SIGN

The green flag at the top-right corner of the Stage ⚑ provides a convenient way to start a Scratch program. You can use it to start many scripts at the same time. Click the green flag to start all scripts that have **when ⚑ clicked** at the top. In Presentation Mode, pressing the Enter key has the same effect as clicking the green flag. The stop sign next to the green flag ⬣ stops all scripts.

WHAT PARTS OF SCRATCH DOES THIS BOOK EMPHASIZE?

The *Script Changers* curriculum for exploring systems thinking and digital storytelling barely "scratches" the surface (if you'll forgive the pun) of the possibilities afforded by the Scratch platform's capacity and tools. In this section, we'll orient you to the most important aspects of the tool for the purposes of digital storytelling, although we have provided "Scratch Challenge Cards" (see Appendix E) for youths interested in exploring even more blocks and other areas of Scratch for their designs.

It's extremely important to allow time to get oriented to Scratch as a tool for digital storytelling. The first challenge of this volume, "Getting Oriented" gives youths a chance to play around with the platform and focus on specific tips and techniques in Scratch. We recommend that you follow along in Scratch as we orient you to the program.

SCRATCH BLOCKS

The Scratch environment includes ten categories of color-coded "blocks"—their name for programming commands—which allow a user to accomplish different types of tasks. Several blocks have white fields on them, which allow you to type in a number or select an option from a drop-down menu. The categories most important to digital storytelling are *Motion, Looks, Sound, Events,* and *Control.* In fact, it's likely that most youths will never need to use the other categories available here (Pen, Data, Sensing, Operators, and More Blocks) unless they decide to experiment with more complex actions.

The *Motion* blocks allow a user to command a sprite to move around the stage in a variety of ways. Here are some commonly used Motion blocks:

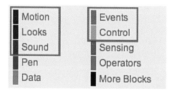

The five categories of Scratch blocks most relevant to the digital storytelling module.

Motion Blocks	Definition
move 10 steps	Moves sprite forward or backward.
turn ↻ 15 degrees	Rotates sprite clockwise (a different block exists to turn a block counterclockwise).
go to x: 0 y: 0	Moves sprite to specified *x* and *y* position on Stage.
glide 1 secs to x: 0 y: 0	Moves sprite smoothly to a specified position over specified length of time.

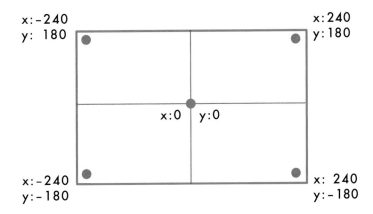

All Scratch projects are based on an x-y grid, with the center of the Stage being the 0,0 coordinate.

Motion blocks can command a sprite to move to a particular set of *X, Y* coordinates, to move a certain number of steps, to point in a certain direction, and a variety of other motion-oriented actions. By clicking the "Rotation Style" buttons that appear when you click the ⓘ in the corner of that sprite's thumbnail in the Sprite list, you can further control how sprites appear when they change direction:

↻	**All around.** The costume rotates as the sprite changes direction.
↔	**Left-right flip.** The costume faces either left or right.
●	**Don't rotate.** The costume never rotates (even as the sprite changes direction).

The *Looks blocks* allow a user to change the visual appearance of sprites and backdrops. Here are some commonly used Looks blocks:

Looks Blocks	Definition
say Hello! for 2 secs	Displays a sprite's speech bubble for a specified amount of time.

Looks Blocks	Definition
think Hmm... **for** 2 **secs**	Displays a sprite's thought bubble for a specified amount of time.
next costume	Changes a sprite's costume to the next costume in the costume list.
switch backdrop to backdrop1 ▾	Changes the stage's appearance by switching to a different background.
switch to costume costume1 ▾	Changes a sprite's appearance by switching to a different costume.
show	Makes a sprite appear on the stage.
hide	Makes a sprite disappear from the stage.

The looks category also includes two of the most important types of blocks for storytelling: the "say" blocks and the "think" blocks. These blocks can be used to create speech and thought bubbles associated with a given sprite. They are key to character interaction within stories, and are often a primary way that ideas and narratives are communicated within a story (in combination, of course with visuals and other story elements).

The *Sound* blocks allow a user to incorporate audio into their Scratch projects in a variety of ways (see page 37 for commonly used Sound blocks). These might look like sound effects associated with a particular sprite, like the sound of a door slamming to go along with an animation of a door slamming in the project, but they also allow for background music that plays throughout a project and isn't associated with a specific moment in the story.

The Scratch Cat sprite speaks when the "say" block is clicked.

Sound Blocks	Definition
play sound meow ▾	Starts playing a sound, selected from a pull-down menu, and immediately goes on to the next block even as that sound is still playing.
play drum 48▾ for 0.2 beats	Plays a drum sound, selected from a pull-down menu, for a specified number of beats.
play note 60▾ for 0.5 beats	Plays a musical note (higher numbers for higher pitches) for a specified number of beats.
rest for 0.2 beats	Rests (plays nothing) for a specified number of beats.
set instrument to 1▾	Sets the type of instrument that the sprite uses for the above "play note" blocks. (Each sprite can play its own instrument.)
stop all sounds	Stops playing all sounds.

The *Events* and *Control* blocks allow a user to determine how all of the blocks above (Motion, Looks, Sounds) come together (see below and the next page for commonly used Events and Control blocks). These blocks help you to control when things happen and allow for the digital story to move forward when a particular key is pressed or with a particular mouse movement. For instance, the "when space key pressed" block when space ▾ key pressed could allow the digital story to start when the space bar is pressed. The "wait" block creates a temporal delay between blocks (e.g., two sound blocks might have a wait block placed in between them to cause a delay or a rest.) A "repeat" block repeat 10 can cycle a certain stack of scripts a number of times, or even forever. Most important for digital storytelling are the "broadcast message" block broadcast message1 ▾ and "when I receive" message block when I receive message1 ▾ , which are used in tandem to sequence together actions within a Scratch project.

Events Blocks	Definition
when ⚑ clicked	Runs an attached script when green flag is clicked.
when space ▾ key pressed	Runs an attached script when specified key is pressed.
when I receive message1 ▾	Runs an attached script when it receives the specified message.

Events Blocks	Definition
broadcast message1 ▾	Sends a message to all sprites, and then continues with the next block.
when backdrop switches to backdrop1 ▾	Runs an attached script when the backdrop is switched to the specified backdrop.

Control Blocks	Definition
wait 1 secs	Waits a specified number of seconds, and then continues with next block.
forever	Runs the blocks inside this bracket over and over.
repeat 10	Runs the blocks inside this bracket a specified number of times.

Later in this section we'll go over particular stacks of blocks that are key to creating digital stories in Scratch, but for now just know that these five categories of blocks—motion, looks, sound, events, and control—are the ones that youth will be using most in the activities we share in this book.

IMPORTING EXISTING MEDIA INTO SCRATCH

The ability to import existing media into Scratch is one of the things that make the platform so powerful for digital storytelling, primarily because it enables youths to incorporate the popular culture content that they find personally meaningful. It also allows participants to create projects much more quickly, because they don't need to spend as much time creating sprites, and youths without drawing skills can easily create projects.

Many youths find the Scratch media library—the images and sounds that come with Scratch—to be a valuable resource for creating projects, and it is entirely possible to make creative and unique projects solely from resources found in the library. At the same time, bringing in content found on the Internet via sources like Google Images has many benefits, including getting youth familiar with many basic web-related literacies including search strategies, understanding how to pull files off of the Internet, and importing images for use in other computational contexts. It also means that youths can bring in more customized content that fits the particular vision of the project they're working on and connect to current trends in popular culture.

To pull an image or sound off the Internet and into Scratch, youths can follow these steps once they find a file they want to use:

1. In a web browser, right-click (Windows) or Control+click (Mac) on an image or sound file; a menu with a number of options should show up.

2. One option should read something like "Save image as" or "Save file as." Selecting this will allow the file to be saved to the computer. It's important to save the file in a folder on the computer that can be easily located again.

3. In Scratch, click an "Import" button for a new sprite or sound and navigate to the folder where the file was saved to select and import it. You can also drag and drop an image from the web or a folder on your desktop directly into Scratch.

Using existing content teaches important web literacies as well as competencies around appropriation and remixing, but also raises issues around authorship and ownership that are increasingly important for youth to think about in a world of easily replicated digital media. If you're inspired, discussing issues around copyright, fair use, and alternative licensing such as Creative Commons can be an important learning moment for those who may not have had any exposure to these ideas. For resources on educating about these issues, you can visit TeachingCopyright.org as well as Common Sense Media's digital literacy curriculum on "Respecting Creative Work" (**commonsensemedia.org/educators/curriculum**). Most important, youth need to understand that although it is often okay to use people's work to create something new, it should be done in ways that are both legal and respectful of the creator. Scratch allows for easy remixing, which creates a context for most of these conversations to emerge naturally during the process of design.

KEY SCRATCH COMPETENCIES FOR DIGITAL STORYTELLING

Just as there are a number of key Scratch blocks that youth need to use to create digital stories, there are also a number of techniques that use those blocks that youth need to be familiar with. In this section, we'll discuss the following:

- How to Coordinate Events
- How to Change Backdrops
- How to Animate Sprites
- How to "Hide" and "Show" Sprites
- How to Create Starting Points

For most of these techniques, you can find relevant Scratch "Building Blocks" cards at the end of Design Challenge 1 that offer step-by-step instructions and can be printed and made available when the youth are working on their projects.

HOW TO COORDINATE EVENTS

Coordinating sprites is a key part of digital storytelling in Scratch. Youths most often communicate many of the big plot ideas and content through dialogue between sprites, so coordinating events, such as turn-taking in a conversation, is a crucial skill for youths to master early on when making digital storytelling projects. Thankfully, it's really easy!

There are two techniques that can be used to get sprites to converse:

1. *The "Wait" Technique:* Use the "say" blocks in conjunction with the "wait" blocks.

2. *The "Broadcast and Receive" Technique:* Use the "say" blocks in conjunction with the "broadcast" and "receive" blocks.

The "Wait" Technique essentially aims to synchronize the *timing* of the interaction between two sprites. Let's say two sprites—a girl and a boy—are having a conversation. The girl begins the conversation by speaking (using a "say" block `say Hello! for 2 secs`), while the boy waits (using the "wait" block `wait 1 secs`). That first "wait" block for the boy will be timed to end just as the first "say" block for the girl ends, at which point

A conversation between two sprites.

the sprites will switch: the girl will have a "wait" block active while the boy has a "say" block active. It's a little bit like a real-life (polite) conversation, with one person waiting to speak until after the other finishes, except in Scratch the listening is programmed in! See the figure below to see what the code would look like for a conversation that uses the "Wait" Technique.

The script combinations used in the boy (left) and the girl (right) when using the "Wait" Technique to create conversations between sprites.

Through simple messing around in Scratch, youth can usually discover this technique easily. However, this technique does have its downsides: If a larger project has many sprites and is edited many times, it can become quite complicated to track the different amounts of time and correctly synchronize all the actions; this can get confusing and frustrating for youth to troubleshoot. The "Broadcast and Receive" Technique avoids this pitfall.

The "Broadcast and Receive" Technique, rather than using timing and waiting to create conversations, uses the "broadcast" and "receive" blocks to *sequence* various commands together across sprites. Let's take those same two sprites from the last example; the girl begins the conversation by speaking (using a "say" block). Then a "broadcast" block is linked to that "say" block, which sends a signal to any "receive" blocks within the project that are assigned its unique signature. One of those receive blocks is waiting in the scripts tab of the boy sprite, and when it receives the broadcast "signal," it responds with whatever blocks follow the receive block, in this case another "say" block. Following that "say" block is another "broadcast" block, with its own unique signature, which is paired with a corresponding "receive" block in the girl, to keep the conversation chain going (see image on the next page).

While slightly more labor intensive to initially create, the broadcast and receive technique allows for easier editing of conversations, because the author can insert new lines of dialogue in the middle, associated with new broadcast and receive blocks,

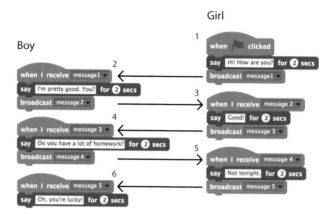

The scripts used in the boy (left) and the girl (right) when using the broadcast and receive technique to create conversations between sprites.

without doing major changes to the existing blocks. Also, when the timing changes or multiple events need to be triggered at one time, using the broadcast and receive commands can be an effective means of communicating multiple sprites and the stage at the same time.

HOW TO CHANGE BACKDROPS

When creating stories that have multiple settings, youths will likely want to have different scenes at different points in their stories. They can achieve this by creating different backdrops and using a "switch backdrop" block `switch backdrop to backdrop1`, which also can trigger scripts in the sprites (e.g., sprites from the previous scene hiding and new ones appearing in designated locations on the stage). Any time you switch the backdrop, it triggers all scripts in all sprites that have the `when backdrop switches to backdrop1` block on top. **Note:** Each of those blocks have pull-down menus for selecting the name of the backdrop.

You can `switch backdrop to backdrop1` to switch backdrops and then continue with the rest of the script. To pause between scene changes, you can use "wait __ secs."

Alternatively, in Scratch 2.0 you can use the "switch backdrop and wait" technique to coordinate scenes and costume changes. The `switch backdrop to backdrop1 and wait` block waits until all scripts that start with `when backdrop switches to backdrop1` finish completely before continuing. The image below shows how to use this technique.

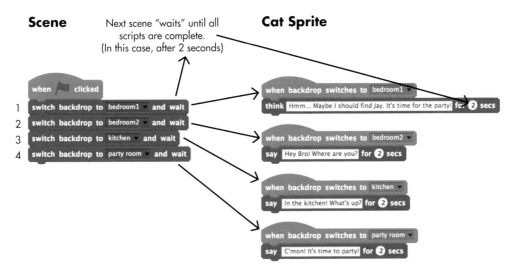

Scene　　Next scene "waits" until all scripts are complete. (In this case, after 2 seconds)　　**Cat Sprite**

Using the "Switch Backdrop and Wait" Technique to switch scenes.

The costume tab for the default sprite, Scratch Cat, with two different costumes that make it appear as if the cat is walking when switched in close succession.

HOW TO ANIMATE SPRITES

While not absolutely necessary for storytelling, animating sprites is often something that youths want to do in their digital stories in Scratch. As mentioned previously, you can "animate" a sprite by programming it to move through a series of costumes. For instance, you can make a sprite look like it is dancing by assigning it a new costume for each position in the dance. Each of the images for the animation is actually a different image stored under the costumes tab associated with that sprite. You can manually click between the costumes to create the appearance of an animated sprite, or create a rotating sequence of costumes using a **next costume** block from the looks palette, nested within a forever block **wait 1 secs** from the control palette. Copying a costume and making a small edit in the paint editor is a good way to get started making your own costumes for an "animated" sprite (see the figure below).

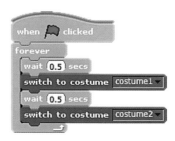

A script combination involving switch costume and wait blocks in order to create an animated sprite.

Once the desired costumes are loaded into the costume tab, the command blocks can be used in combination with the "switch costume" blocks to create the animation (see the figure below).

In the example above, the forever block keeps the animation looping so that the character is continually animated. The wait blocks function to create small pauses in between the costume switching. If they weren't there, the costumes would be switching so fast that it wouldn't be possible to actually see the animation. The timing of the wait blocks can be tweaked depending on the desired effect, and you don't have to use the forever block, either: It can be swapped out for a "repeat" block **repeat 10** if you only want the animation to repeat a certain number of times.

HOW TO "HIDE" AND "SHOW" SPRITES

Creating a digital story in Scratch, youths will often want to have a character only show up later in the story, as opposed to being visible from the start. Similarly, they'll often want to have certain characters leave after a certain scene, or within a given scene. The "hide" and "show" blocks, found under the looks script category, are essential for accomplishing this.

Their usage, while not immediately intuitive, is fairly simple. Just pair either the "hide" hide or "show" show blocks with an events category block to make a sprite appear or disappear at particular times. For complicated scene changes, we recommend using the "switch backdrop and wait" blocks in combination with hide and show commands. The blocks below, for example, enable a particular sprite to be hidden in the kitchen scene but then to appear in the party-room scene.

when backdrop switches to kitchen ▼
hide

when backdrop switches to party room ▼
show

Example of blocks using hide and show when the backdrop switches.

CREATING STARTING POINTS FOR SPRITES

Like using the hide and show blocks, the idea of establishing consistent starting points for sprites isn't entirely intuitive for youth, but it becomes clear as a need fairly quickly when working with Scratch.

Let's say a youth has a story that involves the Scratch cat saying something to a zebra, and then moving across the screen to say something to a little girl. The youth places all of the blocks in the script areas, positions her cat, zebra, and girl in the desired locations, and then hits the green flag to set everything off. It works perfectly; the cat says something to the zebra, it moves across the screen, and then the cat says something to the girl. The youth is thrilled! But when she clicks the green flag again, the Scratch cat is still over by the girl, not by the zebra. This is because nothing has told the Scratch cat sprite that it should be located in a certain place at the start of the project, so it just starts off wherever it was last located.

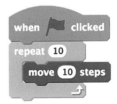

Sample stack of commands without a specified starting point. Each time the green flag is pressed, the sprite will start again wherever it last ended.

Youth will sometimes just drag the sprite back to where it started off, but this is not a sustainable solution, especially if a project has a lot of moving sprites. A simple block combination can sort all this out. Using the green flag event block `when clicked` along with the "go to" motion block `go to x: 0 y: 0` will ensure that the sprites starts off at the same *X, Y* coordinates each time the project is run. To locate the *X* and *Y* coordinates of your sprite, simply open the information about your sprite by clicking on the "i" icon ⓘ, located in the upper left corner of your sprite in the sprite library.

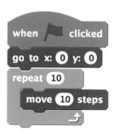

Sample stack of commands with a specified starting point for the sprite by using the `go to x: 0 y: 0` block.

The idea of starting points is also relevant when using the hide and show blocks. It's possible that a certain sprite was visible during the start of a story, and then invisible at the end of the story. In order to make sure that the sprite shows itself again once the story is restarted, youth should create an initial condition using the green flag event block `when clicked` and the "show" motion block `show`. Similarly, a sprite might be visible at the end of the story, but the youth doesn't want it around at the start of the story. A combination of the green flag event block `when clicked` and the "hide" motion block `hide` can take care of this.

GOING DEEPER: INTERACTIVE DIGITAL STORIES

While it's slightly more complicated, one of the wonderful affordances of Scratch is that it allows not only for the creation of simple linear stories that play themselves out the same way each time, but also for *interactive stories* that require input from the "reader." These can be in the form of "Choose Your Own Adventure" stories that involve multiple pathways and endings within the same story, or even small things within an otherwise linear story that asks the reader a question that they need to answer in order for the story to continue.

While we won't go into the nuts and bolts of creating these kinds of stories, certain blocks found in the sensing and operator script categories are particularly useful in order to make these happen. For example, under the sensing category, the "ask and wait" block 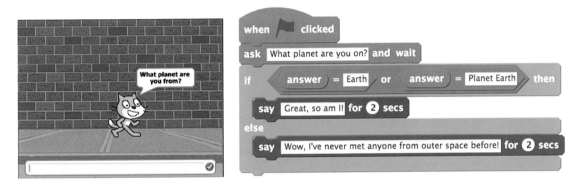 allows the "reader" to be asked a question. This can be paired with a *conditional operator*: something that will only happen depending on if a certain condition is fulfilled. Take a look at the example below, which has the Scratch cat responding differently, depending on the answer the user types, and uses both sensing and operator blocks.

Using operators and sensing to create interactivity in a story.

To create a "Choose Your Own Adventure" story, it's possible to use a combination of sensing blocks and various if/then combinations coming from the control blocks to allow multiple pathways. The example in the script below is very basic, but illustrates how one would approach this kind of interactive story. Depending on what key the user presses, the script will send different broadcasts, which can be linked to various character actions and scene changes.

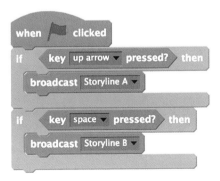

Using conditionals and sensing to create various pathways in a story.

To see more examples of interactive stories and how they're made, go to the Scratch online community on the Scratch website (**scratch.mit.edu**) and check out the stacks of code used in the stories you like. There are also many additional resources found on the Scratch website and ScratchEd community (**scratched.media.mit.edu**). They're all great ways to learn new things!

In addition, there are a host of features to extend youths' creative possibilities in Scratch—ranging from building their own custom Scratch blocks, to using the webcam to detect body movements in the world, to incorporating cloud data into a project (e.g., asking the community to vote on something and having those numbers change something in the project)—among many other possibilities. Guidance for the latest tools and features in Scratch can be found at **scratch.mit.edu/help**.

SUPPORTING YOUTHS' USE OF SCRATCH

Throughout the challenges in this book, youths will mostly learn Scratch by doing, watching, and experimenting, but there are a couple of resources we include to ease and deepen that process.

Scratch "Building Blocks" cards are used to help introduce your youths to the fundamentals of using Scratch to do digital storytelling. You can find them at the end of Design Challenge 1 of this volume. Having a nice selection of the cards available around the room where kids are working can allow easy access and free you from answering the same small questions over and over again, not to mention helping kids who might be too shy to ask for help.

Script Changers Challenge Cards are meant for your kids that want to dive deeper into Scratch. You can find them in Appendix E of this volume. Use these cards to challenge your youths to take their Scratching to the next level! Each of the challenges offers inspiration for open-ended projects and offers hints that will help as kids dive in. Challenge cards can be great for youths who finish in-group projects early, or want to create additional projects outside of meeting time.

USING OTHER STORYTELLING PLATFORMS

While the challenges and resources we offer in this book are oriented specifically to using Scratch as a digital storytelling platform, they can also be adapted for use with a variety of platforms that can support storytelling. For example, instead of creating stories in Scratch, youths might tell stories through creating a podcast or a comic book. In this section, we'll share some possible alternative platforms, as well as some recommendations about what to think about if you do decide to use a different platform.

ALTERNATIVE STORYTELLING FORMS AND PLATFORMS

The number of forms of media and platforms for creating them is proliferating at an amazing rate, allowing so many easily accessible avenues for expression that it's hard to keep track. We offer a list of possible alternative platforms here, but it's by no means exhaustive. If you are considering using other platforms, don't let this list limit you!

- Film/Video

- Storyboards/Dramatization

- Podcasting/Radio/Audio

- Comic book creation (Print or Digital)

- Spoken Word Poetry

- iPad apps like PuppetPals, Toontastic, or other applications

- Blogging

- Photographs accompanied by text or narration

- Multimedia (Powerpoint, Voicethread, HistoryPin, or other interactive multimedia platforms—even simple mashups of audio and photos)

- Good old paper and pen!

When considering other storytelling media and platforms, there are a number of very important questions to consider in terms of adapting the challenges provided in this book. As you consider a platform, ask yourself:

- What do I need to do in order to make sure my youths can effectively express themselves in this platform? What's the learning curve and how can I address that? (For some platforms, youths might already have fluency, but for others they might need to take time to get familiar with the technical aspects of the platform.)

- How much time does the production process take for a given project once youths are conversant with the platform?

- What are a platform's affordances in terms of how it allows youths to share and get feedback on projects they create? Will youths be able to engage in brief pair-and-share feedback structures (a key part of the pedagogical approach taken in design-based learning)?

- What are this platform's capacities in terms of allowing youths to share their work with a broader audience via the web? Are there popular online communities or contexts that allow for easy publication of work?

For any platform that you consider, the answers to these questions will change. Often, it can be helpful to have prior experience with a platform, or conduct some pilot work using the platform with your group to help answer some of these questions before diving into a larger project like those found in *Script Changers*.

DESIGN CHALLENGES OVERVIEW

CONTENTS

DESIGN CHALLENGE 1: GETTING ORIENTED: SCRATCH, SYSTEMS THINKING, AND COMMUNITY-BASED DIGITAL STORYTELLING

Total time: 135 minutes

The goal of this challenge is to briefly orient youths to the idea of systems thinking, the Scratch platform, and how the two will be utilized in the coming challenges to help youths create digital stories about their communities. Youths first engage in an embodied simulation of a paper airplane supply chain—an experience they use to understand some of the basic ideas and language of complex systems. They then consider how community issues might be understood from a systems perspective through briefly looking at the dynamics contributing to homelessness. In the second half of the challenge, the group is introduced to Scratch through a short video and demonstration, followed by the opportunity to view examples of digital storytelling projects from the Scratch community. The challenge closes with group members creating Scratch projects in order to become familiar with some of the core techniques they'll use for digital storytelling.

DESIGN CHALLENGE 2: SYSTEMS, SYSTEMS EVERYWHERE! DIVING INTO SYSTEMS

Total time: 185 minutes

Youths will be introduced to systems thinking concepts through a mini-documentary called *The Story of Electronics*, learning how these concepts relate to communities in general and to their own community specifically. They will then develop a Scratch project that shows a particular function their community performs and the various elements that work together to achieve the goals of that function.

DESIGN CHALLENGE 3: IT'S ALL ABOUT PERSPECTIVE: THINKING BELOW THE WATERLINE ... AND ACROSS THE TABLE

Total time: 365 minutes

This challenge explores how *shifts in perspective* can help us better understand the systems in our world. Learning to understand multiple perspectives—mental models—from various stakeholders is a key habit of a systems thinker. We call this practice "thinking across the table." Youths learn about these mental models by reading the children's novel *A River Ran Wild*, comparing the perspectives present in a commercial for bottled water versus the mini-documentary *The Story of Bottled Water*, and then role-playing various stakeholders involved in an issue in their community. By reading the children's book *Zoom* they look at a system through multiple levels of perspective, understanding that easy-to-spot events are really just the "tip of the iceberg" and are driven by broader patterns, a system's structure, and the mental models of the people involved in the system. We call this practice "thinking below the waterline." As a final project in the challenge, youths will design a Scratch project that explores an issue they're interested in, either through the lens of "thinking across the table" or of "thinking below the waterline."

DESIGN CHALLENGE 4: OUT OF CONTROL: REINFORCING FEEDBACK

Total time: 360 minutes

Reinforcing feedback loops, which often have a "runaway" quality to them, can be an integral part of complex systems. In this challenge, youths will return to the core issue introduced in Design Challenge 1—homelessness—to begin to understand its patterns and why it is so persistent and challenging a problem to resolve. In particular, youths will look for reinforcing patterns that make homelessness a cycle, a reinforcing feedback loop. In order to better understand the idea of reinforcing feedback, youths will explore this core system dynamic through discussion of another children's novel, *The Butter Battle Book*. They'll then use Scratch to model reinforcing feedback loops in the context of homelessness, with the goal of preparing them for a later challenge where they will craft their own story about their community. Additionally, youths will return to the real world to interview another community member as they move toward that final project in Design Challenge 6.

DESIGN CHALLENGE 5: OUT OF BALANCE: BALANCING FEEDBACK AND LEVERAGE POINTS

Total time: 120 minutes

In contrast to *reinforcing* feedback loops, *balancing* feedback loops are processes that bring systems under control and into balance. In this challenge, youths will once again examine the issue of homelessness to explore this concept. They further their understanding of balancing feedback and are introduced to the idea of identifying leverage points by reading the children's short story "The Sneetches." In the final activity youths consider how they might effect maximal change by identifying leverage points in the systems surrounding the issue of homelessness.

DESIGN CHALLENGE 6: MAKE A CHANGE! LEVERAGE POINTS AND UNINTENDED CONSEQUENCES

Total time: ~500 minutes

Understanding the idea of *leverage points*—places where a small change can make a big impact—is critical in order to make effective changes to systems. In this challenge youth explore this concept, as well as the related idea of *unintended consequences*, by reading one more children's novel, *The Lorax,* and identifying possible leverage points in the system of that story. This prepares youths for the final design activity, a Scratch project that depicts using leverage points to make a positive change to a systemic issue in their community.

DESIGN CHALLENGE 1
GETTING ORIENTED: SCRATCH, SYSTEMS THINKING, AND COMMUNITY-BASED DIGITAL STORYTELLING

Total time: 135 minutes

OVERVIEW

The goal of this challenge is to briefly orient youths to the idea of systems thinking, the Scratch platform, and how the two will be utilized in the coming challenges to help youths create digital stories about their communities. Youths first engage in an embodied simulation of a paper airplane supply chain—an experience they use to understand some of the basic ideas and language of complex systems. They then consider how community issues might be understood from a systems perspective through briefly looking at the dynamics contributing to homelessness. In the second half of the challenge, the group members are introduced to Scratch through a short video and demonstration, followed by the opportunity to view examples of digital storytelling projects from the Scratch community. The challenge closes with the group creating Scratch projects in order to become familiar with some of the core techniques the youths will use for digital storytelling.

PRODUCT

Youths will create their first Scratch project as a stepping-stone to more elaborate forms of digital storytelling.

TARGETED SYSTEMS THINKING CONCEPTS

All *systems* are made up of *elements* that form a whole through their *interconnections*, where the whole is always greater than the sum of its parts.

PARTS

PART 1: EMBODYING SYSTEMS: THE PAPER AIRPLANE SUPPLY CHAIN

The group members will collaboratively create a system in the form of a paper airplane supply chain as a means to understand systems concepts in an embodied way, and then discuss the ways that issues in their community might be understood as being part of complex systems.

Time: 45 minutes

PART 2: COMMUNITY ISSUES FROM A SYSTEMS PERSPECTIVE

Following a brief introduction to the language of complex systems in the paper airplane activity, the group will consider how a systems perspective might be applied to a community issue, using homelessness as a grounding example.

Time: 20 minutes

PART 3: SCRATCH INTRODUCTION AND ORIENTATION

The group will be introduced to Scratch via a brief video, and then be given an opportunity to view example stories in the Scratch community.

Time: 30 minutes

PART 4: SCRATCH PROGRAMMING CHALLENGE

Youths will play around with the Scratch platform and practice a technique important to digital storytelling: making two sprites talk with each other. If there's time, the group can modify that project by adding a second scene with new sprites talking to each other.

Time: 40 minutes

KEY DEFINITIONS

SYSTEMS THINKING

Identifying a system. Identifying a system and distinguishing it from other kinds of things that aren't systems. Specifically, a system is a collection of two or more *elements* and processes that *interconnect* to *function* as a whole. The way a system works is not the result of a single part but is produced by the *interaction* among the elements and/ or individual agents within it.

Identifying elements. Identifying the parts of a system that contribute to its functioning.

Identifying behaviors. Identifying the specific actions, roles, or behaviors that an element of a system displays under various conditions.

Identifying interconnections. Identifying the different ways that a system's parts, or elements, interact with each other through their behaviors, and through those interactions, change the behaviors of other elements.

SCRATCH PROGRAMMING

Block. A line of computer code in visual form. You program in Scratch by simply snapping together different types of blocks.

Blocks Palette. Contains all the blocks needed for programming your sprites. Scratch blocks are organized into ten color-coded categories: Motion, Looks, Sound, Pen, Data, Events, Control, Sensing, Operators, and More Blocks. The most frequently used blocks in digital storytelling are the Motion, Looks, Sound, Events, and Control blocks.

Costume. A costume is one of possibly many "frames" of a sprite. Sprites can change their look to any of its costumes. They can be named, edited, created, and deleted, but every sprite must have at least one costume.

Backdrop. *Backdrops* are the images that appear as a background in a Scratch project. All the backdrops are stored in the Stage area.

Script. To tell a sprite what to do, you snap together graphic blocks into stacks, called scripts. When you click on a script, Scratch runs the blocks from the top of the script to the bottom.

Sprite. Objects that perform actions in Scratch. They can serve as characters or items in a digital story, or a wide variety of purposes in a project. All sprites are listed in the bottom left corner of the screen. You can click and edit any of your sprites to change their scripts and costumes.

Stage. Where your sprites move and interact with each other. Just as a sprite can change costumes, the stage can change backdrops.

COMMON CORE STATE STANDARDS COVERED—ENGLISH LANGUAGE ARTS	NEXT GENERATION SCIENCE STANDARDS
• R.6–12.7 (anchor standard)	• 3–5-ETS1–1
• W.6–8.3	• MS-ETS1–1
• W.8.6	
• RST.6–8.3	

MATERIALS OVERVIEW

STUFF TO HAVE HANDY

• Computers for each youth with Internet access and Scratch pre-installed, or accessible via the web (**scratch.mit.edu**)

• Introduction to the Scratch video (**techtv.mit.edu/videos/379-scratch-intro-facilitorial**)

• Sample digital stories studio in Scratch

• Digital projector

• Computer speakers

• ~50–100 sheets of plain 8.5" x 11" paper

• Colored markers (and possibly other art supplies, such as glitter, glitter glue, or puffy paint, at facilitator's discretion)

• Some sort of token that can act as game currency (such as paper circles, buttons, Popsicle sticks—something that can be easily found and distributed as play "wages" for the paper airplane activity)

• Scissors

HANDOUTS

- Scratch "Building Blocks" cards (multiple copies of each to have around the room as youths are working). The cards with asterisks by their name are particularly important in this challenge.

    - Animate It!

    - Glide

    - Broadcast & Receive*

    - Creating a New Sprite*

    - Moving Animation

    - Say Something*

    - Switching Backdrops

    - Hide and Show

OVERALL DESIGN CHALLENGE PREPARATION

- Familiarize yourself with the basics of Scratch described in the "Toolkit" section, especially the section on "How to Coordinate Events" which will help for Part 3 of this challenge.

- Develop a prototype project of the two Scratch programming challenges (making two sprites engage in a conversation and modifying that project to create an additional scene with a new set of sprites engaging in a conversation).

- Prepare computers by making sure they're either loaded with the latest version of Scratch or can access the web-based version of Scratch (both found at scratch.mit.edu).

- Hand out cards so individuals can create and write down usernames and passwords when they save their projects. Store these cards in a central location (or perhaps online.)

- Create or find a studio on the Scratch website that includes examples of digital stories for youths to look to for inspiration. An example with digital stories can be found at scratch.mit.edu/studios/138297.

- Create and print (in color, if possible), the Scratch "Building Blocks" cards. Laminate them for extra durability.

- Start a word wall. This can be helpful for integrating essential vocabulary related to the activities in each challenge. Refer to the vocabulary often and keep the word wall highly visible and clutter-free. Add new vocabulary covered in each unit to the terms already gathered in previous challenges.

PART 1: EMBODYING SYSTEMS: THE PAPER AIRPLANE SUPPLY CHAIN

The group will collaboratively create a system in the form of a paper airplane supply chain as a vehicle for understanding systems concepts in an embodied way. They will then discuss the ways in which their community issues might be understood as parts of complex systems.

Time: 45 minutes

STUFF TO HAVE HANDY

- ~50–100 sheets of plain 8.5″ x 11″ paper
- Colored markers (and possibly other art supplies such as glitter glue, crayons, etc., at facilitator's discretion, used to decorate planes)
- Some sort of token to act as game currency (such as paper circles, buttons, Popsicle sticks—anything that can be easily found and distributed as play "wages" and kept on hand in a big bag)
- Scissors

PLAY: THE PAPER AIRPLANE SUPPLY CHAIN—20 MINUTES

Youths will work within one of the three stations of the supply chain to make it function. They will be paid for their work and receive occasional breaks during which they can spend their wages at the airplane store. The facilitator will act as the "factory boss" throughout. By embodying a system themselves, youths will directly experience how system dynamics form, how systems change over time, and how system elements are deeply interconnected.

10–20 players. For larger groups, create two supply chains, each with about 10–15 players.

SETUP

Set up four stations, each serving as part of a paper airplane supply chain:

1. A *boss station* where the facilitator gives instructions and holds the supplies

2. A *folding station* where the paper airplanes get folded

3. *A design shop* where the folded airplanes get decorated

4. An *airplane store* where the finished products are bought and sold

Station	Role of employees at this station
Boss Station *(Instructor/facilitator)*	This is where the materials (paper, art supplies, and wages) are located, all of which are distributed by the facilitator.
Folding Station *(About 1/3 of the group)*	Youths at this station fold the paper airplanes. They can be subject to various sorts of demands from the "factory boss" at various points (e.g., pressure to speed up production when there's a big inflow of paper resources, to get creative with resources when paper supplies run low, etc.)
Design Shop *(About 1/3 of the group)*	Youths at this station receive folded airplanes from the folding station and are equipped with markers, scissors, and various other supplies for decorating the planes. Just as with paper at the factory station, the shifting amount of art supplies available at a given point in time is controlled by the facilitator.
Airplane Store *(About 1/3 of the group)*	Youths at this station receive completed (decorated and folded) paper airplanes from the decorating station and have to sell the planes to other youths, who buy them with the game currency. Youths at this station should use their judgment to determine the prices, but should be prepared to justify their pricing.

RULES

- Every station must have workers, although the number at each station is up to the facilitator; at some points not as many participants will be at a station, or some stations might not be active, especially at the start of the game. This can highlight how different parts of the system change over time.

- All workers at each station are paid by the factory owner for their work, although the amount paid is regulated by the factory owner, and payment is distributed informally over the course of work.

- Workers must be able to take breaks, during which they can buy paper airplanes. Again, the factory owner can regulate how often breaks occur, and how many workers from each station may take a break at the same time. It's best to keep this informal. Play with giving whole stations their breaks at the same time to have youths see what happens to the system when you do so.

- As the activity unfolds, the facilitator modulates and is able to change the system's dynamics in a variety of ways, for example:

  - Workers might be laid off or given a break just when more paper floods the factory, creating a backlog in the production chain.

  - Some workers might get raises, but also get fewer breaks to spend their money.

  - Art supplies might run out (or be taken from workers by the facilitator to be "saved for later"), just as a lot of folded planes come into the design shop to be decorated.

- All of these events, determined by the facilitator, should not only be visible to the participants, but also be *felt* by them in terms of how they affect what the participants are able to accomplish in the system. This creates an experience and context where clear interconnections, dynamics, and patterns of changes are made clear to youths.

INTRODUCTION

Give the group members a brief overview of the broad idea of the challenges: to begin seeing the world, and especially our communities, as being full of complex systems, and to use digital storytelling in Scratch as a means of making these systems visible, understanding how they work, and figuring out how to change them in positive ways.

Explain that they're going to start with an activity in which they actually create a system themselves.

GAMEPLAY

1. At the start of the activity, explain that today they'll be forming a paper airplane supply chain. See if anyone in the group knows what a *supply chain* is. Explain the overall structure of the game: the various stations and their roles, the role of the facilitator as "factory boss" (feel free to "ham it up," playing the benevolent boss or harsh taskmaster), and how employees will get breaks and wages but could also be re-assigned or even laid off, depending on their performance.

2. Make sure that everyone understands the requirements at each station. In the event that not all youths know how to make a basic paper airplane, do a quick demonstration at the start, or have one of the youths do so.

3. Assign youths to the three stations (folding station, decorating station, and store station). Remember to tell the youths that station assignments may change, so no

one should get too attached! As a modification, let youths choose their own stations; if they end up unevenly distributed, let the activity run as planned but have them see what happens as a result of the uneven distribution of labor. Likewise, ask the youths in each station if they want to spend a minute to plan a strategy for completing their work most efficiently (or even coordinating across stations, if they think of it).

4. Explain that as they participate in the activity, they should keep two questions in mind:

   - How are things interconnected and what sorts of patterns form as a result?

   - How do things change over time in the supply chain?

5. Once everyone is ready, let the supply chain begin! As the role-play proceeds, it's important that the facilitator shifts the quantities of certain elements of the system, including:

   - *Wages* (these can increase or decrease in amount, frequency of distribution, and/or consistency/inconsistency across stations).

   - *Amount of paper* fed into the system over time (play with "flooding" and "draining" the supply, justifying through claims that there are surpluses or shortages in the market for these raw materials).

   - *Amount of art supplies* fed into the system over time (play with "flooding" and "draining" the supply, justifying through claims that there are surpluses or shortages in the market for these raw materials).

   - *Number of workers* at each station.

   - *Frequency of breaks* during which workers can spend their wages.

Note Running this activity well is mostly about actively engaging and tweaking the system so that youths can see how decisions you make as the "boss" affect the way the system plays out and the patterns that form over time. There is no single "right" way for this activity to unfold or an "exact" right way to run it—part of the fun, and part of the lesson, is that it plays out differently every time due to the ways connections and patterns form and groups adapt and use their creativity. Mostly it's important to be attentive, creative, and flexible as the activity unfolds.

MOD THIS ACTIVITY

There are a number of different directions you can take with this activity, depending on the context in which it's going to be used. A couple of easy mods (modifications) are:

- As opposed to having all the participants involved in the various stations of the supply chain, create a "fishbowl" in which a subset of participants (about two-thirds) are working at the stations, with the rest observing and taking notes about what happens to the system as each of the various events occur and how it changes over time. While the observing participants don't get to experience the dynamics themselves, they might be able to more easily observe dynamics since they're not "swept up" in the activity. Adjust the debriefing accordingly.

- Break the participants into 3–4 different supply chains and treat each one differently but in a consistent way within that chain. Shift participants from one supply chain to another so that they can see how the system operates differently when the factory owner treats different elements of the system differently. Adjust the debriefing discussion accordingly.

- Replace paper airplanes with another item that's easy to make quickly, such as greeting cards, if you're worried that participants (younger age groups, perhaps) might be distracted by the paper airplanes and cause a disruption in the space.

- Have certain youths be "assistant managers" in the supply chain, responsible for helping to make decisions about how things operate, as well as for helping to distribute things such as wages, arts supplies, and paper, as these parts of the system change over time.

SHARE: LET'S TALK—25 MINUTES

Following the activity, use this discussion time to orient the participants to the ways that various systems concepts were at play in the activity, particularly attuning them to how the various elements of the system interconnected, what big patterns (or dynamics) formed, and how the system functioned in relation to its goal. The questions in the list below can guide the early part of the discussion:

- What did you think of the activity?

- What do you think the term *systems* has to do with the activity?

- What was one thing in the supply chain that affected something else?

- What were some of the things interconnected in the supply chain? *(Emphasize that there were many different interconnected things in the chain. Some are tangible, such as the amount of different materials like paper or art supplies, the number of workers at a station, or the amount of wages paid. Others are intangible, such as the speed of the airplane folders, the demand for different types of paper airplanes, the creativity of the designers, etc. The most important takeaway is that all of these different elements, and more, are interconnected within the system, with each affecting the others in distinct ways.)*

- Was there anything about these interconnections that surprised you?

- When was the chain was "working" best? When was the opposite true?

- When did the biggest changes happen? What do you think caused these changes?

In the course of the discussion, be sure to introduce four core ideas:

- *System*: a collection of parts, or *elements*, that interact to *function* as a whole, where the whole is always greater than the sum of its parts.

- *Elements*: the individual parts that make up a system. Elements have certain qualities and/or *behaviors* that determine how they relate to other elements, as well as define their role in the system.

- *Behaviors*: the specific ways that elements act within a system.

- *Interconnections*: the different ways that a system's parts, or *elements*, interact with each other through their *behaviors*, and through those interactions, change the behaviors of other elements.

PART 2: COMMUNITY ISSUES FROM A SYSTEMS PERSPECTIVE

Following their brief introduction to the language of complex systems in the paper airplane activity the group will consider how a systems perspective might be applied to a community issue, using homelessness as a grounding example.

Time: 20 minutes

Facilitator's Note   At various points throughout the design challenges, the issue of homelessness is used to ground discussions about systems thinking concepts. The intention is to provide a consistent issue and associated set of ideas that youths can become familiar with and explore from various systems perspectives. We selected homelessness because it's an issue that occurs in many communities, but some facilitators may prefer to substitute a different issue from their community. One consideration when doing so, however, is that for Design Challenges 4 and 5 this alternate issue will need to encompass *reinforcing and balancing feedback loops* and it will require the facilitator to customize background content and context about the issue. Also keep in mind that when involved in the design challenges throughout this book, youths will explore many other issues of their choosing.

1. Review the main points of the airplane activity, reminding the group that a lot of what they'll be doing in the coming design challenges will help them examine community issues from a *systems* perspective. Explain that as a way to get started, they'll talk about the issue of homelessness.

2. Write the word *homelessness* in the center of a chalkboard or whiteboard, and ask if someone in the group can briefly explain what it means to be homeless.

3. Ask how homelessness could be likened to one of those paper airplanes. Building from the group's responses, explain that in the supply chain activity they were able to see how lots of different elements worked together to produce those paper airplanes, and that if they'd just seen the airplanes but not the supply chain in action, it would be difficult to understand the complex processes that produced them. The same is true for homelessness.

4. Ask some initial guiding questions that might get the group to start thinking about homelessness from a systems perspective:

- How does someone become homeless?

- How is someone able to stop being homeless?

- What it might mean to view the issue as something produced through many different sets of interactions? What might be some of the interactions involved in homelessness?

5. Ask the group to brainstorm elements that are involved in, connected to, or that might affect the experience of being homeless. As they share, write the elements up on the board around the word *homelessness*, building a concept web around the topic. Some elements that might be included here are:

- the homeless person
- access to shelter
- access to food
- access to transportation
- access to communication
- mental health
- addiction
- education levels
- familial support/relationships
- amount of time spent being homeless
- gender

- age and ethnicity of the person
- location (urban/rural)
- risk of attack/violence
- laws regarding loitering and panhandling
- interactions with law enforcement and the legal system
- social workers
- shelters
- job training programs
- drug treatment programs

6. Allow about 3–5 minutes for this brainstorming session, and then ask youths to remember their original explanations of what *homelessness* means. Ask volunteers to share if, and in what specific ways, their thinking has changed.

7. Explain that the power of a systems thinking perspective includes how it helps to shift and deepen people's perspectives about how the world works. Throughout these challenges the group will be learning more about how to view the world from a systems perspective.

8. Transition to the next part by reminding group members that they'll be using a computer program called Scratch to tell digital stories about systems in our communities, but first they need to become familiar with what Scratch is and how they can use it.

PART 3: SCRATCH INTRODUCTION AND ORIENTATION

The group will be introduced to Scratch via a brief video, and then be given an opportunity to view already-made stories in the Scratch community.

Time: 30 minutes

STUFF TO HAVE HANDY

- Computers with web browsers bookmarked to **scratch.mit.edu**

- Scratch introductory video URL: **techtv.mit.edu/videos/379-scratch-intro-facilitorial**

- Scratch sample story studio URL: **scratch.mit.edu/studios/138297** (or another one you select prior to the challenge)

- Digital projector

WHAT IS SCRATCH?

Scratch is an exciting new tool and online community used by millions of youths around the globe to create and share their own video games, music, animations, and other forms of digital art. Just like professional artists, youths are combining images, sound, and computer programming to create original, interactive art. Scratch was developed by the MIT Media Lab's Lifelong Kindergarten Group and can be used by youths, educators, and parents for a range of educational and entertainment projects. To learn more about Scratch, consult the Toolkit.

WHAT ARE YOUTHS MAKING WITH SCRATCH?

The projects listed here were created by youths:

Cookie0227Kennedy describes her short film *High School Computers* as an "animation from my social life." Using hand-drawn graphics and a cinematic flair, this programmer transformed her frustration with her school's excessive Internet censoring into a humorous, visually appealing short animation. (**scratch.mit.edu/projects/2652968**)

LilJammerO's remixed music video, *Add yourself riding the Nyan Cat*, recreates the famous Internet meme from 2011 but adds his own character, Lex the Stick Figure, to bounce along atop the cat using custom animation. This project is one of more than 500 "Nyan Cat" remixes where Scratchers add and animate their own characters to ride with Nyan Cat. (**scratch.mit.edu/projects/1781426**)

Two cousins, 8 and 11 years old, collaborated to create their original digital game, Survive the Volcano. Players use the arrow keys to make a hand-drawn dinosaur jump over lava. The game employs commands for movement, score keeping, and a change of "costume" if the dinosaur gets hit by lava. (**scratch.mit.edu/projects/2673605**)

RESEARCH: SCRATCHING THE SURFACE –20 MINUTES

Group members are introduced to Scratch through a brief video and demonstration.

1. Explain that for the remaining activities they'll be using a tool called Scratch to create animations and digital stories about systems that exist in their community.

2. It's often helpful to show an introductory Scratch video like the one found at **techtv.mit.edu/videos/379-scratch-intro-facilitorial**.

3. After watching the video, open Scratch and project it onto a screen that everyone can see easily; move group members close enough to the screen to be able to read text.

4. Conduct a short tutorial by demonstrating how to use Scratch with a sample project. Here's a step-by-step sample, but feel free to adapt it to fit a specific teaching style and/or group abilities.

    a. Note: Be sure to react to questions youths may have when proceeding through this introduction, and if adapting the activity, don't forget to introduce key vocabulary, marked in italics. This type of short introduction will usually be enough to get youths started on their first Scratch projects.

    b. Launch Scratch to see the *stage* with the Scratch cat on it. In the middle of the screen is the programming *blocks palette*. Drag any of the *blocks* in the programming palette into the Scripts area (on the right side of the screen) to begin to program the Scratch cat (or any other sprites; note that any character or object in Scratch is called a *sprite*). Blocks can snap together into stacks, called *scripts*, which tell the sprites what to do.

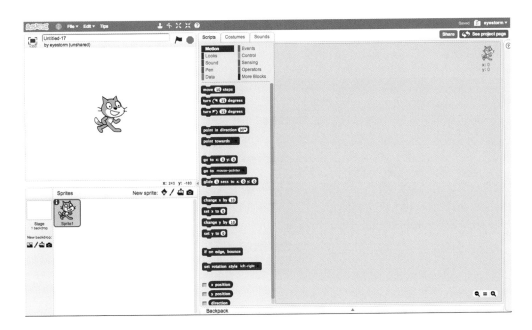

c. Try a block like "move 10 steps" from the motion palette. Then try adding on others like the "turn 15 degrees" block into the scripts area to connect with your first block. The two blocks will snap together to look something like this:

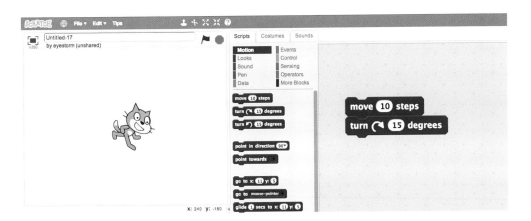

d. Click on the blocks to make the cat move. What happens by continuing to click?

e. Now try to add some of the other kinds of blocks to the script, like Looks or Sound blocks in the Motion category to see what happens. Here's one idea that will change the color of the cat every time the user clicks on a script with the "change color effect by 25" block. What happens to the color of the cat?

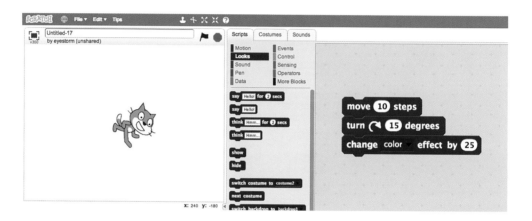

f. Tired of clicking the script to get things started? Click on the Control blocks and try dragging out a "forever" block. Drop it on top of the script to put the old blocks in the mouth of the "forever" block. Now the script will run forever (or at least until the user presses the stop button in the upper right corner)!

g. The user can also start the program by a simple key press, like the space bar or any other key on a keyboard. Try snapping on the "when space key pressed" block, and then press the space key on the keyboard. Now what happens? The cat should spin in a circle and rapidly change colors.

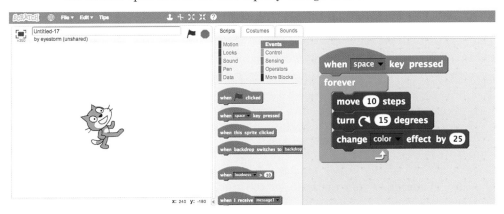

h. Want to add new sprites or change the background for a project? To add new sprites, click on one of the four boxes below the stage to upload a sprite from the library, paint an individual sprite, choose a new sprite from a file on the computer or from the scratch library, or to use the computer's webcam to take a picture for the sprite! To change the background, users can click on the Stage and go to the Backdrops tab to go to the library and then draw or import their own backdrop, or similarly use their computer's webcam.

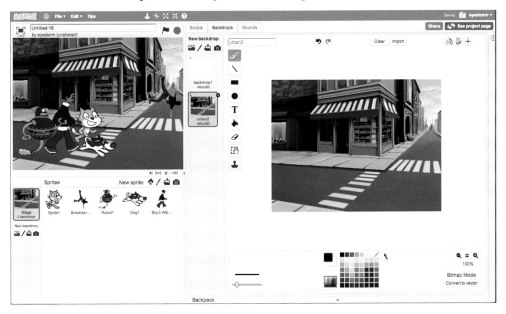

i. Now allow youths to take turns at the projected computer to play with some of these features. Encourage them to think aloud so that others learn from what they are discovering.

PLAY: GETTING TO KNOW SCRATCH STORIES—10 MINUTES

The next part of this activity is designed so that youths have the opportunity to check out existing Scratch stories on their own to see what's possible in Scratch.

1. Direct group members to view a sample stories studio on the Scratch website that were put together or found prior to the challenge. For example, the Scratch development team has created a studio with digital stories; explore those examples at scratch.mit.edu/studios/138297.

2. Encourage youths to pay attention to the project itself but also click the "See Inside" button to view the sprites and Scratch blocks that make up the story. They can even click the "Remix" button to begin to edit the project to make it their own (this function requires that youths have an account created and are able to log into Scratch).

PART 4: SCRATCH PROGRAMMING CHALLENGE

The goal of this part is to allow youths to play around with the Scratch platform and practice a technique important to digital storytelling: making two sprites talk with each other. If there's time, ask the group to modify that project by adding a second scene with new sprites talking to each other.

Time: 40 minutes

STUFF TO HAVE HANDY

- Computers with web browsers bookmarked to **scratch.mit.edu**
- Digital projector

HANDOUTS

- Scratch Building Blocks cards

CREATE: MAKING SPRITES TALK TO EACH OTHER—40 MINUTES

There are two basic skills in creating a story in Scratch: (1) to coordinate events so that they occur in the proper order, and (2) to show sprites thinking or talking through conversation bubbles. In this challenge youths will practice these skills by creating a Scratch project that includes two sprites carrying on a conversation.

VOICES FROM THE FIELD

Youths see that after one action happens, another should react to it. I point out and say, "Awesome, I can tell that you are using systems thinking to make this conversation happen. Let's look at what commands we could use." I think youths have an idea of systems thinking, but when it comes to visually making it happen with Scratch, they need guidance to put what they are thinking into the program.

—JENILYNN REDILA, CHICAGO QUEST

---

1. Explain that the group will be spending time engaging in a Scratch conversation challenge.

2. State the challenge: *Make two sprites have a short conversation with one another.*

3. Pass out the Scratch "Building Blocks" cards to youths or place them around the room. Alert youths that the (a) "Broadcast & Receive," (b) "Creating a New Sprite," and (c) "Say Something" cards will be particularly useful today. Note that individual youths won't need a copy of each card; the cards serve merely as reference materials, available as needed.

4. You may want to model in some way a sample conversation in Scratch (perhaps with a project of your own) or have group members work on a sample group project so they have a better idea of what it might mean for the sprites to "have a conversation."

As an introduction to making a first project, we have often used a "Scratch-go-round" where a large group works on one project. To get started, I usually have the group collectively decide on a simple idea for a project. Then we use and project from one central computer, so that the entire room can see the work as it's evolving. As the instructor, I get the group started by doing one small thing to begin the project. For example, if we were to create a simple dialogue between Jack and Jill in the classic nursery rhyme, I might start by importing a new sprite to be "Jill." As I do so, I use the 'think aloud' technique to articulate my thinking process, saying something like, "Okay, so for this project we're going to need two new sprites, so I'm going to import an image form the Scratch library. [I open the Scratch library and describe what I'm doing.] 'This one looks like a great Jill! Voila! We now have a new sprite! Okay, now it's someone else's turn to contribute to our project." Then I step away and have the next person come up to the computer to add one thing to the process. It's important that each task is nothing large and that youths continue to think aloud as they work—adding one command, importing a sound, changing the color or look of the sprite, and so forth—so that everyone or almost everyone has a chance to try something in front of the group, and everyone benefits from each step. I also try to refrain from giving answers. Rather, I encourage the group to offer suggestions; sometimes there is someone knowledgeable in the audience but oftentimes the group will just make a suggestion based on what they have seen in Scratch so far. If the group truly gets stuck, I offer oral directions to the person at the computer (rather than taking the mouse and doing it myself). This seems to encourage a playful atmosphere where risk taking and tinkering are valued over knowing the solution.

—KYLIE PEPPLER, INDIANA UNIVERSITY'S LEARNING SCIENCES PROGRAM

5. As youths begin to figure out these processes, assist where necessary. Throughout the activity, encourage group members to help each other when they can. In general, try not to "fix" their projects when they can't get them to work; encourage them to try to debug them themselves, trying various techniques to see what works.

6. After all youths have had a chance to get started on their individual projects, ask if anyone has figured out how to make the sprites talk with one another, and if so to share the findings. If youths are working individually or in pairs, have one partner play the project via the digital projector and show the Scratch blocks that make it work. Talk about the strategies that the project used and how the blocks supported that approach.

7. Ask if group members used a different approach. If so, ask those individuals or pairs to share their approach to the group.

8. At the end of the activity, demonstrate via the digital projector how to save projects. The exact manner of doing this will depend on whether group members are using the downloaded or cloud-based version of Scratch. Note that in order to save a project to the website, youths must be logged into a Scratch account.

9. Encourage youths to share or publish their projects in Scratch as often as possible. Let them know that they can continue to edit their project but make sure they understand that sharing is an important part of membership in the Scratch community.

10. At the end of the activity, explain that in the next challenge they will start to explore the idea of systems.

MOD THIS SESSION

Some youths will finish the first programming challenge fairly quickly, or it may be wise for the whole class to spend more time figuring out Scratch techniques. In either case, propose a second challenge:

- Add a new scene to the existing project so that after the first conversation ends, a new set of sprites in a different setting show and have a conversation that's related to the first.

- Essential blocks to complete this challenge that youths likely didn't use in the first challenge would be the "hide" and "show" blocks, along with the "switch to backdrop___" blocks.

A MIDDLE-WAY APPROACH TO SUPPORTING NOVICE SCRATCHERS

As youths begin to figure out the basics of Scratch, one of the often-challenging things for educators is to figure out what kind of support to give them. The level of support can be seen as existing on a spectrum—on one end, having youths rely completely on just messing with the program until stuff starts to click, and on the other end, totally taking over the keyboard the minute a kid asks for help. As with most things, a middle-way approach works best. Obviously, youths are never going to learn to Scratch if every time they hit a bump in the road someone pushes them over it. At the same time, giving no help isn't good either—pointing to resources when they're stuck can help them clear up misunderstandings and help them successfully overcome challenges. When youths are developing their understanding of Scratch as an expressive medium and hit snags in that process, a combination of probing questions, pointing to scaffolds like Scratch "Building Blocks" cards, or even just recommending that they persist for a little bit with figuring things out before asking someone else how to do something can be effective. This leads to good Scratching, and good learning habits in general.

YOUTHS' SAMPLE PROJECTS: FIRST CONVERSATIONS

Conversation between two football players in a sports-themed narrative. User imported personal images into their project. (Credit: by Arturo)

Dialogue between two sprites. (Credit: by Daryl)

A project showing three sprites engaged in a conversation. (Credit: by Tammy)

DESIGN CHALLENGE 1, PART 2:

SCRATCH BUILDING BLOCKS CARDS

HIDE & SHOW

GET READY

Choose at least one sprite

New sprite:

TRY THIS CODE

when b ▸ key pressed
show

when a ▸ key pressed
hide

DO IT

Click the A and B buttons to make your sprite show and hide.

EXTRA TIP

Remember if a sprite is hidden at the end of a program, to add a show block at the beginning so it shows when it plays again.

broadcast Go! ▾

Also, hide and show blocks can be paired with other orange control blocks, like broadcast and receive blocks.

when I receive Go! ▾

Original content provided by the Scratch Team from the MIT Media Lab

---

SCRATCH
HIDE & SHOW

Show and hide a sprite so it only appears when you want

SCENE 1:

SCENE 2:

http://scratch.mit.edu

GET READY

Click to open the sprite library

New sprite:

Choose a sprite that has 2 or more costumes

New costume:
1 parrot-a 171×143
2 parrot-b 132×135

TRY THIS CODE

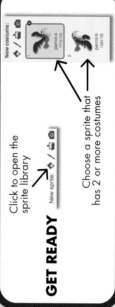

when 🏳 clicked
forever
  next costume
  wait 0.5 secs
  move 5 steps
  if on edge, bounce

EXTRA TIP

Does your sprite look upside-down?
You can change its rotation style

Parrot3

Click the ℹ️

Parrot3
x: 147 y: -60 direction: 90°
rotation style: ↻ ↔ •
can drag in player:
show: ☑

↻ all around
↔ left-right
• don't rotate

SCRATCH
MOVING ANIMATION

Animate a character as it moves

http://scratch.mit.edu

SCRATCH

SWITCHING BACKDROPS

Sometimes when you're telling stories in scratch, you have different scenes and settings in different parts of the story

BACKDROP 1:

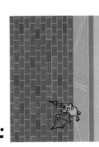

BACKDROP 2:

SWITCHING BACKROUNDS

GET READY

Click on the "stage" area near where the sprites are located

Import or paint a new backdrop

TRY THIS CODE

```
when space ▾ key pressed
next backdrop
```

DO IT

Hit the space bar to change your backdrop!

EXTRA TIP

Different combinations of the orange "when" control blocks and purple "looks" blocks can also make backdrop changes happen!

```
when this sprite clicked
next backdrop
```

```
when clicked
change color ▾ effect by 25
```

```
when I receive Go! ▾
switch backdrop to brick wall1 ▾
```

GLIDE

GET READY

Import a costume or paint your own

Scripts Costumes Sounds

ghost1

New costume:

TRY THIS CODE

Try different numbers

Vertical position

when ⚑ clicked
glide 1 secs to x: 20 y: 80
glide 1 secs to x: 10 y: -20
glide 2 secs to x: -110 y: -110

How long

Horizontal position

DO IT

Click on the geen flag to start

EXTRA TIP

To see a sprite's x and y position

Click the ℹ

Sprites

Ghost1

The x position is shown here

Ghost1
x: 27   y: 20   direction: 90°
rotation style: ↺ ↔ •
can drag in player: ☐
show: ☑

Here are the x and y positions on the stage

x: 0 y: 0

x: -240 y: 180
x: 240 y: 180
x: -240 y: 180
x: 240 y: 180

Original content provided by the Scratch Team from the MIT Media Lab

---

GLIDE

Move smoothly from one point to another

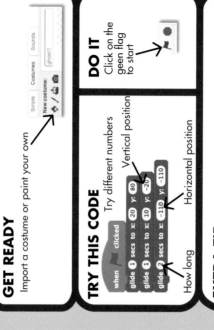

GET READY

Select a sprite

New sprite:

TRY THIS CODE

```
when this sprite clicked
say Hey! I didn't know hippos could fly! for 2 secs
```

EXTRA TIP

Click on the sprite to start

Original content provided by the Scratch Team from the MIT

Media Lab

SCRATCH

SAY SOMETHING

**What do you want
your sprite to say?**

Hey! I didn't know hippos could fly!

http://scratch.mit.edu

TRY THIS CODE

```
when       clicked
say  Hey!!  for  2  secs
broadcast  Say Hi ▾  and wait
```

```
when I receive  Say Hi ▾
say  Hi! How are you?  for  4  secs
```

DO IT

Press the green flag to watch the story unfold!

EXTRA TIP

Use the drop-down menu in the broadcast block to create new commands that can be linked to other scripts. You can also use broadcast blocks to change a sprite's costume, change backdrops, or to start different set of scripts you've set up.

SCRATCH

BROADCAST AND RECEIVE

Use broadcast and receive blocks to make sprites have a conversation

Hey!!

Hi! How are you?

http://scratch.mit.edu

SCRATCH

CREATE A NEW SPRITE

Add any character to your project

http://scratch.mit.edu

CREATE A NEW SPRITE

You can draw your own Sprite

Use a Sprite from the existing library

You can import your favorite pictures, or even use a webcam to create a character!

ANIMATE IT

GET READY

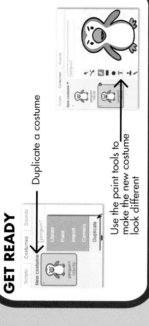

Duplicate a costume

Use the paint tools to make the new costume look different

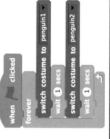

TRY THIS CODE

when ⚑ clicked

forever
  switch costume to penguin1 ▸
  wait 1 secs
  switch costume to penguin2 ▸
  wait 1 secs

DO IT

Click on the geen flag to start

Original content provided by the Scratch Team from the MIT Media Lab

---

SCRATCH
ANIMATE IT

Make a simple animation

http://scratch.mit.edu

USING STORIES TO EXAMINE SYSTEMS

The activities we share in this book all focus on using existing children's stories and the medium of digital storytelling as lenses through which kids can come to describe, understand, design, and intervene within systems. But why *stories* and *storytelling*? There are a number of established ways to engage kids in systems thinking, including mathematical modeling, simulations, and interactive group activities, among others. Stories and storytelling, though, have many unique features that make them effective platforms for exploring systems.

In the introduction to her book about systems thinking and children's stories, *When a Butterfly Sneezes*, Linda Booth Sweeney quotes scientist Fritjof Capra, who shares that "stories ... are the royal road to the study of relationships. What is important in a story, what is true in it, is not the plot, the things, the people in the story, but the relationships between them" (Sweeney 2001). Sweeney's book inspired us to create a set of systems thinking activities that focus on stories, because stories are about connecting parts of wholes and exploring the relationships within them. They're a means to weave together and make meaning across disparate events and factors that affect our lives. Good stories can describe change over time in a way that's compelling, accessible, and memorable. Consider the ways that we described the major concepts associated with systems thinking in the preceding sentences. For each we shared a number of examples, small stories in and of themselves that gave life to otherwise inert concepts in ways that were (hopefully!) meaningful. In our work teaching systems thinking to youths, we have found that stories provide an accessible avenue into a complex world.

We share activities in this book that were inspired by the work that Linda Booth Sweeney did in identifying powerful children's stories across cultures, and we wanted to extend her vision to others. We aimed to create lessons that built on and leveraged those stories to highlight powerful systems thinking ideas and with those powerful ideas in hand, then put kids in the driver's seat as systems storytellers.

Stories offer compelling metaphors and contexts for understanding systems, and putting kids in the storyteller's role means that they are becoming the purveyors of insight themselves. The process of using storytelling to describe systems that kids see in the world provides a means for them to make sense of that world from a systemic standpoint in a familiar format. In addition, as they consider the connections between these stories and the "real world" in which they live, youths can use these stories to advocate for change in the systems most important to them. Research on framing and storytelling around current events shows that stories that holistically approach issues and show how systemic structures are at play are the ones most likely to effect policy and community change (Iyengar, 1991). Part of our hope in using storytelling to learn about systemic issues is that young people will build identities as individuals who don't just understand these issues, but are vocal advocates for them as well.

USE WITH CARE: A POTENTIAL CAUTION IN USING STORIES TO TEACH SYSTEMS

One caution to keep in mind, though, when using stories and storytelling to understand systems, is that sometimes it's easy to miss the forest for the trees. One aspect of stories that makes them powerful—their narrative structure and ability to create rich detail that pulls an audience in—can also be a challenge when it comes to seeing and describing larger systemic patterns at play. People in general, and not just young people, can latch onto small details, characters, and other emotional hooks and sometimes miss the structures present in a story. This is why the role of the facilitator is crucial—to help youths establish some distance from the stories so that they can come to see the systemic connections at play within the reading and storytelling process.

SUPPORTING YOUTH TO TELL STORIES ABOUT SYSTEMS

I write entirely to find out what I'm thinking, what I'm looking at,
what I see, and what it means.

—*Joan Didion*

Script Changers is at its heart about supporting youth to use systems thinking to see, understand, and tell stories about the complexities in their communities. But telling stories about complex systems is no easy task, even for adults. What are the things that we can do to support young people in this process?

A good place to start is to *have youths experiment with writing about and representing systems in low-stakes contexts.* While the long-term idea in *Script Changers* is for youths to write about systemic issues for authentic audiences such as peers and community members, it's important that they have safe spaces to hone their skills before doing so. Throughout the design challenges, after youths read about systemic issues through various stories, there's always some sort of composition exercise where they get to practice representing some of the systems ideas in the story. Often, these are modeling activities such as creating diagrams, but it's possible to add ways for youths to write short vignettes about the systems stories they're reading.

As systems ideas are shared throughout the design challenges, it's always a good idea to *make systems concepts and concrete examples visible in the youths' writing space.* One approach that we've used a lot is to create a "word wall" of important concepts that are discussed throughout the design challenges. Additionally, if you use chart paper for group brainstorms about different issues and what elements connect to them, you can keep these posted around the room. You can also find online the classic poster called "Habits of a Systems Thinker" from the Waters Foundation and put it up in the project room. While doing their own writing, youths can then easily reference the ideas posted in the space to see if they might be applicable in their stories.

When they get started writing their own stories about systems, *have the group members ask themselves some regular systems-oriented questions as part of a prewriting heuristic* to ensure that they're zooming in systemic issues, such as:

- What's the problem or issue they're concerned with?

- What are the "big trends" associated with the issue? How has the issue changed over time?

- What are the key elements of the system? How are they connected to one another?

- What would the community look like if the problem was solved?

- What kinds of changes would make that solution possible?

If you're working with older youths and teens who might be able to think in more nuanced ways about storytelling, *encourage them to think about balancing* episodic *storytelling with* thematic *storytelling.* The process of *episodic storytelling* focuses almost exclusively on stories about individuals who are encountering challenges. The challenges might be the result of systems out of balance, but usually the structures and patterns leading to those challenges are invisible in episodic storytelling. The result is that readers often end up blaming the individual or believing that dealing with the problem is just up to those affected by it. *Thematic storytelling* aims to make visible the structures and patterns that lead to events, and those tend to focus less on an individual encountering a problem and more on the context behind that problem and the ways it manifests for many people. Thematic stories are always "thinking below the waterline"— beyond the most visible events in a system—to focus on what led to those events. Combining episodic and thematic storytelling often allows readers to empathize with sympathetic characters that embody what it means to encounter a systemic problem in a personal way, but also provides the bigger picture that led to the individual episode.

You can look to most of the mentor texts that we include in the design challenges as good examples of stories that combine episodic and thematic approaches. Think of *The Lorax*: it creates a compelling narrative around the individual characters of the Once-ler and the Lorax, but it uses these characters as a means of revealing all of the structural issues and effects involved in the kind of environmental degradation that can happen when natural resources are viewed from an exploitative, rather than interdependent, perspective. This kind of combined approach generally results in stories that are more likely to have readers engage in advocacy around systemic problems.

So, to wrap up, it's always good to keep these strategies handy as kids tell stories about systems:

- Create low-stakes contexts where youths can experiment with this sort of writing before they share it publicly.

- Make systems thinking concepts and examples visible in youths' writing spaces through things like word walls or posters.

- Have youths ask themselves a regular set of systems-oriented questions in their pre-write phase to make sure that their drafting is connecting to systems ideas.

- Encourage youths to think about balancing *episodic* storytelling that focuses only on characters with *thematic* storytelling that focuses on structures and patterns that drive systems.

Telling stories about systems is a tall task, but with these strategies in mind, kids are able to create narratives that are both powerful and revealing.

DESIGN CHALLENGE 2
SYSTEMS, SYSTEMS EVERYWHERE!
DIVING INTO SYSTEMS

Total time: 185 minutes

OVERVIEW

Youths will be introduced to systems thinking concepts through a mini-documentary, *The Story of Electronics*, learning how these concepts relate to communities in general and to their own community specifically. They will then develop a Scratch project that shows a particular function their community performs and the various elements that work together to achieve the goals of that function.

PRODUCT

Youths will create a Scratch project that explores how one *function* of their community is carried out, illustrating how various *elements* of the community are *interconnected* in ways that help to achieve the *goal* of that function, or possibly in ways that prevent that goal from being achieved.

TARGETED SYSTEMS THINKING CONCEPTS

All systems are made up of elements that interact to function as a whole, where the whole is always greater than the sum of its parts. The structure of a system determines how its parts form interconnections and broader patterns of *system dynamics*. Sometimes a system functions in a way that aligns with the goals people have for that system, but sometimes it doesn't. It's often hard to see whether a system is working in the ways we want unless we look at a system with an appropriate *time horizon* and incorporate *time delays* into the ways we think about systems.

PARTS

PART 1: DIVING INTO SYSTEMS: THE STORY OF ELECTRONICS

Youths are introduced to more of the core ideas concerning systems and the big idea of this module: seeing their local community as a system, identifying points where change might occur, and making digital stories in Scratch about how to bring about each change.

Time: 45 minutes

PART 2: COMMUNITIES AS SYSTEMS

Drawing on the conversations and ideas about systems that youths engaged within the context of *The Story of Electronics* and the paper airplane supply chain activity (Design Challenge 1), the group members will begin to apply systems thinking to their local community. They will identify various systems in their community, the systems' individual parts, what goal the systems are trying to meet, and how well the systems are functioning to meet that goal.

Time: 50 minutes

PART 3: SCRATCH DESIGN CHALLENGE: SYSTEMS IN MY COMMUNITY

Youths choose one goal of a system in their community, and create a Scratch project about it. In the project, they describe what things (elements) are connected to or affect this goal, and how they might help or hinder in achieving this goal.

Time: 90 minutes

KEY DEFINITIONS

Identify the way a system is functioning. The *function* of a system describes the overall behavior of the system—what it is doing or where it's going over time. A system's function might emerge naturally based on interconnections among elements, or it might be the result of an intentional design. Regardless, the function of a system is the result of the dynamics that occur among interconnected elements.

Distinguishing the goal of a system. The *goal* of the system is what a system was intentionally designed is to do. Sometimes this might be the same as the function of the system … other times the goal and the function are not aligned.

Nested systems. Systems that are a smaller part of other systems. Almost all systems are nested within larger systems. With nested systems, a larger system will affect the way that a subsystem behaves, and the subsystem will affect the way that the larger system behaves. The nature of systems as nested within one another means that it's usually possible to zoom in or out of systems in order to see systems that are either around them (if those systems are bigger) or within them (if those systems are smaller).

Time delays. The time lag between an action in a system and the evidence of its effects.

Time horizons. The overall period of time that you look at something in order to understand it.

OTHER ESSENTIAL VOCABULARY

- Identifying systems
- Identifying elements
- Identifying behaviors
- Identifying interconnections

COMMON CORE STATE STANDARDS COVERED—ENGLISH LANGUAGE ARTS	NEXT GENERATION SCIENCE STANDARDS
• R.6–12.7 (anchor standard)	• 3–5-ETS1–1
• RI.7.3	• MS-ETS1–1
• W.6–12.2 (anchor standard)	• MS-ETS1–4
• W.8.6	• MS-ESS3–3
• W.6–12.7 (anchor standard)	
• RST.6–8.3	
• RST.6–8.7	
• SL.7.2	
• SL.6–12.4 (anchor standard)	

MATERIALS OVERVIEW

STUFF TO HAVE HANDY

- A computer for each person with Internet access, as well as Scratch pre-installed or accessible via the web (**scratch.mit.edu**)

- *The Story of Electronics* video, found at:

  - Web version: **storyofstuff.org/movies/story-of-electronics**

  - Download link: **storyofstuff.org/wp-content/uploads/movies/Story%20of%20Electronics.zip**

- Digital projector

- Computer speakers

- Chart paper (optional)

- Markers (optional)

HANDOUTS

- "Finding Systems in Our Community"

- "Mission: Community Member Interview"

- "Telling Stories about Systems: Key Questions"

HOW FAMILIAR ARE YOUR YOUTHS WITH SCRATCH?

As you start this design challenge, assess how competent and confident you think your group is with the Scratch platform. Depending on how Design Challenge 1 went, you may want to integrate some open-ended Scratch design sessions throughout this challenge, so that all participants are well prepared for the final culminating project.

PART 1: DIVING INTO SYSTEMS: *THE STORY OF ELECTRONICS*

Youths are introduced to more of the core ideas concerning systems and the big idea of this module—seeing their local community as a system, identifying points where change might occur, and making digital stories in Scratch about how to bring about that change.

Time: 45 minutes

STUFF TO HAVE HANDY

- *The Story of Electronics* video, found at:
  - Web version: **storyofstuff.org/movies/story-of-electronics**
  - Download link: **storyofstuff.org/wp-content/uploads/movies/Story %20of%20Electronics.zip**
  - Computer & Digital Projector
- Chart paper and markers (optional)

RESEARCH: *THE STORY OF ELECTRONICS*—25 MINUTES

In this part of the challenge, group members extend and deepen their understanding of core systems thinking concepts and how they are at play in community contexts by watching and discussing *The Story of Electronics*.

VOICES FROM THE FIELD

The great thing about using a video clip like *The Story of Electronics* is that it provides an immediate connection with youth and is also a springboard for them to explore other possibilities they may not have considered before. This video gave youth a quick introduction to what systems are and how elements within a system create problems which need a solution.

—TRINA WILLIAMS, GREAT BEAR WRITING PROJECT

1. Take time to watch *The Story of Electronics* video (8 minutes).

2. Conduct a debriefing conversation about the video by asking questions such as the following:

   - What did you think of the video?

   - What do you think the concept of "systems" has to do with the video? (*It might help to locate and freeze the video at the point—about 75 seconds into the story—where the narrator describes what "designed for the dump" means, and showing the line of buildings with labels:* extraction, production, distribution, consumption, *and* disposal. *Use the graphic to guide discussion about the formation of the system.*)

   - What was one thing in the video that affected something else?

   - What were the different things that were connected to electronics in the video? (*Emphasize that electronics were connected to all kinds of things in the story like the consumer, the toxins, the designers ... the electronics didn't exist in a vacuum.*)

   - Was there anything about these different connections that surprised you?

3. During the conversation, at an appropriate moment, reintroduce the core systems concepts (system, elements, behaviors, and interconnections), and add a couple to the list: *system function* and *system goal*. Note that *there will be other opportunities later in the challenge to introduce and define some of this vocabulary, so it is not necessary to cover all of them at this point.*

    - *System*: a collection of parts, or *elements*, that interact to *function* as a whole, where the whole is always greater than the sum of its parts.

    - *Elements*: the individual parts that make up a system. Elements have certain qualities and/or *behaviors* that determine how they relate to other elements, as well as define their role in the system.

    - *Behaviors*: the specific ways that elements act within a system.

    - *Interconnections*: the different ways that a system's parts, or elements, interact with each other through their behaviors, and through those interactions, change the behaviors of other elements.

    - System *function*: the overall behavior of the system—what it is doing or where it's going over time. A system function might emerge naturally based on interconnections among elements, or it might be the result of an intentional design (in which case, we might also call refer to the function of a system as its goal).

    - System *goal*: what a system that was intentionally designed is intended to do.

4. Explain that a system is made up of interconnected parts (elements) and that we can't understand a system by examining only one individual part. Instead, to understand a system you must look at how all parts are connected to one another in unique ways and what it is they all work together to achieve, intentionally or not.

5. Ask group members if they see any systems at play in the video. For example, the electronics themselves are systems, but they're nested within a larger system of a consumption-oriented economy, which is itself nested within a larger system of the earth's environment. If your youths are older or more advanced, you may want to add in the terminology of *nested systems*.

    - *Nested systems* are a smaller part of other systems. Almost all systems are nested within larger systems. With nested systems, a larger system will affect the way a subsystem behaves, and the subsystem will affect the way the larger system behaves. The nature of systems as nested within one another means that it's usually possible to zoom in or out of systems in order to see systems that are either around them (if those systems are bigger) or within them (if those systems are smaller).

- If the group seems ready for this level of conversation, explore how each of those nested systems has unique goals that are coming into conflict, causing the systems to be out of balance.

IMAGINE: MAPPING *THE STORY OF ELECTRONICS* — 20 MINUTES

The group brainstorms elements of the system described in *The Story of Electronics* video. This serves to model the kind of brainstorming/diagramming of system elements and behaviors that will occur throughout the course of the module.

1. Mention again that systems have many parts—called elements—which are interconnected with one another in unique ways, and that a key role of the systems thinker is to make sense of those interconnections. Explain that group members will be using a technique called a "connection circle" to help figure out those connections.

2. Brainstorm with group members all the elements of the system they can think of that are associated with electronics in the video. Record them for everyone to see

(i.e., on a chalk or whiteboard, chart paper, or via the digital projector). Examples of elements include the use of the "design for the dump" technique, the amount of profits, the companies' growth, the amount of toxins or pollutants in the environment, the consumer demand, health of foreign workers, and so on.

TIPS FOR BRAINSTORMING ELEMENTS

Make sure youths avoid identifying only concrete elements (like profits, or amount of electronics) but also consider nontangible elements (like consumer demand or desire for profits), as they are also important elements driving how a system functions.

Also, the most important elements in a system are often the ones that change over time, usually because they're the ones that are connected to one another and to the main issues or problems going on in a system. For instance, in the case of *The Story of Electronics*, the amount of pollution in the air increased as consumers threw away more electronics, and the amount of new electronics consumers bought went up as the ease of repairing electronics went down. So when you brainstorm elements, try to focus on the elements that are centrally connected to an issue or problem and that change over time.

---

3. After the group has brainstormed a good number of elements for this system, draw a big circle on the board, and have the group members choose what they think are the most important elements in the system. Use the Connection Circle Technique to help them make visible the interconnections between elements in the system. See "Tools for Making Systems Visible" (p. 143) for a full explanation of how to facilitate the connection circles technique.

4. Here's an example of what a connection circle for *The Story of Electronics* might look like:

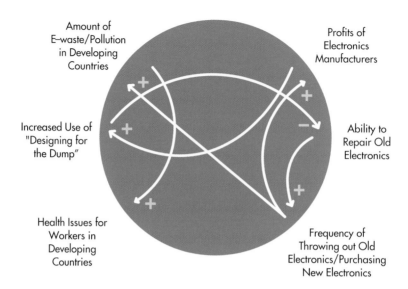

Amount of E–waste/Pollution in Developing Countries

Profits of Electronics Manufacturers

Increased Use of "Designing for the Dump"

Ability to Repair Old Electronics

Health Issues for Workers in Developing Countries

Frequency of Throwing out Old Electronics/Purchasing New Electronics

5. As group members create the connection circle, focus on having them deliberate and discuss their theories for what is causing what in the system; this sense-making process, rather than a rapid review of the connections, is the most powerful part of the connection circle tool.

6. As an option, you might introduce two additional systems concepts at this point: time horizons and time delays. Ask the group if there were any important things that happened in the system, but took a while to show their effects. A good example here is the relationship between the decreasing ability to repair electronics and the eventual effects on health for workers in developing countries. Explain that a common phenomenon in systems is called a time delay:

- *Time delays*: the time lag between an action in a system and the evidence of its effects. Because of time delays the "time window" through which we look at a system, be it a week, a month, a year, or even longer, has a major effect on what we think is going on in that system. That time window is called a time horizon:

- *Time horizons*: the overall period of time that you look at something in order to understand it. Ask group members if they can think of situations where, if you just looked at things for a short period of time, you'd miss the "big picture" and possibly miss something important that happened.

7. To close the overall activity, prompt the youths to think about examples of other systems that have many interconnected parts. They've thought about homelessness, and now manufacturing, from the standpoint of complex systems; where else are systems present in our world? Some examples to share here might be economies, large companies, ecosystems, the human body, schools, transportation systems, computers, political systems, the global climate system and, of course, local communities.

8. Explain that many of our world's problems, like the one they saw in *The Story of Electronics*, are a result of systems that are *out of balance*, and that is one of the reasons it's becoming more and more important to look at the world like a systems thinker.

PART 2: COMMUNITIES AS SYSTEMS

Drawing on the conversations and ideas about systems that youths engaged within the context of *The Story of Electronics*, the group will begin to apply systems thinking to the local community. Youths will identify various systems in their community, the parts they're made up of, what goal they're trying to achieve, and how well the systems are functioning to meet that goal.

Time: 50 minutes

STUFF TO HAVE HANDY

- Digital projector
- Chart paper and markers

HANDOUTS

- "Finding Systems in Our Community"

RESEARCH: BIG IDEA OF THE PROJECT—5 MINUTES

In this next part of the design challenge, the group moves more deeply into the big idea of the full curriculum: looking at our local community as a system and attempting to find ways to positively influence that system.

1. Reintroduce the big ideas of *Script Changers*: the group members will be looking at the local community as a system, identifying issues in the community that arise because of the ways these systems are structured and interact, finding ways to change those systems, and creating digital stories in Scratch about that investigation.

2. Explain that throughout their design process, they will talk to people in their community to find out more about the community and what people think might need changing.

IMAGINE: SYSTEMS IN OUR COMMUNITY—30 MINUTES

Through brainstorming and conversation, youths will begin to see how various goals are met, or not, by systems that exist in their community. In the process, they come to distinguish a designed system's goal from how it's actually working—the way it's functioning.

1. Explain that the first step in thinking about systems within communities is to figure out the goals of the designed systems in a community, and whether or not the way those systems are actually functioning is meeting those goals. The next step is to identify interacting elements in a given system within a community and whether those elements interconnect with one another to help achieve those goals.

2. Brainstorm with the group the goals of different systems in their communities, recording these on a large sheet of chart paper. Examples can include: educating people, creating jobs, keeping community members safe, providing housing and shelter, helping people get from one place to another, and providing sources of entertainment and recreation. Encourage youths to think broadly; list every goal they can think of that a community might try to achieve!

3. Once you have a long list, pick *one* goal, and briefly identify different elements of a community that help to achieve it. You can use the a whiteboard or another sheet of chart paper to create a concept map, writing the goal in the center and listing around it the elements that affect it. **Note:** To control this discussion, it's easier to focus on only one goal. For example:

- *Housing and shelter* are provided through the interactions of real estate developers, landlords, the amount of available land, construction companies / contractors, governmental housing programs, community boards that deal with zoning laws, and so on.

- *Education* might be achieved through a combination of available schools and associated school boards, state and federal policies that govern the schools, parent/teacher associations, libraries, museums, afterschool clubs, children, teachers, youth workers, and more.

4. After the activity, post the sheet of chart paper on which you listed the community goals somewhere in the space. Youth will return to this list as a reference throughout the unit.

IMAGINE AND PLAY: INTERCONNECTION IN OUR COMMUNITY—15 MINUTES

Using the "Finding Systems in Our Community" handout and working in small groups, youth will identify a goal in their community and explore how various different elements are connected to it and work together in order to achieve it, or fail to do so.

1. Break up into small groups of two or three.

2. Distribute the "Finding Systems in our Community" handout.

3. Instruct each group to come up with a goal that their community achieves (or maybe that it doesn't, but they believe it should), one that hasn't been deeply explored yet in the previous discussion. Refer to the chart-paper list posted in the space for ideas.

4. Ask for a volunteer to share one of the goals that their group came up with and how various elements interconnect in order to achieve that goal.

WHAT TO EXPECT

This is not an exhaustive list, but rather an overall sense of the ways that youths who are new to these ideas might think about them, as opposed to those who have had opportunities to think about these ideas in more depth. Note that moving from novice to expert is a process, so it's possible that group members will not be complete "novices" or "experts."

	Novice	Expert
Understanding community (questions 1 and 2)	• Struggles to identify a goal that a community might have. • Unsure how to identify the elements that work together to realize a goal OR identifies elements but doesn't talk about why those elements are relevant.	• Identifies goal (or multiple goals) and can explain how they impact (or why they are important to) a community. • Understands which elements contribute to the achievement of that goal. • Is able to explain how those elements might connect with one another.
Systems thinking concepts (questions 3 and 4)	• Thinks causally (rather than interactively) about elements (if you want bullying to stop, suspend the bullies from school). • Believes that the only way to reach the overall goal or changing the system is to make major changes in the ways elements interconnect, rather than small changes that can have big systemic effects. • Doesn't understand how elements of the system interact.	• Sees the overall system as being based on interactions among elements … so changing one element only changes the system's ability to achieve its goal to the extent that it impacts the interconnections with other elements. • Recognizes that sometimes a small change to an element can make a significant impact on the overall behavior of the system. • Can describe how elements of the system interact and impact one another.

DESIGN CHALLENGE 2, PART 2

FINDING SYSTEMS IN OUR COMMUNITY

1. What goal of your community are you addressing?

2. What are the different parts of your community (the elements) that interconnect in order to achieve that goal?

3. How do those elements interact with one another in order to achieve that goal? Describe in words *and* pictures. Consider using a connection-circle diagram to illustrate the interconnections.

4. What would happen to the goal if one of the elements disappeared? Give one example.

PART 3: SCRATCH DESIGN CHALLENGE

Youths choose one goal that exists in their community, and create a Scratch project about it. In the project, they describe what things (elements) are connected to or affect this goal, as well as how those elements either help or hinder the achievement of the goal.

Time: 90 minutes

STUFF TO HAVE HANDY

- Computers with web browsers bookmarked to **scratch.mit.edu**
- Digital projector

HANDOUTS

- "Mission: Community Member Interview"
- "Telling Stories about Systems: Key Questions"

CREATE AND PLAY: INTERCONNECTIONS—60 MINUTES

Youths are given the design challenge of creating a Scratch project that explores how one *goal* of their community is carried out, illustrating how various *elements* of the community are *interconnected* in ways that either help or hinder the achievement of the goal.

1. Explain that for the next hour, they'll be doing a Scratch Design Challenge. The challenge (which you might write on chart paper and hang on a wall for continual reference) is: *Create a project or story that explores one goal that your community carries out, or fails to carry out, that you think is important. The project or story should show how different elements of the community are connected to this goal, and how those elements either help or hinder the achievement of the goal.*

2. Let youths know that they may explore a goal that they came up with in their small groups or come up with something new.

3. Distribute the "Telling Stories about Systems Handout," which contains general questions to guide the design of the project. Make sure that Scratch Building Blocks cards are available if needed. Encourage youths to assist each other in Scratch as they work through their designs.

4. At the end of the design period, remind youths to save often, and encourage them to publish their project online in the Scratch community if they feel that it's ready

for public viewing. Encourage youths to continue to revise and improve their project if they don't feel like it's ready to share more broadly.

SHARE—25 MINUTES

Use the digital projector to share individuals' projects to discuss as a whole group.

1. Ask for volunteers who are willing to share their Scratch projects with the group on the digital projector (either by connecting the volunteer's computer to the projector, by putting the project on a flash drive and transferring to a computer already connected to the projector, or by some other means).

2. As youths are sharing, encourage them to explain (if it's not evident in the project) the ways in which the project illustrates how one goal of their community is achieved (or not) through the interaction of various parts of the community.

SAMPLE PROJECTS: COMMUNITY INTERCONNECTIONS

This selection of projects seek to illustrate how different elements in a community are coordinated to either accomplish or prevent the achievement of a community's goal.

The design of this story highlights several relationships among elements in a community: people in the community, the trash on the ground, and the animals. The story is intended to illustrate the interconnections between these elements and the consequences of littering. (Credit: by Jeffrey)

This story highlights the relationships among elements in a community: people in the community, communal or private property, and health. The story is intended to illustrate the interconnections between these elements and the consequences of how new housing developments create adverse health effects.

This story highlights relationships when things are working together well in a community. In this example the people in the community come together to share information about a local crime and decide to report the information to the police. The story is intended to illustrate the interconnections between these elements and the positive consequences of working together as a team.

RESEARCH: TONIGHT'S MISSION: COMMUNITY MEMBER INTERVIEW—5 MINUTES

Youths are given the mission of interviewing a member of their community to start to get a feel for the issues facing the community. They will use this information in further investigations in future challenges.

1. Explain that everyone will have a mission tonight (or at another specified non-meeting time) to interview a member of their community (this could be a parent or guardian, a local shopkeeper, a neighbor, etc.) about five things:

    • How the community has changed over time in positive ways.

    • How the community has changed over time in negative ways.

    • What they think the most important parts (elements) of the community are and how these parts are connected to one another.

    • What they think are good goals for the community, or the purposes that the community should serve.

    • What they think are the most important issues, challenges, or opportunities facing the community.

2. Hand out the "Mission: Community Member Interview" sheet, explaining that they can record the answers to their interview there.

DESIGN CHALLENGE 2, PART 3

TELLING STORIES ABOUT SYSTEMS: KEY QUESTIONS

As you draft and create your stories, keep these questions in mind to make sure that you're thinking about things from a systems perspective:

- What's the problem or issue you're concerned with?

- What are the "big trends" associated with the issue? How has the issue changed over time?

- What are the key elements of the system? How are they connected to one another?

- What would the community look like if the problem was solved?

- What kinds of changes would make that solution possible?

DESIGN CHALLENGE 2, PART 3

MISSION: COMMUNITY MEMBER INTERVIEW

Name: _____

Date: _____

Instructions: Your mission is to go into your community and talk to people to find out more about it and what people think might need changing. Interview a member of your community (this could be parent, a local shopkeeper, a neighbor, etc.), focusing on these five questions. Use the back (or a separate sheet of paper) if you need more room for notes.

NAME AND TITLE OF THE COMMUNITY MEMBER YOU INTERVIEWED:

- How has the community changed over time in positive ways?

- How has the community changed over time in negative ways?

- What are the most important parts (elements) of the community, and how are these parts connected to one another?

- What are good goals for the community, or the purposes that it should serve?

- What are the most important issues, challenges, or opportunities facing this community?

DESIGN CHALLENGE 3
IT'S ALL ABOUT PERSPECTIVE: THINKING BELOW THE WATERLINE ... AND ACROSS THE TABLE

Total time: 405 minutes

OVERVIEW

This challenge explores how *shifts in perspective* can help us better understand the systems in our world. Learning to understand multiple perspectives—mental models—from various stakeholders is a key habit of a systems thinker. We call this practice "thinking across the table." Youths learn about these by reading the children's novel *A River Ran Wild,* comparing the perspectives present in a commercial for bottled water versus the mini-documentary *The Story of Bottled Water*, and then by role-playing various stakeholders involved in an issue in their community. By reading the children's book *Zoom* they look at a system through multiple levels of perspective, understanding that easy-to-spot events are really just the "tip of the iceberg" and are driven by broader patterns, a system's structure, and the mental models of the people involved in the system. We call this practice "thinking below the waterline." As a final project in the challenge, youths will design a Scratch project that explores an issue they're interested in, either through the lens of "thinking across the table" or of "thinking below the waterline."

PRODUCT

Youths produce a skit in the form of a role-play to display the mental models of various stakeholders associated with an issue.

Youths create a Scratch project that explores a given issue by first "thinking across the table" (showing how different stakeholders think about and relate to that issue), then by "thinking below the waterline" (showing how events, patterns, system structures, and mental models are interconnected in that issue).

TARGETED SYSTEMS THINKING CONCEPTS

Systems thinkers work differently by shifting their perspective on situations. They learn to consider the *mental models*, or sets of ideas and assumptions, held by stakeholders involved in a system (perspective taking, or "thinking across the table"). And they examine, test, revise, or even discard their own mental models by looking at a system from multiple *levels of perspective* ("thinking below the waterline").

PARTS

PART 1: THINKING ACROSS THE TABLE

Youths consider the ways that an individual's mental model shapes how he or she behaves in a system and how that behavior affects it. The idea of mental models is explored through watching and discussing a commercial for bottled water and then contrasting it with the mini-documentary *The Story of Bottled Water*, highlighting very different perspectives on an everyday issue.

Time: 45 minutes

PART 2: OUR COMMUNITY, FROM MULTIPLE PERSPECTIVES

The group will explore one issue that arose in their interviews with community members (conducted at the end of Design Challenge 2) through writing and performing a skit that illustrates how various *stakeholders* involved in that issue might view it and what different mental models of the issue might look like depending on where someone stands in relation to an issue.

Time: 130 minutes

PART 3: SCRATCH DESIGN CHALLENGE: ALL ABOUT PERSPECTIVE

Youths create the first scene of a Scratch project that explores a given issue through "thinking across the table," demonstrating how different stakeholders might think about and relate to that issue.

Time: 100 minutes

PART 4: THINKING BELOW THE WATERLINE

Youths are introduced to levels of perspective that shape the way that we look at issues by reading and discussing the children's book *Zoom*. After the reading the book, the group discusses the metaphor of the iceberg, which is used to illustrate different levels of perspective they can take when looking at systems: events (which are the most visible), patterns (recurring sets of events), structures (ways the elements are set up in a system which give rise to regular patterns), and mental models (which shape systems structures).

Time: 20 minutes

PART 5: SCRATCH DESIGN CHALLENGE—ALL ABOUT PERSPECTIVE (CONTINUED)

Youths continue the Scratch project from Part 3, adding a new scene that enriches their story by "thinking below the waterline." In this process, youths will aim to show how events, patterns, structures, and mental models are interconnected in their story.

Time: 110 minutes

KEY DEFINITIONS

Mental model. An evolving set of ideas and assumptions about a system and how it works. Consciously or not, people use their mental models of how a system works when they decide how they're going to act in a system. When someone's mental model changes, the ways that they relate to and act within systems change with them. From a systems perspective, mental models are important because any "map" we create of a complex system is essentially a map of our mental models. The more clarified our mental models, the closer to reality (that is, the closer to representing a complex set of interconnections) the map will be.

Considering how mental models shape action in a system. The ability to consider the assumptions, ideas, and intentions that a given actor might have in relation to a system, and how these affect that actor's behavior within the system. Mental models are often correct about what elements are included in a system, but frequently draw wrong conclusions about a system's overall behavior.

Looking at a system from multiple perspectives. The ability to understand that different actors in a system will have different mental models of the system and consider each of these perspectives when engaging in action within a system. This is also called "thinking across the table."

Considering multiple levels of perspective. The ability to move fluidly between different levels of perspective within a system, from events, to patterns to system structures, to mental models. The most visible level of systems is *events,* visible instances of elements interacting in a system. Using the metaphor of a system as an iceberg, events are "above the waterline"—they're easy to see. When we start to think "below the waterline," we start to see three other levels of perspective: *patterns* (recurring sets of events), *structures* (ways the elements are set up in a system which give rise to regular patterns) and *mental models* (which shape systems structures.) Switching between different levels of perspective when looking at a system deepens understanding of how a system operates.

Considering the role of system structure. Understanding how a system's *elements* are set up in relation to one another gives insight into the *behavior* of a component. A system's structure affects the behaviors of its elements and the overall *dynamics* and *functioning* of a system. For instance, how a city's highway system is structured affects overall traffic patterns and car movement within it. Being able to see a system's structure gives insights into the mechanisms and relationships that are at the core of a system, which can be leveraged to create systemic changes.

OTHER ESSENTIAL VOCABULARY

- Behaviors
- Elements
- Interconnections
- Stakeholders
- Patterns

COMMON CORE STATE STANDARDS COVERED—ENGLISH LANGUAGE ARTS	NEXT GENERATION SCIENCE STANDARDS
• R.6–12.3 (anchor standard)	• 3–5-ETS1–1
• R.6–12.7 (anchor standard)	• 3–5-ETS1–2
• RI.7.3	• MS-ETS1–1
• W.6–12.2 (anchor standard)	• MS-ETS1–2
• W.8.6	• MS-ETS1–4
• W.6–12.7 (anchor standard)	• MS-ESS3–3
• W.6–12.9 (anchor standard)	
• RST.6–8.3	
• RST.6–8.7	
• SL.7.2	
• SL.6–12.4 (anchor standard)	
• SL.7.5	
• WHST.6–8.7	

MATERIALS OVERVIEW

STUFF TO HAVE HANDY

- Homework from Design Challenge 2 ("Telling Stories about Systems: Key Questions" handout)

- "Stakeholder Skit Planning Worksheet"

- A computer for each youth with Internet access and Scratch pre-installed, or accessible via the web (scratch.mit.edu)

- Digital projector

- Computer speakers

- Copies of the children's book *Zoom* (Ideally one for each group member, but fewer copies can be shared in pairs or one copy read to the whole group)

- Blank sheets of paper

- Scratch Cards

- Commercial for Poland Spring bottled water: www.youtube.com/watch?v= A3uDEnk2QpU

- *The Story of Bottled Water* video, found at:

  - storyofstuff.org/movies/story-of-bottled-water

  - storyofstuff.org/wp-content/uploads/movies/SoBW-167MB.mov .zip (available for download)

Additional items to have available include (optional):

- Chart paper

- Chalkboard or whiteboard

- Markers

- Sticky notes

- Colored stickers

HANDOUTS

- "Stakeholder Skit Planning"

- "The Iceberg: Looking below the Waterline"

OVERALL CHALLENGE PREPARATION

- Familiarize yourself with the various resources associated with the challenge, including the Poland Spring commercial, *The Story of Bottled Water,* and *Zoom.*

- Preload a computer with the links to the Poland Spring commercial and *The Story of Bottled Water.*

PART 1: THINKING ACROSS THE TABLE

Youths consider the ways that an individual's mental model shapes how he or she behaves in a system and how that behavior affects it. The idea of mental models is explored through watching and discussing a commercial for bottled water and then contrasting it with the mini-documentary *The Story of Bottled Water*, highlighting very different perspectives on an everyday issue.

Time: 45 minutes

STUFF TO HAVE HANDY

- Computer with Internet access
- Digital projector
- Computer speakers
- Blank sheets of paper
- Chart paper and markers (optional)

RESEARCH: THINKING ACROSS THE TABLE—DIFFERENT PERSPECTIVES ON BOTTLED WATER—45 MINUTES

In this activity, youths explore what it means to understand an issue through multiple perspectives by watching a commercial for bottled water and a mini-documentary that refutes the benefits of bottled water, and then contrasting the mental models behind each.

1. Open the activity by asking if anyone in the group has ever had bottled water. (In all likelihood most of them have.)

2. Ask what the reasons are for drinking bottled water versus tap water. Responses might include thirst, convenience, taste, or health benefits.

3. Watch the Poland Spring commercial for bottled water (~30 seconds): www.youtube.com/watch?v=A3uDEnk2QpU.

4. Open a discussion about the commercial, focusing on how group members might view the act of drinking bottled water from a systems perspective. Introduce the idea of a *mental model* (i.e., a set of assumptions, priorities, and mindsets), and how the ways they *think about a system* can dramatically change the kinds of actions they take in it. As you discuss what sorts of things might be interconnected

in this process, begin creating a list on a whiteboard, chalkboard, or chart paper. The following questions can guide the discussion:

- What's the main message of the commercial?

- If you were going to think about bottled water just from the information in the commercial, who and what would be involved in the "system" of bottled water? What would the elements be? (e.g., *the person drinking the water, the water itself, desire for water / thirst, the water source, the company bottling the water, the bottle*).

- What would be the most important interconnections? (e.g., *the water gets consumed by the person drinking the water, the company gets the water from the water source and then bottles it, the bottle carries the water, the water source provides the water*).

5. Explain how you're going to show a short video that might provide different perspective on bottled water. Encourage group members to look particularly for anything they might add to their mental model of what's involved in bottled water. Watch *The Story of Bottled Water* (8 minutes, **storyofstuff.org/movies/story-of-bottled-water**).

6. Follow up with a discussion that focuses on how the video changes and deepens the perspective on the issue by looking at where the water in bottled water actually comes from, what is involved in the production process, how demand is "manufactured," and the impacts of bottled water. The following questions can help guide discussion:

    -   What did you think of the video?

    -   Was there anything that was surprising in the video?

    -   After watching the video, do you think we should add anything new to the mental model we created about drinking water? (*Potential things to include could be: oil for making the bottles, which adds to energy usage involved; the tap water sources that often taste better but are getting underfunded; landfills where the empty bottles go, advertising that manufactures demand, the ocean where many bottles end up, local water sources that get polluted by water manufacturing plants, etc.*)

    -   After watching the video, did anything change in the way you think about the act of drinking bottled water?

    -   What do you think the differences are in the mental models of the people who created *The Story of Bottled Water* and the people who created the commercial? Did they have the same view of the system? Did they have the same priorities in the system?

7. Close the discussion by emphasizing that systems thinkers may form better mental models by "thinking across the table." When we think across the table, we aim to understand how different people involved in a system see that system, what their assumptions are, what their priorities are, and how they might act in a system as a result. If we can have a good sense of the stakeholders' perspectives and how they might act, we can make better decisions about how to push that system in a positive direction. The more we think across the table, the better we'll be able to think about a system.

PART 2: OUR COMMUNITY, FROM MULTIPLE PERSPECTIVES

The group will explore one issue that arose in their interviews with community members (conducted at the end of Design Challenge 2) through writing and performing a skit that illustrates how various *stakeholders* involved in that issue might view it and what different mental models of the issue might look like depending on where someone stands in relation to an issue.

Time: 130 minutes

STUFF TO HAVE HANDY

- Homework from Design Challenge 2
- Sticky notes and colored stickers (optional)
- Whiteboard and markers (optional)

HANDOUTS

- "Stakeholder Skit Planning"

OVERVIEW

This activity involves the following sequence of activities:

- Sharing issues from youths' interviews
- Selecting one issue on which to focus the role-play
- Brainstorming the key stakeholders associated with the issue
- Breaking into teams that will role-play the different stakeholders' perspectives
- Researching the issue from the viewpoint of the group's stakeholder
- Conducting the role-play
- Debriefing the role-play
- Considering with the group what it would look like to view the issue from a systems perspective

Note This activity will vary according to the unique perspectives of the stakeholders chosen. As the process unfolds, have youths adapt and focus on concepts and related issues that emerge from the way the stakeholders interact. This will focus attention on mental models and the assumptions that perspectives force upon various stakeholders.

IMAGINE: SELECTING AN ISSUE AND BRAINSTORMING STAKEHOLDERS—25 MINUTES

In this activity group members are introduced to the overall community role-play activity. Following that, they share some of the community issues they encountered when they interviewed community members. From this collective list, they then vote to explore one issue through a role-play. Once group members have selected an issue, they brainstorm the stakeholders that are connected to the issue.

1. Share with the group members that they'll be doing a community role-play around an issue that came up in their interviews from Design Challenge 2, and briefly overview what to expect in the activity (sharing from the interviews, voting on an issue, researching that issue, doing the role-play, debriefing).

2. Ask for volunteers to share what issues came up during their interviews with community members. It can be useful to have youths focus on the questions that dealt with how the community has changed over time in negative ways and assess the most important issues, challenges, and opportunities the community faces.

3. As the issues are shared, post them on a board or chart paper.

4. Once a good number of issues are up on the board, conduct an informal vote to determine which issue the group would like to focus on for the role-play. This can involve multiple rounds of voting, with "finalists" that the group narrows down until a consensus is reached. Alternatively, you can create a simple bar graph by asking individuals to place a sticky note above the issue they are most interested in. The issue with the most notes wins.

5. When the issue is selected, create a concept web by writing the issue in the middle of the board or chart paper and brainstorming people or groups who might be interested in or connected to that issue, writing their names around it. Explain that these people are called *stakeholders* because they hold a "stake" or personal interest in the issue in some way. While obviously every issue is different, likely stakeholder categories might include governmental representatives or regulatory actors, private industry in the form of large or small business, community groups

such as parents or nonprofit organizations, political parties, public services (law enforcement, education, etc.). A given issue might involve multiple stakeholders in each of these categories, each with different interests.

RESEARCH: ISSUE INVESTIGATION AND RESEARCH—45 MINUTES

In this activity, groups select stakeholders to research online, paying particular attention to the ways that the stakeholder might hold a particular mental model, or set of assumptions, about the issue. **Note:** Prior to this activity, determine which of the stakeholders will be most productive to focus on for the role-play. Ideally, all groups should work on a stakeholder who has a large "stake" in the issue. Depending on how familiar you are with the issue, it can be helpful to conduct your own research in order to facilitate this set of activities ahead of time. It's also important for youths to explore topics that are personally meaningful to them. If some youths feel strongly about a different issue that wasn't the center of the discussion in earlier parts of this challenge, allow them to focus on a different issue in their story.

1. From the list of stakeholders that were brainstormed in the last activity, help the group to select the most important ones, those most connected to the issue. Then create teams of 3–5 members, with each team focusing on a different stakeholder.

2. Explain that during this research period, each of the teams should investigate the issue from the perspective of the stakeholder they will be representing, focusing on the mental model that those stakeholders might have in relation to the issue. To help youths focus their research efforts, post the following guiding questions or turn these into a handout that team members can reference:

   • Who is your stakeholder, and what stake does that person or entity hold in the issue? Why does your stakeholder care about this issue?

   • What goals do you think this stakeholder has?

   • What kinds of assumptions does your stakeholder have when it comes to the issue?

   • What elements of the issue are either unknown or unimportant to your stakeholder? (In other words, what kinds of things might be *missing* from the stakeholder's mental model?)

   • If your stakeholder were explaining the issue to someone, what approach do you think the stakeholder would take? What kinds of things would the stakeholder focus on, and what kinds things would the stakeholder explain? What *wouldn't* the stakeholder say?

   • How do you think your stakeholder views some of the other stakeholders? What kinds of relationships does your stakeholder have with others?

3. Have teams conduct research on the Internet, helping them to think about what sources would most likely contain information about the issue (e.g., local news sites, community discussion boards). **Note:** Teams can share computers depending on what you think would be most productive for your group.

4. Encourage teams to take notes about the issue in general and this stakeholder's role in it specifically.

CREATE: COMMUNITY ISSUE ROLE-PLAY—30 MINUTES

In this activity, the stakeholder teams share out their research findings in the form of a role-play that evidences how their group thinks about the issue and what's important to them in terms of the issue.

1. Inform the group members that during this activity they'll be working in their teams to turn what they've uncovered in their research into a small role-play presentation that will be brief, entertaining, and informative for the rest of the group.

2. Explain that each team will have 30 minutes to come up with a skit of about three minutes, during which team members help the audience understand: (a) something about the systemic nature of the issue, and (b) the role their stakeholder has in it. Have groups leverage the "Stakeholder Skit Planning" worksheet to help them map out their skits.

3. As the teams plan, encourage them to make sure that their role-play is informative, but also give these tips to make their skits entertaining:

   • Ham it up! Get into characters, and give them personalities that might fit with their role and their point of view on the issue.

   • Remember that not all characters need to speak in the skit—some group members can play inanimate objects, forces of nature, and so on. *But* each member must be knowledgeable about the stakeholder, as there will be a round of audience questions at the end of each skit!

   • Try to identify types of language that say something memorable about their stakeholder group or about their attitude toward the issue.

SHARE: PERFORM THE COMMUNITY ISSUE ROLE-PLAY—30 MINUTES

In this activity, the teams perform their skits and debrief what they learned, both as actors and audience.

1. Have each team present its skit. Keep an eye on the clock; you may need to cut a team short if it goes too far beyond the three-minute limit.

2. At the end of each role-play, ask each team to field questions from the other stakeholder groups, staying "in character" (look for fun ways to get the "inanimate" objects involved in this question session, too!). Add your own questions to help guide this discussion.

3. Once all skits have been performed, open up a discussion to the group, focusing first on getting general reactions to the activity and what differences people noticed in terms of the ways different stakeholders related to the issue. The following questions can guide the discussion:

   • What was it like to try to "get inside the head" of your stakeholder?

- Were there any big differences between the ways the stakeholders thought about the issue?

- Did any of the stakeholders have a specific goal that they're trying to achieve on this issue?

- Did any of the different stakeholders hold similar mental models? If so, why do you think that is?

WHAT TO EXPECT—COMMUNITY ISSUE ROLE-PLAY

You can use a combination of the skits themselves as well as the skit-planning sheet to infer how well youths are engaging with systems thinking concepts and practices using the rubric below. This is not an exhaustive list, but rather an overall sense of the ways that youths who are new to these ideas might think about them, as opposed to those who have had opportunities to think about these ideas in more depth. Note that moving from novice to expert is a process, so it's possible that they will not be complete "novices" or "experts."

	Novice	Expert
Systems thinking concepts	• Struggles to identify a particular stakeholder group that holds a perspective on the issue. • Unable to identify stakeholder's priorities in relation to an issue. • Conveys the community issue in a simplistic, rather than, systemic, way. • Doesn't understand how elements in the system connected to the issue interact.	• Identifies a clear stakeholder group in relation the community issue identified. • Able to clearly articulate the stakeholder group's priorities in relation to the issue. • Explores how their stakeholder group might relate to another stakeholder group. • Presents the overall system related to the issue as being based on interactions among elements … so changing one element only changes the system's ability to achieve its goal to the extent that it impacts the interconnections with other elements. • Can describe how elements of the system interact and impact one another.

CHALLENGE 3, PART 2:
STAKEHOLDER SKIT PLANNING

In order to create a short skit about various perspectives on a community issue, take a moment to "get inside the head" of your particular stakeholder. Consider how you can use your research to teach the audience (a) something about the systemic nature of the issue and (b) the role your stakeholder has in it.

1. What is the community issue being addressed in your skit?

2. Which stakeholder are you representing?

3. What is your stakeholder's general relationship to the issue? What's that person or entity's "stake" in it?

4. From your stakeholder's perspective, what is the root cause of the issue?

5. From your stakeholder's perspective, what are some good next steps to either help solve the issue or make sure things stay exactly as they are?

6. Where and when will your skit take place (present-day or as an event in the past that laid the foundation for the current community issue)?

7. Besides the main stakeholder, what other characters will appear in your skit? Why are you including them?

8. What does your stakeholder think about some of the other characters?

9. What events will happen in your skit? How will your stakeholder or the other characters react to them? What do their reactions tell the audience about the issue and each character?

10. On the back of this paper, draft your script: a short dialogue and actions that will take place during the beginning, middle, and end of the skit as well as who is playing what role.

PART 3: SCRATCH DESIGN CHALLENGE: ALL ABOUT PERSPECTIVE

Youths create the first scene of a Scratch project that explores a given issue through "thinking across the table," demonstrating how different stakeholders might think about and relate to that issue.

Time: 100 minutes

STUFF TO HAVE HANDY

- Digital projector
- Scratch cards
- Internet-connected computers with Scratch pre-loaded or accessible via the web

IMAGINE: DIGITALLY DRAMATIZING AN ISSUE—5 MINUTES

Youths will use their stakeholder skits from Part 2 to guide the design of the first scene of a digital story in Scratch. **Note:** Depending on the size of your group and the number of available computers, youths can work in small groups of 2–3 or individually.

1. Outline the general guidelines for their Scratch project: Group members will translate their skits from the previous part of the challenge into a Scratch project. Engage youths in a discussion about how a digital story might differ from a live dramatization of the same topic. What can they do in a digital story that is impossible in a live skit?

2. Individually or in small groups, have youths brainstorm what techniques in Scratch they'll need to employ for the characters, setting, dialogue, and actions.

CREATE: INITIAL DESIGN PERIOD—75 MINUTES

Youths begin the preliminary programming work on the first scene of their Scratch project.

1. Let youths know that they'll have an initial period of 75 minutes to program their designed scene in Scratch. At the end of the 75-minute design period there will be a peer feedback session.

2. Monitor the youths closely as they work in Scratch. Keep an eye out for any who seem to be spending too much time on some tasks—such as creating elaborate

sprites, sounds, or backgrounds—as some youths focus on these specifics to the point that they aren't able to complete the assigned task. **Note:** If you feel it might help, create a timetable for specific task benchmarks (e.g., 5 minutes for choosing character sprites, 5 minutes to select a background, 40 minutes to program conversations).

SHARE: PAIR, SHARE, AND FEEDBACK ON FIRST DRAFTS—20 MINUTES

Youths work in pairs to give each other feedback.

1. Have the group work in pairs to take turns sharing their projects. Ask partners to make sure to give both "warm and cool" feedback (see the Introduction to this volume). The feedback generally begins with a few minutes of warm feedback, which may include comments about how the work presented seemed to meet the desired goals. Then it moves on to a few minutes of cool feedback, sometimes phrased in the form of reflective questions. Cool feedback may include possible disconnects, gaps, or problems that youths see in their peers' projects. Often during this time, ideas or suggestions for strengthening the work are presented.

2. Instruct partners to pay particular attention to how well the project:

   • Holds together as a narrative (look for interesting dialogues and actions.

   • Demonstrates "thinking across the table").

   • Shows good Scratch programming technique (comment on how the project uses Scratch blocks to help tell a story). Offer technical assistance, advice, or support if your partner asks for it.

3. After 10 minutes, have pairs reverse roles so that each has the opportunity to give and receive feedback on this first scene.

VOICES FROM THE FIELD

The youths eventually began to see that if the elements were not connected, the system could not operate in the manner in which it was made to operate. Their projects began to demonstrate that understanding clearly and powerfully. It is a great idea to encourage the youths to try new things in Scratch. Some thought that when things didn't work well, that they made a mistake, but they were encouraged to see these "mistakes" as being creative. One student confided in me that he liked Scratch, but he didn't like making mistakes. I told him that these are great learning opportunities.

—JANIE BROWN, GREAT BEAR WRITING PROJECT

SAMPLE PROJECT: GRAPPLING WITH MULTIPLE PERSPECTIVES (SCENE 1)

The story depicts a new big-box business opening up in a small town. This first scene gives multiple views of the situation. Depicted here, the local business owner on the left is considering dropping prices to match those of the big business. Others in the local community are excited for the discounts and to have a large store like SaveSmart in their local community.

PART 4: THINKING BELOW THE WATERLINE

Through reading and discussing the children's book *Zoom*, youths are introduced to the idea of *levels of perspective* shaping the way that we look at issues. After the reading the book, the group discusses the metaphor of the iceberg, which is used to illustrate different levels of perspective they can take when looking at systems: events (which are the most visible), patterns (recurring sets of events), structures (ways the elements are set up in a system, which give rise to regular patterns) and mental models (which shape system structures).

Time: 20 minutes

STUFF TO HAVE HANDY

- Copies of the children's book *Zoom* (ideally one for each group member, but fewer copies can be shared in pairs or one copy read to the whole group)
- Blank sheets of paper
- Scratch cards
- Chart paper and markers (optional)

HANDOUTS

- "The Iceberg: Looking below the Waterline"

RESEARCH: READING *ZOOM*—IT'S ALL IN HOW YOU LOOK AT IT!—20 MINUTES

In this activity youths read the book *Zoom* and are introduced to the idea of *levels of perspective* when looking at a system and how different levels can change our understanding of how a system works.

1. Share the text-free picture book *Zoom*, which uses pictures to demonstrate how your understanding of a thing changes as you change your perspective. **Note:** The way you share the book with youths will depend on the number of copies you have available, but make sure everyone understands how each new picture alters their perceptions of what they are looking at.

2. Have a short discussion about the book. The following questions can be used to guide the discussion:

    - What pattern did you notice in the book? (*Encourage and explore answers that focus on the way that each scene was embedded in larger scenes, and that what the reader saw in each scene was never the full picture.*)

- Did you change the way you thought about one of the scenes in the book when you saw that it was part of a larger scene?

- What do you think the book is saying about the way that we look at things?

- Have you ever looked at a situation, and seen it in a certain light, and then later realized that you didn't have the "full picture"?

3. Introduce the idea of *levels of perspective*, and how a person's point of view can often shift between different levels in order to gain greater insight into a system. Every system can be viewed from different levels. The most visible level is the level of *events*—visible instances of elements interacting in a system.

4. Post or project the iceberg image on "The Iceberg: Looking below the Waterline" handout as you explain how the iceberg can serve as a metaphor for a system:

- Events are "above the waterline"; they're easy to spot.

- But looking deeper, you could say that we're looking "below the waterline," noticing other levels of perspective: *patterns* (recurring sets of events), *structures* (ways the elements are set up in a system, which give rise to regular patterns), and *mental models* (which shape systems structures).

- Switching between different levels of perspective when looking at a system deepens understanding of how a system operates.

DESIGN CHALLENGE 3, PART 4

THE ICEBERG
Looking below the Waterline

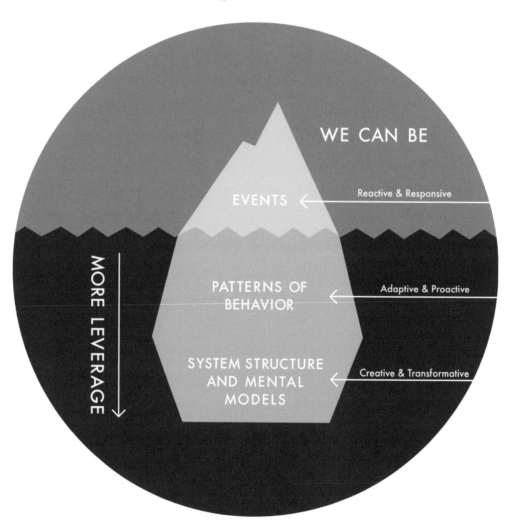

PART 5: SCRATCH DESIGN CHALLENGE: ALL ABOUT PERSPECTIVE (CONTINUED)

Youths continue the Scratch project from part 3, adding a new scene that enriches their story by "thinking below the waterline." In this process, youths will aim to show how events, patterns, structures, and mental models are interconnected in their story.

Time: 110 minutes

STUFF TO HAVE HANDY

- Digital projector
- Internet-connected computers with Scratch pre-loaded or accessible via the web

IMAGINE: "ZOOMING OUT / ZOOMING IN" ON THE STORY—10 MINUTES

Youths will brainstorm a second scene of the digital story they began in part 3 of this challenge, based on their new understanding about "thinking below the waterline" of an issue. In this new scene, they are required to show how events, patterns, system structures, and mental models are interconnected in that issue.

1. Brainstorm how *events*, *patterns*, and *system structures* can be illustrated in a digital story. What are some examples that they've seen represented in books, plays, television shows, or movies?

2. Individually or in small groups, have youths sketch out what they want to happen in the next scene of their digital story if they "zoom out" or "zoom in" to a story, including events, setting, and dialogue. If they need help getting started, have them consider the following questions:

    - What are the key events that happen when looking at this issue?
    - What patterns drive those events?
    - Are there ways that things are structured so that those patterns happen regularly?
    - What mindset led to the structures that are in place around the issue?

DIGITAL STORYTELLING SUGGESTION

Suggest that youths use a narrator—a sprite in the corner of the screen with a thought bubble, or simply a box with text in the top or bottom of the screen, comic-book style—for plot points that may be difficult to convey in dialogue or action.

ITERATE AND PUBLISH—75 MINUTES

During this design period, youths take into account the feedback they received in the previous session and use it to inform the way they build out the next scene of their story. If time permits, they can even make changes to their first scene. The "Scene Change" Scratch card may prove particularly useful for the creation of a second scene in the digital story.

1. Remind youths to consider incorporating the feedback they previously received into their projects. Point out that this *iterative* process of drafting, getting feedback, and revising based on that feedback is how most if not all authors, game designers, and artists work.

2. Let them know that they'll have another 75 minutes to work on their projects until the group share-out at the end of the day.

3. At the end of the iteration period, encourage youths to share their project on the Scratch website if they feel like it's ready to be shared with a broader audience.

SHARE: GROUP SHARE-OUT—25 MINUTES

Youths publicly share their Scratch stories, explaining them for the group.

1. Once the design period is complete, ask for volunteers who are willing to share their Scratch projects with the group via the digital projector (by connecting their computers to the projector, by putting the projects on a flash drive and loading onto a computer already connected to the projector, by navigating to it as published on the Scratch website, or by some other means).

2. As youths share, encourage them to explain (if it's not evident in the project), how the project illustrates ideas around "thinking across the table" and "thinking below the waterline," what their inspiration for the project was, and what challenges they encountered during the design process.

SAMPLE PROJECT: ZOOMING IN OR ZOOMING OUT IN THE STORY (SCENE 2)

Scene 2 of this story builds on the first scene about a big business entering a small town, but "zooms out" to a different level of perspective (in this case the viewpoint of the corporate headquarters). In this case, the large-scale corporation is pleased to be saving average citizens money on groceries and prescriptions that they can then use for other purposes. Other viewpoints could be explored in additional scenes, such as the impact on local customers, the impact on local shop owners, or the impact on the business economy of the small town.

INTRODUCTION AND TOOLS FOR THE ADVANCED DESIGN CHALLENGES

Up to this point, your youths have gone through activities that help them get a handle on Scratch as a storytelling tool (Design Challenge 1), understand the basic concepts associated with systems thinking (Design Challenge 2), and take on some of the habits of mind associated with systems thinkers (Design Challenge 3). In the second half of the design challenges, youths dive more deeply into the process of understanding *systems dynamics*, that is, how systems change over time and the sorts of patterns that involves. To help them in this complex process, we introduce a new set of analytic tools that help to make it a lot easier. We used one of these in a limited way in Design Challenge 2. In this section, we take you through the system modeling techniques of *connections circle and causal loop diagrams*, central approaches used in the latter set of challenges for making systems visible.

TOOLS FOR MAKING SYSTEMS VISIBLE: CONNECTIONS CIRCLE AND CAUSAL LOOP DIAGRAMS

As they author their own systems stories, youths delve deeply into examples of systems to begin to understand how they operate. As this process evolves, they engage in activities that help them develop the systems thinking skill of *making systems visible* for themselves and others. In doing so, they gain a greater sense of how these systems work, what the connections are within them, and how they unfold over time. Within the context of Design Challenges 4 through 6, we use a number of tried-and-true tools, beyond general discussion, to uncover the systems at play in stories and communities. Specifically, we look to *connection circle diagrams* and *causal loop diagrams*. Each of these tools helps to attune youths' existing mental model to include increasingly specific patterns and relationships that drive the way a system is functioning.

In this section, we'll be describing the specifics of how these two inquiry tools work and the way they relate to one another. There are times where it makes sense to use just one of these tools in the course of analyzing a system, and times where both can be helpful. When you come across a place in the coming design challenges where we suggest the use of these tools, refer back to this section and adapt each tool to the specific context at hand within the challenge.

CONNECTION CIRCLE DIAGRAMS

Connection Circles, a tool developed by Rob Quaden and Alan Ticotsky, is an approach to analyzing systems that focuses on mapping the causal relationships within a system. The process of using this visual tool allows youths to more easily see the dynamics that are driving a system, especially *feedback loops*.

At first glance the tool can look a little complicated, but once you get going with it, it's actually pretty easy to pick up. Let's use "The Sneetches," Dr. Seuss's short story that we'll read in Design Challenge 5, as an example of how it looks in practice.

First, a quick overview of what happens in "The Sneetches." The story centers on the theme of prejudice, and how in-groups and out-groups get maintained through consumerism. Some "Sneetches" have stars on their bellies, which they decide is a good reason to exclude the "Plain-Belly" Sneetches from their fun activities. These Plain-Belly Sneetches consequently feel bad. Seeing an opportunity, an entrepreneur named Sylvester McMonkey McBean creates a machine that adds stars to Sneetches' bellies, which he proceeds to successfully market and sell to the Plain-Belly Sneetches. With the Plain-Belly Sneetches no longer so plain-bellied, the original Star-Belly Sneetches need a new way to tell who's who in order to know which Sneetches should actually be coming to their exclusive social events. Lo and behold, McBean has another machine to *remove* stars from bellies. The story proceeds with each of the groups going back and forth between having stars on their bellies and not, and McBean walks away with a pretty penny out of the deal. Eventually, the two groups of Sneetches get completely confused as to who's who, and come to realize that it makes more sense to live together peacefully rather than play the in-group/out-group game, which has only served to part them from their money.

So, after the youths in your group read the story and you've talked about the big trends and relationships that are going on in the story, shift into the connection circle activity. The discussion of big trends and what elements in the story change over time allows kids to focus on *what* happened, and the connection circle aims to help them unpack *why* it happened. It makes visible the causal chains that led to the overall *patterns* in the story.

Below we outline the basic steps to conducting the connection circle, adapted from the original in Rob Quaden and Alan Ticotsky's book *The Shape of Change.* The tool can of course be adapted in a number of ways, and we'll describe some of those after we go over the basics.

1. Start by drawing a nice big circle on the board.

2. Have youths in your group brainstorm *elements* that they saw changing (increasing or decreasing) over time in the story that relate to the core issue or problem.

Note The main criteria of what to list are *things that can increase or decrease.* For example, some elements might be tangible and visible (like the numbers of various Sneetches in each group that have stars, or McBean's profits), and others might be intangible but still important (like Plain-Belly Sneetches' desire to participate, and the Star-Belly Sneetches' desire for exclusivity). No matter what, these should be things that are nouns or noun phrases.

3. Once you have a good number of elements, maybe 5–10, write these brainstormed elements around the outside of the circle. Here's a sample of what this might look like:

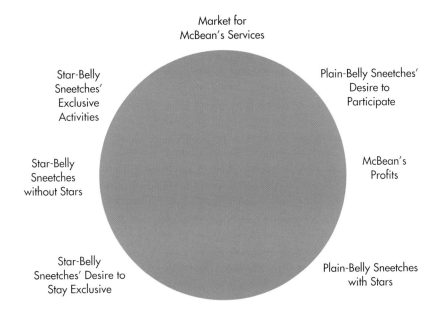

4. Once the elements are identified, work with your group to start to draw connections between them, specifically *connecting one element that causes another element to increase or decrease*. This is the substance of the activity:

- If something causes another thing to increase, draw an arrow from it (to indicate the causal direction) and a *plus sign* trailing the head of that arrow (to indicate that it caused an increase).

- If a change in one element causes another to decrease, put a *minus sign* near the head of the arrow instead.

An initial pathway from the above circle could look like this:

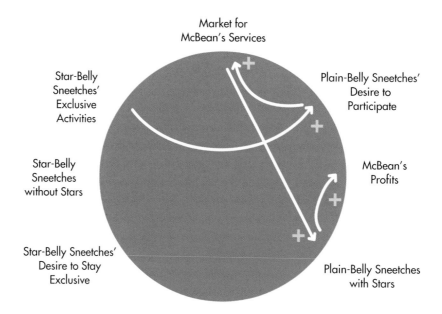

Let's break that down a little, starting at the beginning:

➢ The Star-Belly Sneetches' exclusive activities caused an increase in the desire of the Plain Belly Sneetches to participate …

    ➢ This created a market for McBean's star-adding services …

        ➢ Which led to an increase in "Plain-Belly Sneetches with stars" …

            ➢ Followed by an increase in McBean's profits.

The connections, of course, don't end there—there are still other elements that we haven't included. Below we continue to map the connections:

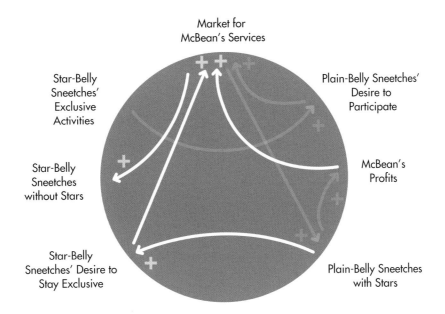

The grayed-out lines are the ones we already established—let's pick up the story from there:

> The increase in McBean's profits expanded his ability to offer his services.

  ❖ At the same time, the increase in the number of Plain-Belly Sneetches with stars increased the Star-Belly Sneetches' desire to stay exclusive … just in time too, since McBean had just expanded his product line!

    > The Star-Belly Sneetches, usage of McBean's services led to an increase in "Star-Belly Sneetches *without* stars."

If we continue to connect the dots, we see how the cycle starts itself over again:

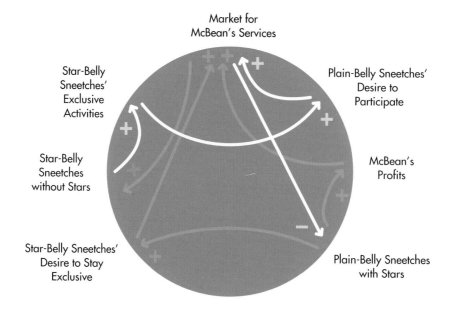

❖   The Star-Belly Sneetches, now lacking stars, can resume their exclusive activities.

    ➢   Now, those Plain-Belly Sneetches want to be "in" again, and so want to get rid of their stars …

        ➢   Leading to an increase in usage of McBean's services, and a decrease in the number of Plain-Belly Sneetches with stars.

The cycle continues from here, looping back onto itself and oscillating as the two groups add and remove stars from their bellies.

IS THERE A "RIGHT" OR "WRONG" CONNECTION CIRCLE DIAGRAM?

Yes and no. It's a good bet that if you'd gone and read "The Sneetches," had already been familiar with connection circles, and made your own diagram, it would probably look somewhat different than the example that we shared here. There are lots of ways to map connections for the same situation, and in that sense there's no one "right" connection circle diagram of a situation. The places where you'd want to "correct" a diagram like this are if youths can't explain why they've drawn an arrow from one element to another or if the reasoning they gave doesn't seem to hold up. In that case, the tool still does its job of clarifying the way things are working in a system, and of making youths' thinking visible. The point of the connection circles, as the creators of this tool emphasize, is to provide *thinking tools* that attune young people to causal connections, as opposed to some visual aids that act as *definitive* maps of a system. It is the *process* of mapping those connections that's at the heart of this approach.

Establishing the connections in this way helps us to visualize when there are processes that are looping back on themselves—feedback loops that recur and drive the behavior of the system over time. This leads us to the other tool we'll share here for making systems visible and clarifying our understanding of how they operate: *causal loop diagrams*.

CAUSAL LOOP DIAGRAMS

Causal loop diagrams aim to map the core dynamics that feed back on themselves and cause a system to act in particular ways. In contrast to the Connection Circles tool, which was developed in order to help kids make sense of systems, causal loop diagrams have been used by professionals in the field of systems dynamics for many years *to make complexity visible.* Unfortunately, asking youths to jump right into making these after having looked at a system can be too much complexity for them to grasp, so Rob Quaden and Alan Ticotsky often position the creation of causal loop diagrams as the final part of the connection-circle process, with the original connection circle serving as a scaffold.

Let's pick up at the last step of connection circles. Through the primary activity there has now been an opportunity to create a general map of the connections. Once those connections are mapped, have the group look for "closed loops"—recurring processes that loop back on themselves and drive behavior in the system over time. For example, if an arrow goes from element A to element B, and another from B to C, and then a third from C back to A, then you've got a *closed loop of causality*, which means you probably have a feedback loop on your hands. What's wonderful about the connection circle is that any time you look at that mess of lines and are able to make out a "closed loop" of arrows, there is most likely a feedback loop going on.

In the case of "The Sneetches," almost all of the elements involved are part of a closed loop, and we can even collapse some of them together in order to create a clear causal loop diagram about the central oscillating dynamic at play in the story between the two groups of Sneetches:

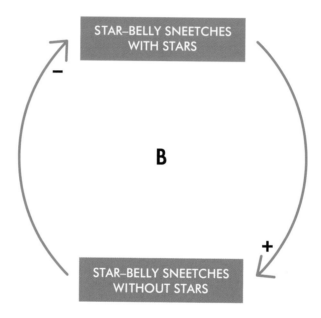

Because the dynamic is maintaining an equilibrium (for a while), we can identify this as a *balancing* feedback loop, putting a (B) in the center to indicate this. Balancing loops are a little complicated to represent in a static way, because the little plus and minus signs in reality are switching back and forth after each cycle. In the case of the Sneetches, a decrease in the "Plain-Belly Sneetches with stars" leads to an increase in "Star-Belly Sneetches without stars," which then leads to an increase "Plain-Belly Sneetches with stars"... and so on.

We can take another story from the design challenges, *The Butter Battle Book,* to show how a causal loop diagram can be boiled down to a simpler, more expressive form once you've created a connection circle diagram. *The Butter Battle Book* tells the story of two hostile cultures, the Yooks and the Zooks, which live on opposite sides of a long, winding wall. The dispute between the two cultures is rooted in the fact that the Yooks eat their bread butter-side up, while the Zooks eat their bread butter-side down. One day, a Zook provokes a member of the Yook's border patrol by breaking the guard's weapon. Outraged, the Yooks develop a larger and more dangerous machine to guard the wall. In response, the Zooks create an even larger machine to overpower the Yooks' weapon. The conflict leads to an escalating arms race involving military generals on each side of the wall competing to make bigger and better weapons to outdo the other. By the end of the book, each side possesses an extremely destructive red bomb that neither the Yooks nor the Zooks has any defense against, resulting in the threat of mutually assured destruction. Take this example of a connection circle diagram based on *The Butter Battle Book*:

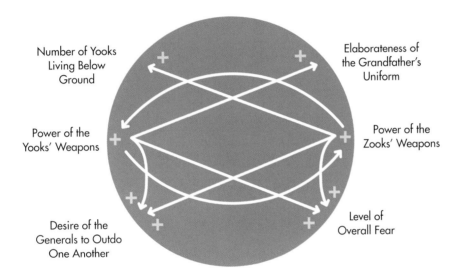

There's a lot going on in there, but really the core dynamic driving the whole system is the relationship between *the power of the weapons*, which we can highlight within the connection circle:

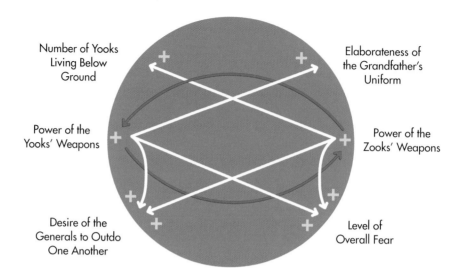

Once we've identified that reinforcing feedback loop, we can simplify the whole thing into a causal loop diagram like this one:

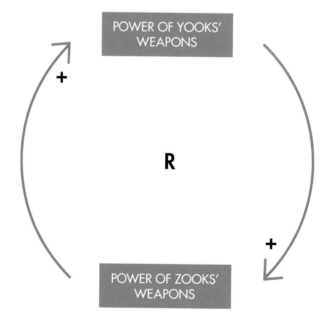

The causal loop diagram aims to strip away all of the extraneous details in the story and get to the heart of the matter: the escalation cycle that fed the arms race. We can insert an (R) in the center of the diagram to indicate that it's a *reinforcing* feedback loop.

Just like with the connection circle diagram, using little plus and minus signs near the arrowheads helps to indicate increases and decreases. As mentioned earlier, in the case of a balancing loops, these are constantly switching (an element will increase in one cycle of the loop, and then decrease in the next, as part of the oscillation process), but having them there can sometime help visualize at least one "cycle" of the process.

In the real world, multiple feedback loops often interact with one another. Take this example of adoption of new technologies:

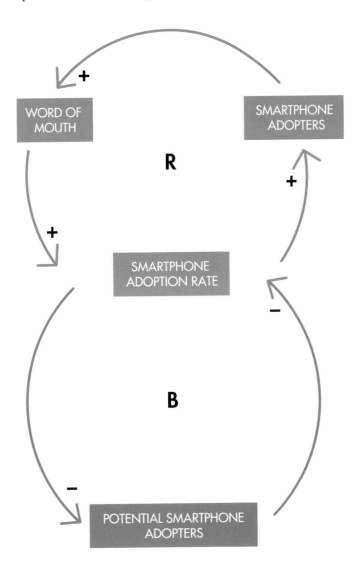

There's often a snowball effect occurring on one hand, with the smartphone adopters increasing the word of mouth, the word of mouth increasing the adoption rate, which leads to more adopters. However, because that adoption rate has increased, the number of *potential* adopters goes down, which in turn tempers the adoption rate.

As you can probably tell by now, working with causal loop diagrams can be challenging; however, through training with connection circles, it is possible to get youths to the point where they can start to skip directly to creating them after they've taken a look at a text. At the same time, depending on the age range of your group, you might choose to stick with connection circles. Good luck as you move into this next set of exciting design challenges!

MODDING THESE TOOLS

What we provided in this section is really just a quick flyover of how these tools work to make systems visible. We didn't go into the many ways that you can structure and adapt these tools for different situations. It will sometimes be useful to have youths engage in different steps of these practices in small groups or on their own, and other times whole-group discussions and processes are more effective. Switching back and forth so that a small group or individual can modify the model they're creating can also add value. For example, if your group gets familiar with creating connection circles, you can ask them to create their own after reading or writing a story, and then have a handful of volunteers share their diagrams with the room to use as a basis for discussion. Or you can start off with a whole-group process around connection circles, and then move to a small-group process to have youths create causal loop diagrams.

For more resources on using these tools, look to *The Shape of Change* classroom activities by Rob Quaden and Alan Ticotsky, available at the Creative Learning Exchange at CLExchange.org.

Total time: 360 minutes

OVERVIEW

Reinforcing feedback loops, which often have a "runaway" quality to them, can often be an integral part of complex systems. In this challenge, youths will return to the core issue introduced in Design Challenge 1—homelessness—to start to try to understand its patterns and why it is such a persistent problem that is so challenging to permanently resolve. In particular, they will look for reinforcing patterns that make homelessness a cycle—a reinforcing feedback loop. In order to better understand the idea of reinforcing feedback, youths will explore this core system dynamic through discussion of *The Butter Battle Book*. They'll then use Scratch to model reinforcing feedback loops in the context of homelessness, with the goal of preparing to think about crafting their own story about their community in Design Challenge 6. Additionally, they'll go out into their community again to interview another community member as they move toward a final project in Design Challenge 6.

PRODUCT

Youths create a story in Scratch to model how reinforcing feedback loops operate in the context of homelessness (or another topical issue of interest to the group).

TARGETED SYSTEMS THINKING CONCEPTS

The notion of *reinforcing feedback loops* is central to understanding how systems can sometimes get out of control. They are self-perpetuating dynamics that often cause a system to move out of a state of balance through repetition and growth of certain behaviors, though these behaviors always exhaust themselves eventually. Sometimes a reinforcing loop can be helpful in terms of the overall goals of a system. This is called a *virtuous cycle*. Often though, reinforcing loops can destabilize a system in a way that prevents it from meeting its goal. In this case, they're called *vicious cycles*.

PARTS

PART 1: WHY IS IT SO DIFFICULT TO STOP BEING HOMELESS?

Youths will consider the question of why it can be challenging to stop being homeless. They will read some first-person stories written by homeless (or formerly homeless) people, and examine the factors that appear to contribute to homelessness. In particular, they will look for patterns in relationships among those factors (or elements), with the goal of beginning to understand and see the ways that some patterns are actually *reinforcing*.

Time: 45 minutes

PART 2: OF YOOKS AND ZOOKS AND REINFORCING LOOPS

Here youths further their understanding of the concept of reinforcing feedback loops, which take the forms of *vicious* and *virtuous* cycles. Dr. Seuss's *The Butter Battle Book*, an allegory about the arms race of the Cold War, serves to illustrate a reinforcing loop that is a vicious cycle, much like the problem of homelessness that was addressed in part 1.

Time: 65 minutes

PART 3: SCRATCH DESIGN CHALLENGE: REINFORCING FEEDBACK LOOPS

Youths will brainstorm and storyboard ideas for Scratch projects that illustrate a homeless person's experiences and that model reinforcing feedback. After receiving and responding to feedback from their peers, youths will have a chance to create, iterate, and publish their Scratch stories, as well as share with the whole group.

Time: 250 minutes

KEY DEFINITIONS

Reinforcing feedback loops. Circular cause and effect processes that create growth, such as in escalation cycles, or decay, such in resource drain cycles. Reinforcing feedback loops are important to understand because they're the engines of growth or decline and are often at the heart of what are described as "out of control," experiencing a "snowball effect" or "out of balance." Reinforcing feedback loops rarely occur in isolation—often when you find them you'll also find balancing feedback loops.

Vicious cycle. Reinforcing feedback loops that cause a negative outcome in terms of the perceived goal of the system. It's important to understand that sometimes reinforcing feedback loops can be considered good or positive, depending on where you stand in relation to a system.

Virtuous cycle. Reinforcing feedback loop that causes a positive outcome in terms of the perceived goal of the system. It's important to understand that sometimes reinforcing feedback loops can be considered bad or negative, depending on where you stand in relation to a system.

OTHER ESSENTIAL VOCABULARY

- Elements
- Behaviors
- Interconnections
- System dynamics

COMMON CORE STATE STANDARDS COVERED—ENGLISH LANGUAGE ARTS	NEXT GENERATION SCIENCE STANDARDS
• R.6–12.3 (anchor standard)	• 3–5-ETS1–1
• R.6–12.7 (anchor standard)	• 3–5-ETS1–2
• RI.7.3	• 3–5-ETS1–3
• W.6–12.2 (anchor standard)	• MS-ETS1–1
• W.8.6	• MS-ETS1–2
• W.6–12.7 (anchor standard)	• MS-ETS1–4
• W.6–12.9 (anchor standard)	• MS-ESS3–3
• RST.6–8.3	
• RST.6–8.7	
• SL.7.2	
• SL.6–12.4 (anchor standard)	
• SL.7.5	
• WHST.6–8.7	

MATERIALS OVERVIEW

STUFF TO HAVE HANDY

- A computer for each youth, with Internet access and Scratch pre-loaded
- Digital projector
- Computer speakers
- Copies of *The Butter Battle Book* (if possible, one copy for each youth)
- Blank paper (two sheets for each youth)
- Pens (one for each youth)
- Reinforcing Feedback Scratch projects:
  - Vicious Cycle: scratch.mit.edu/projects/1811225
  - Virtuous Cycle: scratch.mit.edu/projects/1900642

Additional items to have available (optional):

- Chart paper
- Markers

HANDOUTS

- "Telling Our Stories: What Homelessness Feels Like"
- "Mission: Community Member Interview"
- "Reinforcing Feedback Loop Examples"
- "Feedback Form: Reinforcing Loops Project"
- "Scratch Project Storyboard"
- "Connection Circle"

OVERALL CHALLENGE PREPARATION

- Read *The Butter Battle Book* and pinpoint for yourself the reinforcing feedback loops that are present in all the texts. (These are highlighted in the activities outlined in the challenge.)
- View the *Vicious Cycle* Scratch project: scratch.mit.edu/projects/1811225.
- View the *Virtuous Cycle* Scratch project: scratch.mit.edu/projects/1900642.
- Familiarize yourself with the connection circle technique and make yourself sample connection circles for the two texts.
- Familiarize yourself with storyboarding as a technique authors use to create a draft for a story, as well as the "Scratch Project Storyboard Worksheet" handout. You might find it useful to search for examples of storyboards online to see how people use these tools.

PART 1: WHY IS IT SO DIFFICULT TO STOP BEING HOMELESS?

Youths will consider the question of why it can be challenging to stop being homeless. They will read some first-person stories written by homeless (or formerly homeless) people and examine the factors that appear to contribute to homelessness. In particular, they will look for patterns in relationships among those factors (or elements), with the goal of beginning to understand and see the ways that some patterns are actually *reinforcing*.

Time: 45 minutes

STUFF TO HAVE HANDY

- Digital projector
- Blank sheets of paper
- Chart paper and markers

HANDOUTS

- "Telling Our Stories: What Homelessness Feels Like"
- "Connection Circle"

RESEARCH: HOMELESSNESS AND JOBS—15 MINUTES

Remind youths of the problem of homelessness that you discussed in Design Challenge 1. Then explain that you want to try to focus on one particular aspect of homelessness: why it can be so difficult to overcome it.

1. Distribute the "Telling Our Stories" handout. Review the accounts, either in small groups or as a whole class. Make sure that students are thinking about the following:

- What are the key *elements* of the system of homelessness?
- What *interconnections* can you identify among the elements?
- Do you notice any patterns that might emerge between any of the interconnections?

CREATE AND SHARE—15 MINUTES

In this next exercise, youths will use the connection circle as a tool for identifying the key elements in the story as well as the interconnections between them.

1. Distribute the "Connection Circle" handout. Ask youths to work in groups to create the diagram by identifying the elements of the stories and mapping how they think they are *interconnected*.

2. As a whole group, review a subset of the connection circles that youths have developed. In your whole-group discussion, be sure to emphasize the ways that particular factors build on each other. Examples you might want to highlight include:

- *The challenge of getting a job*: Being homeless often means that you have limited access to facilities that would allow you to be clean and groomed. Even if you are in a shelter, you are unlikely to have a range of clothing that would be considered "professional." As a consequence, when you go to an interview for a job—even a low-wage job—you might appear to be unreliable or uninterested in it (appearance matters!). This makes you less competitive for a job than other candidates who might have homes, which leaves you out of work, which causes you to remain homeless ... and perpetuates the problem of not having access to those things you need to look more professional. *Elements: appearance, likelihood of getting hired, income for / access to clothing.*

- *The challenge of transportation*: Being homeless usually means that you lack the resources for independent transportation. In many cities public transportation is unreliable or scattered. As a consequence, you may be ineligible for

particular jobs or be late or miss work (because you cannot get to work on your own). This makes it difficult for you to either secure or maintain a job, which means that you lack income, which means that you cannot purchase independent transportation. *Elements: transportation, reliability, income.*

• *The challenge of work records*: Many people become homeless because of a catastrophic event in their life that made it impossible to work for a long period of time, and that shows up on their employment record. A big gap between jobs is considered a red flag by many hiring agents, which makes it harder for a homeless person to get a job, which contributes to their spotty work record. *Elements: work record, likelihood of employment.*

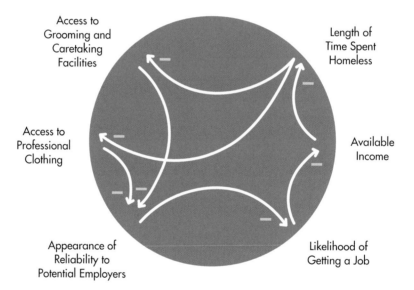

Sample connection circle diagram representing one potential reinforcing dynamic that makes escaping homelessness so challenging.

3. At this point, you will want to introduce the idea of *reinforcing feedback*, and explain that reinforcing feedback describes a situation where one element causes another element to increase, which feeds back to the original element, increasing it again, and so on, creating to an escalation cycle in the system. Note that this could also happen in the opposite direction, with something decreasing again and again until it disappears.

• *Reinforcing feedback loops* are circular cause-and-effect processes that create *growth* (e.g., escalation cycles) or *decay* (e.g., resource drain cycles). Reinforcing feedback loops are important to understand because they're the engines of growth or decline. When you hear something described as being "out of control," "out of balance," or experiencing a "snowball effect," a reinforcing feedback loop is probably at the heart of the problem.

IMAGINE: REINFORCING FEEDBACK LOOPS BRAINSTORM—15 MINUTES

In this brainstorm youths think of other examples of where reinforcing feedback might be at play in the world.

1. As a whole group, brainstorm other examples of situations like the one in *The Butter Battle Book*, where events escalate until they become out of control. Try to identify which of the suggested examples might be due to a reinforcing feedback loop in action. Then try to identify how those loops work. Keep in mind that reinforcing feedback can be characterized not only by rapid escalation, but also rapid diminishment.

EXAMPLES OF REINFORCING FEEDBACK

- *Microphone feedback:* A microphone screech is caused by the microphone picking up some sound that its speakers played. That sound is then amplified when it goes out through the speakers again, which is then picked up by the microphone the next time around, and the sound keeps getting louder.

- *Bank runs:* During the Great Depression in the United States, a bank run occurred when depositors feared that they would not be able to withdraw their money and remove their holdings. They pulled their money out because of that fear, which weakened the banks, which led to bank closures, which reinforced the fear of bank instability, starting the cycle again.

- *Gossip:* Somebody tells a bit of "news" to a couple of friends, and then each of the friends tells it to a couple of their friends … and the gossip spreads faster and faster within a community.

- *Interest on savings*: When money is put in a bank, it accrues a certain amount of interest, based on the amount of money that is deposited and the current interest rate. That interest is added to the original amount of money, which then increases the amount of money earning interest, increasing the base amount again … a self-reinforcing cycle.

---

2. Using multiple computers or a computer with a projector, share the following Scratch project to illustrate how a digital story can represent a reinforcing dynamic. In this digital story, two youths are engaged in one-upping each other by buying newer and fancier technology: scratch.mit.edu/projects/1811225.

DESIGN CHALLENGE 4, PART 1

TELLING OUR STORIES: WHAT HOMELESSNESS FEELS LIKE

WHY DON'T HOMELESS PEOPLE JUST GET JOBS AND STOP BEING HOMELESS?
IT SEEMS LIKE IT WOULD BE EASY, JUST GET A JOB AND GET OFF THE STREET, RIGHT?

By Kylyssa Shay, Yahoo! Contributor Network

Many people believe that homelessness is a choice, that all a person needs to do is get a job to stop being homeless. The fact is that it isn't that simple, either to get a job when homeless or to get out of homelessness even with a job. For one thing, getting a job while homeless presents a set of difficulties a homed person might not suspect. For another, a job isn't always enough to get a person off the street.

Unemployment rates are high and jobs are scarce. Even for those who have homes, it's hard to find a job. As to why homeless people have more difficulty getting jobs, there are multiple reasons.

Many people become homeless due to unemployment or illness, both of which create gaps in job history many employers find unacceptable. Homeless people lack regular addresses and may not even have cell phones, making them too much trouble for prospective employers to contact. Homelessness makes staying clean and tidy enough for job interviews nearly impossible. Transportation is also a major issue for homeless people. Many job listings specify: "dependable transportation required." While some homeless people have cars, not all of them do.

In some areas, homelessness itself is illegal, resulting in jail time and a criminal record, which tends to look bad on a job application. Even without a criminal record, the stereotype of homeless people as drug-using criminals prevents many employers from even considering anyone they suspect might be homeless.

On top of those problems, there's another barrier to employment that many homeless people face when looking for work—credit checks. Many employers perform credit checks now in their employee-screening process. As you can imagine, not having an address or recent income, and probably having past evictions and medical bankruptcies or past-due bills on your record, destroys your credit rating.

That covers reasons why homeless people who are capable of working may not have jobs—there are also those who are not able to hold a job due to illness, mental or physical.

Many homeless people are physically disabled by illness or age. That's right, some homeless people are senior citizens whom someone ought to be caring for, and others are very sick people unable to support themselves.

Then there is another category, a surprisingly large one—employed homeless people, often called the working poor. Anywhere from one-third to one-half of homeless Americans have jobs. They simply do not earn enough to get off the streets due to excessive debts such as medical bills, student loans, alimony or child support, or due to the lack of a living wage.

MY STORY—FALL, 2001

By Anonymous

My story is simple, but you won't like it. I had a job and I made $9 an hour. But one-third of what I had went to the childcare center and nearly half went to rent. The rest went to food and regular bills. I got five kids. I got no other money. You can't make it on that. It's just plain and simple. I got skills. I went to school and learned to be a cook. I work good restaurants. I did what I was supposed to do. You just can't have kids and make it on $9 an hour. When my daughter got pneumonia I had insurance, but the co-pay was high and the hospital wanted me to pay out $300 a month. I couldn't give them but $20 or $30 and they took me to court. Then my boyfriend got married and wanted to get custody of my kids. I had to fight him in court. I paid $200 a month for a lawyer and he didn't do nothin'. I had to get all the witnesses and do all the legwork. Then my car needed a new exhaust. And that was $1,000. Comes a point where something's gotta give. With the car—I had to have that to work. The lawyer wouldn't stop getting after me for the money I owed him. There's just no way. I fell behind a little on my rent and got kicked out. Ain't no way you can do it. You figure the math. They tell you, you got a skill and you be making $9 an hour. You can pay your bills—*just* pay your bills. Then anything come up and you're flat. You can't do it.

They say here that they will help me, and they do. But I can't just convince them of the obvious. I'm off the streets now, but I'll be back. Ain't no way you can do it. I could do like these other women and sell a little pot, but I ain't raising my kids in that environment. So I do it the way they say. Ain't no way it can work. Do the math.

I'm trying now to find a job that will pay me just a little more, but so far no good. The good salad and grill jobs are way out by Waukesha. Then I'd have to have a better car and spend hours traveling and my daycare wouldn't keep the kids that late. I don't know what the solution is. I feel like it's just no use. All I can do is get me some boyfriend that will bring a little money into the house. But then I have to feed him too.

DESIGN CHALLENGE 4, PART 1

CONNECTION CIRCLE

Use the circle below to map connections within the system.

1. First, list the important elements of the system around the outside of the circle. Keep in mind that your elements should be things that increase or decrease over time in the system.

2. Then use arrows to start mapping the connections between the elements in terms of one causing another to increase or decrease. Remember to:

   a. Use arrows to indicate the "direction" of the relationship (which element is causing, which element is being affected).

   b. Use plus (+) and minus (–) signs near the heads of the arrows to indicate whether the relationship is causing an increase or decrease in the affected element.

PART 2: OF YOOKS AND ZOOKS AND REINFORCING LOOPS

Here youths further their understanding of the concept of *reinforcing feedback loops*, which take the form of *vicious cycles* and *virtuous cycles*. Dr. Seuss's *The Butter Battle Book*, an allegory about the arms race of the Cold War, serves to illustrate a reinforcing loop that is a vicious cycle, much like the problem of homelessness that was addressed in part 1.

Time: 65 minutes

STUFF TO HAVE HANDY

- *The Butter Battle Book*
- Digital projector
- Blank sheets of paper
- *Vicious Cycle* Scratch project: **scratch.mit.edu/projects/1811225**
- *Virtuous Cycle* Scratch project: **scratch.mit.edu/projects/1900642**
- Chart paper and markers

HANDOUTS

- "Reinforcing Feedback Loop Examples"
- "Mission: Community Member Interview"
- "Connection Circle"

RESEARCH: READING *THE BUTTER BATTLE BOOK*—15 MINUTES

Now that we've seen how reinforcing feedback can work in our communities in the issue of homelessness, it's time to explore how such a system dynamic can play out in other situations. In this activity youths will read a story that also illustrates a reinforcing feedback loop. Distribute copies of *The Butter Battle Book* and let youths read on their own or as part of a group read-aloud. Encourage youths to ask themselves how they might visualize the events of the story from a systemic perspective.

CREATE: GRAPHING THE BUTTER BATTLE—10 MINUTES

In this activity youths will graph the events of *The Butter Battle Book* as a first step in making visible the elements of a feedback loop. The goal is for students to be able to see that as one group escalates so too does the other group.

1. Ask the group what they saw happening in the story. It's best to start the discussion broadly with a question like, "What did you see in the story that was interesting to you?" and then follow up with a question like, "How does this story get at ideas of interconnectedness in a unique way?" Discuss until there's a general understanding among the group of the story's big ideas and patterns.

2. Remind the group that every system has *elements*, which interact with each other to form larger patterns called *system dynamics*.

3. Using a whiteboard or chart paper, brainstorm the different elements at play in *The Butter Battle Book*. Remind youths to focus on elements that increase or decrease over the course of the story as they interact with other elements. These elements should all be connected to the central problem in the story.

Examples of key elements in *The Butter Battle Book*

- Power of the Yooks' weapons
- Power of the Zooks' weapons
- Safety of the Yooks
- Safety of the Zooks
- Animosity between Yooks and Zooks
- Size of the Wall
- Number of Yooks living above ground

4. As a group, draw a graph of the key patterns in the story. One example is shown below, but note that this is just one of many possible representations your group might create. The goal is for group members to be able to visualize the escalation that occurs between the Yooks and the Zooks:

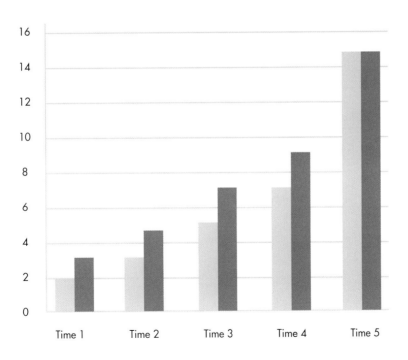

CREATE: DIAGRAMMING CONNECTIONS IN THE BUTTER BATTLE—15 MINUTES

Having established what the big patterns are in the story, in this activity youths work in small groups and use the connection-circle diagramming tool to unpack the relationships that led to those patterns. Refer back to the extended description of the connection circles technique, found in *Introduction and Tools for the Advanced Design Challenges,* when conducting this activity.

VOICES FROM THE FIELD

The diagramming process was a useful visual moment to see where the youths' thinking was. To have the small groups discuss, draft, and explain their diagrams to the entire class, I believe, helped the whole group with their understanding of systems.

—JENILYNN REDILA, CHICAGO QUEST

1. Now that we have a "big picture" of what went on in the story, we're going to dive deep into the nitty-gritty of how that big picture came about, by making what are called *connection circle diagrams*.

2. Have youths form groups of two or three, and give each group a copy of the "Connection Circle" handout. Review the guidelines for how to create the diagrams:

   • Include only the most important elements of the story that change over time.

   • Use arrows to indicate *direct* causal connections between elements, and plus and minus signs to indicate increases and decreases in elements.

   • Notice any "closed loops" among a set of arrows (i.e., where two or three elements are connected by arrows looping back—going in both directions).

3. Allow 5–7 minutes to create their diagrams, and provide assistance as needed.

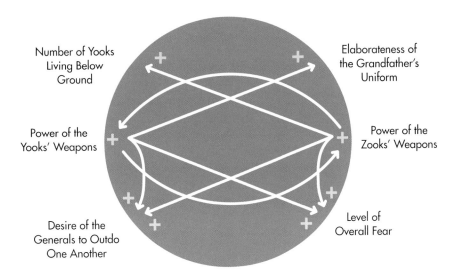

Sample Connection Circle Diagram for *The Butter Battle Book*.

4. Ask for two or three groups to share their diagrams, explaining the decisions they made about what to include, what not to include, and how they connected elements to one another. Have the broader group provide feedback on the decisions that the partners made. Throughout the presentations, highlight times when groups depicted closed loops—sets of arrows that looped back on themselves in some way.

Optional: Depending on how advanced your group is, you may choose to have them transition from their connection circle diagrams into traditional *causal loop diagrams*. For a full description on using causal loop diagrams, see *Introduction and Tools for the Advanced Design Challenges*.

VOICES FROM THE FIELD

There might be a strong need to scaffold some youths' understanding if they cannot see the bigger dynamic between the weapons and how the escalation of the "battle" came about between the Zooks and Yooks in *The Butter Battle Book*.

—JANIE BROWN, GREAT BEAR WRITING PROJECT

RESEARCH AND SHARE: REINFORCING FEEDBACK LOOPS
DISCUSSION—10 MINUTES

By this point, the graphing and connection circle diagramming has likely highlighted the key ideas in the story around escalation. In the following discussion, youths will become oriented toward the idea of reinforcing feedback loops so that they understand this dynamic as a regular feature of many systems.

1. Continuing from the discussion that emerged as groups were presenting their diagrams, invite the group members to see if they, from their diagrams, can identify one key pattern that kept the story going. If the group isn't already attuned to the arms race, gently guide the discussion toward the escalating dynamic between the power of the Yook's weapons and the power of the Zook's weapons.

2. Remind students about the language of reinforcing feedback loops at the appropriate point in the discussion:

- *Reinforcing feedback loops* are circular cause-and-effect processes that create *growth* (e.g., escalation cycles) or *decay* (e.g., resource drain cycles). Reinforcing feedback loops are important to understand because they're the engines of growth or decline. When you hear of something described as being "out of control," "out of balance," or as experiencing a "snowball effect," a reinforcing feedback loop is probably at the heart of the problem.

3. Apply the idea of reinforcing feedback loops to *The Butter Battle Book*. Possible prompts include:

- What elements of the system affected other elements, feeding on each other? (One side arming themselves caused the other side to get better arms, which in turn caused the original side to arm more).

- Why might we call what happened in the story a *reinforcing* process?

- Could this process go on forever? Why or why not? What kinds of resources fueled this dynamic?

VOICES FROM THE FIELD

Helping youths understand the terminology is always easier when it is related to their background knowledge. For those who have no background to connect to, the teacher should be prepared to build that background.

—JANIE BROWN, GREAT BEAR WRITING PROJECT

RESEARCH: REINFORCING GOES BOTH WAYS—COMPARING VICIOUS AND VIRTUOUS CYCLES—10 MINUTES

Now youths are introduced to the idea of *vicious and virtuous cycles*—reinforcing feedback loops with positive and negative effects—and the fact that the reinforcing feedback loop in *The Butter Battle Book* was of the *vicious* variety.

1. Write the term *vicious cycle* on the board or chart paper and ask if anyone can guess what it might be.

2. If no one guesses, explain that vicious cycles are reinforcing feedback loops that cause a *negative* outcome in terms of the perceived goal of the system.

- Point out that in *The Butter Battle Book*, the goal of the grandfather was to keep the Yooks safe, but instead he ended up making them less safe and more at risk of being destroyed because of the escalation dynamic that emerged. This is why we could call this a vicious cycle; it goes against the grandfather's goal.

- Discuss the similarities between the systems in *The Butter Battle Book* and the problem of homelessness. Ask students to identify in each which elements are interacting to create the reinforcing dynamic.

3. Hand out the Reinforcing Feedback Loop Examples handout, and explain how some reinforcing loops actually help a system meet its goal, and as such create good outcomes. We call these *virtuous cycles*.

- Explore together the examples from the handout of virtuous cycles: positive peer influence and saving money.

- Help youths understand that virtuous cycles are reinforcing feedback loops that cause a positive outcome in terms the perceived goal of the system.

4. Be sure to leave space and time for fielding questions from the group and clarifying the difference between virtuous and vicious cycles for those that might be having trouble with them.

5. Help your group to understand that these ideas are complex and can be hard to grasp, but the reason they're useful is that they can help us think about how things are (or aren't) working in our communities and how we can change things in the world that we care about.

WHAT TO EXPECT

A common misconception to look out for after group members have learned about vicious and virtuous cycles is that youths sometimes walk away with the idea that *anything good* happening in a system is a virtuous cycle, and *anything bad* is a vicious cycle, forgetting that the terms "vicious" and "virtuous" here only relate to feedback loops. Continue to point out the "snowball effect" and "self-reinforcing" nature of virtuous and vicious cycles to help youths develop a systemic mindset and to differentiate between events that are good or bad *in general* versus *reinforcing feedback loops* that are good or bad for the system.

	Novice	Expert
Systems thinking concepts	• Thinks causally (rather than interactively) about the system (one element causes another, rather than one element interacts with another to produce system behavior). • Struggles to predict how the behavior of an element will be impacted by a change to another element. • Understands the idea of interconnections between multiple elements, but struggles to understand how those interconnections are reinforcing.	• Sees the overall outcome of the system as the result of interactions among multiple elements. • Can describe how those elements interact in a way as to reinforce one another. • Has a sense of how elements of the system interact and impact one another, and can predict these changes. • Understands the differences between vicious and virtuous reinforcing systems.

RESEARCH: MID-CHALLENGE MISSION—5 MINUTES

For homework ask youths to find a new community member and conduct another interview using the "Community Member Interview" handout. Ask them to pay particular attention to the question about the "most important, issues, challenges, or opportunities facing the community." **Note:** The responses to this question will help youths when they develop their final Scratch project in Design Challenge 6.

DESIGN CHALLENGE 4, PART 2

REINFORCING FEEDBACK LOOP EXAMPLES

Reinforcing feedback loops are circular cause and effect processes that create growth, such as in escalation cycles, or decay, such in resource drain cycles. Reinforcing feedback loops are important to understand because they're the engines of growth or decline and are often at the heart of that are described as "out of control," experiencing a "snowball effect" or are "out of balance." Reinforcing feedback loops rarely occur in isolation—often when you find them you'll also find balancing feedback loops.

Vicious Cycles

Definition

A *vicious cycle* is a reinforcing feedback loop that causes a negative (bad) outcome in terms of the perceived goal of the system. (*Note:* Don't forget that sometimes reinforcing feedback loops can be considered good, depending on where you stand in relation to a system. In that case they aren't vicious.)

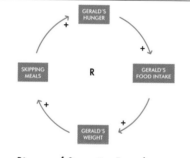

Diagram of Overeating Example

Examples

Overeating

Gerald wants to lose weight and is under the impression that if he only eats twice a day (instead of three) he will lose weight. Unfortunately, when Gerald skips breakfast he experiences an increased feeling of hunger at lunch. As a result, Gerald eats more than he should at lunch, taking in more than his body actually needs between lunch and dinner. This causes Gerald to slowly gain weight, which leads him to think that he needs to continue to skip meals, starting the cycle over again.

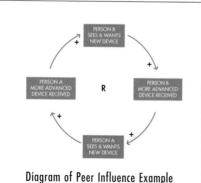

Diagram of Peer Influence Example

Peer Influence

Tiffany just got an iPod as a gift for her birthday and she brings it to school to show her friend Jayden. After Jayden sees Tiffany's iPod, he tries to convince his parents that he needs one, despite having a working CD player. As a result, on Jayden's birthday his parents buy him an iPod that comes with more memory than Tiffany's iPod. When Tiffany's parent's bought hers, iPods came with 2 gigabytes of memory, but when Jayden's parents buy his, most iPods come with 10 gigabytes of memory. After learning that Jayden's iPod has so much more memory, Tiffany tries to convince her parents that she needs an iPod with more memory.

Virtuous Cycles

Definition

A *virtuous cycle* is a reinforcing feedback loop that causes a positive (good) outcome in terms the perceived goal of the system. (*Note:* Don't forget that sometimes reinforcing feedback loops can be considered bad, depending on where you stand in relation to a system. In that case they aren't virtuous.)

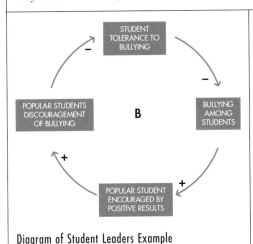

Diagram of Student Leaders Example

Examples

Student Leaders

Mr. Johnson, a high school principal, notices that his more popular students have begun to speak out against bullying when they witness it. He also notices that more students are beginning to look down upon casual bullying. This has led to less acts of bullying observed among students, which the popular students take as feedback that their words have an effect, which in turn further encourages his popular students to increase their efforts to speak out against bullying.

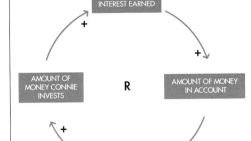

Diagram of Saving Money Example

Saving Money

Every two weeks, Connie puts some of the money from her paycheck into the bank. Over time, the money she invests grows interest, which increases the total amount of money in her bank account. Connie notices that the more money she invests, the greater amount of interest she earns. This encourages Connie to put as large a portion of her paycheck as possible into her account.

DESIGN CHALLENGE 4, PART 2

MISSION: COMMUNITY MEMBER INTERVIEW

Name: _____

Date: _____

Instructions: Your mission is to go into your community and talk to people to find out more about it, and to inquire what people think might need changing. Interview a member of your community (this could be parent, a local shopkeeper, a neighbor, etc.) about the five things below. Record your answers on this sheet, and use the back (or a separate sheet of paper) if you need more room.

Community member you interviewed:_____

How has the community changed over time in positive ways?

How has the community changed over time in negative ways?

What are the most important parts (elements) of the community, and how do they interact with one another?

What do you think are good goals for the community, or the purposes that it should serve?

What are the most important issues, challenges, or opportunities facing our community?

DESIGN CHALLENGE 4, PART 2

CONNECTION CIRCLES

Use the circle below to map connections within the system.

1. First, list the important elements of the system around the outside of the circle. Keep in mind that your elements should be things that increase or decrease over time in the system.

2. Then, use arrows to start mapping the connections between the elements in terms of one causing another to increase or decrease. Remember to:

   a. Use arrow to indicate the "direction" of the relationship (which element is causing, which element is being affected).

   b. Use plus (+) and minus (-) signs near the heads of the arrows to indicate whether the relationship is causing an increase or decrease in the affected element.

PART 3: SCRATCH DESIGN CHALLENGE: REINFORCING FEEDBACK LOOPS

Youths will brainstorm and storyboard ideas for Scratch projects that illustrate a homeless person's experiences and that model reinforcing feedback. After receiving and responding to feedback from their peers, youths will have a chance to create, iterate, and publish their Scratch stories, as well as share with the whole group.

Time: 250 minutes

STUFF TO HAVE HANDY

- Digital projector

- Blank sheets of paper

- Chart paper and markers (optional)

HANDOUTS

- "Scratch Project Storyboard," several copies per youth

- "Feedback Form: Reinforcing Loops Project"

IMAGINE: REINFORCING FEEDBACK LOOP STORY / PROJECT DRAFTING—20 MINUTES

Youths brainstorm ideas for their Scratch project on reinforcing feedback loops in the homeless community.

1. Break into small groups of three or four youths.

2. Explain that each small group will be writing stories that illustrate examples of reinforcing feedback loops in homeless communities. The stories will eventually be created in Scratch.

3. Hand out blank paper. Direct them to record all their ideas.

4. Post the following question where everyone can see it: How might you tell a story in Scratch to show a reinforcing feedback loop related to homelessness? Remind youths that reinforcing feedback loops can be either positive (virtuous) or negative (vicious).

5. Encourage groups to brainstorm ideas freely, and ask individuals to list the ideas that arise on their sheets of paper.

6. Have the groups discuss which ideas they think might make the most interesting Scratch stories.

RESEARCH AND IMAGINE: GOING FROM AN ISSUE TO SCRATCH—20 MINUTES

In this discussion, the whole group will work together to explore how a story might be developed in Scratch that illustrates reinforcing feedback dynamics.

1. Ask each group to share just one of its brainstormed ideas about an aspect of homelessness that they might explore through storytelling. List each idea on the

board or chart paper. After all small groups have shared their ideas, take an informal vote to choose one to explore together.

2. Analyze the chosen story first in terms of the *elements* and the *interconnections* they have with one another. Be sure to remind students to keep the ultimate outcome of these interconnections in mind.

3. Ask what kind of dynamics or relationships are occurring within the story, and particularly, how they see interconnections generating *reinforcing feedback loops*. **Note:** You might find it helpful to do some diagramming on the board of the system being discussed.

4. Brainstorm with the group how someone might represent this story in a Scratch project. Ask youths to think about what sort of sprites and backgrounds the project could use, what the scene could look like, what kinds of commands would be helpful, and so on. The general idea here is to model how to get from a community issue to an actual project in Scratch. Also explain to the students that the primary way they are going to be able to communicate reinforcing feedback is through dialogue—through the story that the characters tell.

IMAGINE: CONTINUED STORY/PROJECT DRAFTING—20 MINUTES

Youths select one story idea and begin fleshing it out. They then begin to convert this draft into a storyboard for their project.

1. Have the group continue drafting based on what they started to write up during the initial story-drafting activity.

2. Once youths have gotten their drafts to a point where they're fairly well set about their story idea, distribute the "Scratch Project Storyboard" handout so that they can convert the idea they have for the project into a storyboard. **Note:** Keep several copies per youth available.

Tip   Show youths a sample of completed storyboards to help them visualize the tool's usefulness. Storyboards related to popular culture genres they're familiar with, such as comic strips, cartoons, movies, or animé, make this more accessible to this age group. An Internet search should produce many examples you might use.

3. Remind youths to consider how their project or story idea illustrates feedback loops such as the ones discussed in part 1.

4. Encourage youths to be as detailed as possible in their storyboards, including their main characters, the sequence of events, and dialogues. The "Scratch Project Storyboard" handout will guide them in thinking through every aspect of their project.

SHARE: PAIR, SHARE, AND FEEDBACK ON STORYBOARDS—20 MINUTES

Youths work in pairs to receive feedback on their drafts, each partner filling out a feedback form and giving advice about the two projects.

1. As youths finish their storyboards, create feedback pairs to share their projects.

2. Pass out the "Feedback Form: Reinforcing Loops Project" to each partner. This will help them clarify their own thinking as well as provide concrete feedback to their partners. **Note:** You might want to consider collecting these to assess the group's understanding about reinforcing feedback.

3. Ask each partner to give both warm and cool feedback (See Tools for the Advanced Design Challenges) and advice on the following:

   • *General flow of the story*: Comment on the narrative structure and how well the story holds together.

   • *Illustrating systems concepts*: Comment on how well the story illustrates a reinforcing feedback loop of some sort.

MODELING CONSTRUCTIVE DESIGN FEEDBACK

Before dividing the group into pairs, it's helpful to model how to provide constructive feedback. Consider role playing—with you, the facilitator, taking the role of the partner receiving feedback. Ask for a volunteer to give you examples of unhelpful feedback. Process with the group why that type of feedback is unhelpful, then brainstorm the kinds of feedback sentences that might be more constructive. (e.g., "Have you thought about ...?," "What were you thinking when you ...?" "I was confused when ... can you help me understand?")

---

4. Have partners switch after 10 minutes so that both partners receive feedback on their projects.

WHAT TO EXPECT

The open-ended questions at the bottom of the worksheet are where you can begin to see how youths are thinking about the systems-thinking elements of the project. Youths who are struggling to understand reinforcing feedback might have a harder time explaining how the feedback system works. *Expert systems thinkers recognize that feedback is the result of interconnections among multiple elements and can explain how the behaviors of those elements serve to create a reinforcing dynamic.*

	Novice	Expert
Systems thinking concepts	• Thinks causally (rather than interactively) about the system (one component causes another, rather than one component interacts with another to produce system behavior). • Struggles to predict how the behavior of a component will be affected by a change to another component. • Understands the idea of interconnections between multiple elements, but struggles to understand how those interconnections are reinforcing.	• Sees the overall outcome of the system as the result of interactions among multiple elements. • Can describe how those elements interact in a way as to reinforce one another. • Has a sense of how elements of the system interact and affect one another, and can predict these changes. • Understands the differences between vicious and virtuous cycles.

CREATE: DESIGN TIME IN SCRATCH—85 MINUTES

Youths engage in project creation in Scratch during this primary design period for the project.

1. Ask youths to open (or log in to) Scratch and begin drafting the projects they have planned.

2. Let youths know that they'll have more than an hour to begin their design, followed by a peer feedback period, and then another 45 minutes to continue designing the project.

3. Provide support and assistance as needed. Look for common areas where new programmers often spend too much time, such as in the creation of elaborate sprites, sounds, or backgrounds. Many youths pay so much attention to these elements that the story suffers; poor time management results in incomplete projects with highly detailed sprites and backgrounds!

SHARE: PAIR, SHARE, AND FEEDBACK ON FIRST SCRATCH DRAFTS—20 MINUTES

Youths pair up to give feedback on their project drafts prior to the final design period.

1. As youths finish their drafts, create feedback pairs to share what they've accomplished so far in their reinforcing feedback loop Scratch stories. (If desired, pair the youths in the same initial feedback groups that they were in earlier. This can help youths see the evolution of their peers' projects, and also means that a person giving feedback has more context coming into the feedback process.)

2. Ask each partner to give both warm and cool feedback (see *Introduction*) and advice on the following:

    a. *General flow of the story*: Comment on how well the story holds together, the flow of the narrative.

    b. *Illustrating systems concepts*: Comment on how well the story illustrates a reinforcing feedback loop of some sort.

    c. *Scratch technique*: Comment on how the project uses Scratch blocks to tell a story. Invite partners to offer any technical assistance, advice, or support.

3. Have pair groups switch after 10 minutes so that both partners receive feedback on their projects.

ITERATE AND PUBLISH: MAKING REVISIONS—45 MINUTES

During the final design period, youths consider the feedback they received and determine how much to incorporate into a revision of their projects.

1. Have youths return to Scratch and begin polishing their projects. Remind them to consider incorporating the feedback they just received. Point out that this *iterative* process of drafting, getting feedback, and revising based on that feedback is how most authors, game designers, and artists work, but remind them that they are the ultimate designer and the amount of advice they choose to use is up to them.

2. Allow 45 minutes to work on projects, leaving time for a group share out before the session end.

3. As they finish, encourage youths to share their project on the Scratch website if they are ready for it to be viewed by a broader audience.

SHARE: GROUP SHARE-OUT—30 MINUTES

Youths share their Scratch stories with the group.

1. Ask for volunteers to use the digital projector to share their Scratch projects so that the whole group can see it as the designer reads the dialogue aloud.

2. Encourage each volunteer designer to explain (if it's not evident in the project):

    *   How the project illustrates feedback loops related to homelessness.

    *   The source of their inspiration.

    *   The challenges they encountered during the design process.

3. Allow as many volunteers as you have time for before the end of the session.

SAMPLE PROJECT: REINFORCING LOOPS

In this project, a youth depicts a common reinforcing feedback loop in the form of a viral campaign: more people will hear about a protest, which will spur them to protest as well, keeping the cycle growing and escalating. This could be considered a virtuous cycle. (Credit: by Anthony)

DESIGN CHALLENGE 4, PART 3

FEEDBACK FORM: REINFORCING LOOPS PROJECT

Designer's name: _____ Consultant's name: _____

Circle a number in each category to give the designer your feedback on their project.

Interest: How interesting is the story?

1..........................2.............................3............................4............................5

A bit boring   Fascinating!

Plot: How well does the story hold together?

1..........................2.............................3............................4............................5

It's confusing   I completely understand

Feedback: How well does the story demonstrate a reinforcing feedback loop?

1..........................2.............................3............................4............................5

Not Well   Very well

Type of Reinforcing Feedback: Is this story about a vicious or virtuous cycle? (circle one)

                    Vicious   Virtuous

Describe the reinforcing feedback loop that is being shown in the story. What are the elements of the feedback loop and how do they work together?

What suggestions do you have to improve the story?

What suggestions do you have to help the story illustrate a reinforcing feedback loop more clearly?

DESIGN CHALLENGE 4, PART 3

Name: _____ Date: _____ Topic:_____

Working Title: _____

SCRATCH PROJECT STORYBOARD

SCENE#

Scratch Code	Sketch
Description	**Dialogue**
_____	_____
_____	_____
_____	_____
_____	_____
_____	_____
_____	_____
_____	_____
_____	_____
_____	_____
_____	_____
_____	_____
_____	_____

Use as many copies of this storyboard as needed to plan your story.

DESIGN CHALLENGE 5
OUT OF BALANCE: BALANCING
FEEDBACK AND LEVERAGE POINTS

Total time: 120 minutes

OVERVIEW

In contrast to reinforcing feedback loops, balancing feedback loops are processes that bring systems under control and into balance. In Design Challenge 5, youths once again examine the issue of homelessness to further their understanding of balancing feedback and are introduced to the idea of identifying leverage points by reading a children's short story, "The Sneetches." In the final activity youths consider how they might effect maximal change by identifying leverage points in the systems surrounding the issue of homelessness.

PRODUCT

Youths analyze and create connection circle diagrams to identify potential leverage points in the context of homelessness (or another topical issue of interest to the group).

TARGETED SYSTEMS THINKING CONCEPTS

Balancing feedback loops are relationships where two or more elements of a system keep each other in balance, with one (or more) elements leading to increase, and one (or more) elements leading to decrease. These processes keep a system at a state of equilibrium. Usually, balancing feedback processes stabilize systems by limiting or preventing certain processes from happening. Having a sense of how balancing feedback loops operate can give a person a sense of what will make a system stable. *Leverage points* are particular places within a system where a small shift in one thing can produce big changes in everything. Not every place in a system is a leverage point—sometimes changing one thing in a system will produce only small effects that aren't felt throughout the system.

PARTS

PART 1: LOOKING FOR STABILITY

By returning once more to the problem of homelessness, youths consider the ways that the systems can stay in balance—in other words, how to understand the problem of chronic homelessness. Youths will read a story from the *New Yorker* that details the context of the chronically homeless and a potential solution to that problem. In analyzing the story of Murray, youths will begin to look for patterns of interconnections that lead to *balance* in a system.

Time: 30 minutes

PART 2: BALANCING FEEDBACK IN "THE SNEETCHES"

Through the story of "The Sneetches," youths further explore the idea of *balancing feedback loops*, another feature of complex systems, which help them stay balanced and achieve their goals. The goal of this activity is for youths to translate the concept that they encountered in part 1 into a new context, so that they can start to focus on how elements work together to create balance (rather than conflating the specifics of Murray's situation with what balancing feedback is).

Time: 45 minutes

PART 3: WHERE TO DIRECT CHANGE: EXPLORING LEVERAGE

Revisiting the *New Yorker* article read in part 1, youths consider how to determine effective points to intervene in a system in order to evoke maximal change. This opens discussions of the idea of *leverage points* and their related potential problem, *fixes that fail*. Additionally, an optional activity involves having the youths pair up to discuss what community issue they think they'll want to focus on for their final project in Design Challenge 6.

Time: 45 minutes

KEY DEFINITIONS

Perceiving dynamics. Perceiving a system's dynamics involves looking at a higher level at how the system works. Dynamics in a system are often characterized by circles—patterns that feed back on another. These are called feedback loops.

Balancing feedback loops. Relationships where two or more elements of a system keep each other in balance, with one (or more) elements leading to increase, and one (or more) elements leading to decrease. These processes keep a system at a state of equilibrium. Usually, balancing feedback processes stabilize systems by limiting or preventing certain processes from happening. Having a sense of how balancing feedback loops operate can give a person a sense of what will make a system stable.

Leverage points. Particular places within a system where a small shift in one thing can produce big changes in everything. Not every place in a system is a leverage point—sometimes changing one thing in a system will just have small effects that aren't felt throughout the system.

Fixes that fail. Any kind of solution to a problem that fixes the problem temporarily but fails to fix it in the long term, and might even make it worse over time. Fixes that fail are often put in place quickly, usually without much reflection on what consequences they'll have for the system.

OTHER ESSENTIAL VOCABULARY

- Interconnections

COMMON CORE STATE STANDARDS COVERED—ENGLISH LANGUAGE ARTS	NEXT GENERATION SCIENCE STANDARDS
• R.6–12.3 (anchor standard)	• 3–5-ETS1–1
• R.6–12.7 (anchor standard)	• 3–5-ETS1–2
• RI.7.3	• 3–5-ETS1–3
• W.6–12.2 (anchor standard)	• MS-ETS1–1
• W.6–12.7 (anchor standard)	• MS-ETS1–2
• W.6–12.9 (anchor standard)	• MS-ETS1–3
• RST.6–8.3	• MS-ETS1–4
• SL.7.2	• MS-ESS3–3
• SL.6–12.4 (anchor standard)	

MATERIALS OVERVIEW

STUFF TO HAVE HANDY

- A computer for each youth with Internet access and Scratch pre-loaded

- Digital projector

- Computer speakers

- Copies of "The Sneetches," from the book *The Sneetches and Other Stories* (at least one per small group)

- Copies of the *New Yorker* magazine article "Million Dollar Murray" (see links below, provide one for each group member)

- Blank sheets of paper (one for each group member)

- *Balancing Feedback* Scratch project: **scratch.mit.edu/projects/1900511**

HANDOUTS

- "Connection Circle"

- "Balancing Feedback Loop Examples"

- "Finding Balance in Our Community" (optional)

OVERALL CHALLENGE PREPARATION

- Download "Million Dollar Murray" from either the companion website for this book series: Interconnections (**digitalis.nwp.org/gnl**) or at the author's website (**gladwell.com/million-dollar-murray**). Alternatively, you can conduct an Internet search for the title "Million Dollar Murray" for a printable PDF. The article is readily available online.

- Duplicate one copy of the article (about 9 pages) for each youth.

- Read "The Sneetches" to understand how it illustrates balancing mechanisms. Then read the magazine article "Million Dollar Murray" to explore a balancing feedback loop in the context of chronic homelessness, as well as the leverage points that are identified by the power-law theory of homelessness.

PART 1: LOOKING FOR STABILITY

By returning once more to the problem of homelessness, youths consider the ways that the systems can stay in balance—in other words, how to understand the problem of chronic homelessness. Youths will read a story from the *New Yorker* ("Million Dollar Murray") that details the context of the chronically homeless and a potential solution to that problem. In analyzing the story of Murray, youths will begin to look for patterns of interconnections that lead to *balance* in a system.

Time: 30 minutes

STUFF TO HAVE HANDY

- Digital projector
- Copies of the magazine article "Million Dollar Murray," downloaded and duplicated previously (one for each person)

HANDOUTS

- "Connection Circle"

RESEARCH: INTRODUCTION—15 MINUTES

The goal of this activity is to explore another aspect of homelessness—chronic homelessness, those people who live on the streets for years rather than coming and going—and identify the factors that are at work in keeping some people permanently on the streets.

1. Either read the first two pages of "Million Dollar Murray" aloud, or ask youths to read it in pairs or independently, depending on your group's reading skills. **Note:** The *New Yorker* is written at an adult reading level. The article will eventually need to be read in its entirety, but the first two pages are all that are needed to focus the first activity.

2. Write the term *chronic* on the board and ask for volunteers to define it (lasting for a long period of time or frequently recurring.) Discuss what is going on in Murray's life and why he is *chronically* homeless. Encourage youths to identify the *elements* and *interconnections* that they can pick out. Specifically, some key ideas that should emerge include:

    a. Murray had a significant drinking problem.

    b. It was very easy for him to get alcohol.

c. This problem was persistent (lasting at least 15 years).

d. Given opportunity and structure, Murray showed that he could be substance-free and show up reliably to work.

e. Picking up people like Murray could take half of a policeman's time.

f. When someone like Murray passes out, an ambulance is called (which includes a team of four), and the person often spends significant time in the hospital.

IMAGINE AND SHARE: MAPPING THE STORY OF MURRAY—15 MINUTES

Youths will use the "Connection Circle" handout to map the story of Murray.

1. Ask youths to think about Murray's chronic homelessness by linking specific elements via interconnections: in other words, can they figure out how the elements work together to keep Murray chronically homeless? Start by brainstorming the specific elements in the story that they think are central to Murray's problem *and* can increase or decrease over time (use nouns or noun phrases).

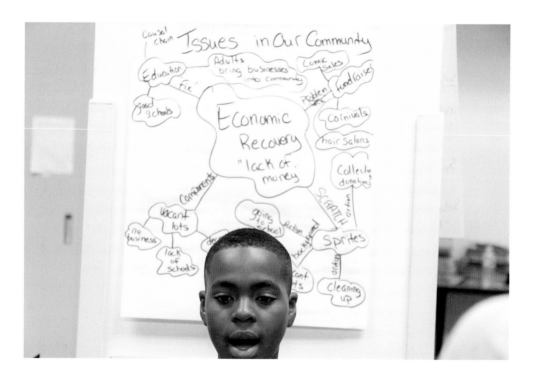

2. Once you have a list, pass out the "Connection Circle" handout and have them work in groups to complete a connections circle about Murray, using the elements they just brainstormed in order to create interconnections in their diagrams.

3. Next ask volunteers to share their understandings of the interconnections in Murray's connection circle. It would be particularly useful to identify connection circles that appear to model some of the balance that can be found in the system. One relationship that is important for youths to see involves the relationship between being homeless, receiving services, improving, having services removed, and then becoming homeless again.

- Specifically, providing Murray with support structures and services allows him to stay sober and employed, which makes people think that he is better, which makes them remove the structure, which makes him spiral into drunkenness (and, subsequently, homelessness), which then puts him back on the street and makes him eligible for social services once again.

- This type of loop, which returns full-circle to the beginning, is called a *balancing feedback loop*. Note how this differs from a *reinforcing feedback loop*, which continues to escalate (or decay). Balancing loops return to the status where they began.

4. Explain that *balancing feedback loops* are relationships in which two or more elements of a system *keep each other in balance*, with one element (or more) leading to increase, and one element (or more) leading to decrease. These processes keep a system at a state of equilibrium. What is tricky about this example of balancing feedback loops is that the equilibrium is not necessarily a positive state (though often it is)—this is important to make clear to group members.

DESIGN CHALLENGE 5, PART 1

CONNECTION CIRCLE

Use the circle below to map connections within the system.

1. First, list the important elements of the system around the outside of the circle. Keep in mind that your elements should be things that increase or decrease over time in the system.

2. Then, use arrows to start mapping the connections between the elements in terms of one causing another to increase or decrease. Remember to:

    a. Use arrows to indicate the "direction" of the relationship (which element is causing, which element is being affected).

    b. Use plus (+) and minus (-) signs near the heads of the arrows to indicate whether the relationship is causing an increase or decrease in the affected element.

PART 2: BALANCING FEEDBACK IN "THE SNEETCHES"

By reading the story "The Sneetches," youths further explore the idea of *balancing feedback loops*, which help them stay balanced and achieve their goals. The goal of this activity is for youths to apply what they learned in part 1 to a new situation, so that their focus remains firmly on how elements work together to create balance in any situation, not just Murray's.

Time: 45 minutes

STUFF TO HAVE HANDY

- Digital projector

- Copies of "The Sneetches," from the book *The Sneetches and Other Stories* (at least one per small group)

HANDOUTS

- "Connection Circle" (on p.196)

- "Balancing Feedback Loop Examples"

RESEARCH: INTRODUCTION AND OVERVIEW—5 MINUTES

The goal of this activity is to further youths' understanding of *balancing feedback*, which causes systems to change over time. This activity will build on the understandings they developed in part 1 of this challenge.

1. Share a new example of balancing feedback with the group by using a real-world example:

   - What often happens if you have a busy day and don't have time to eat lunch at the usual time? When that happens, your body starts to feel an uncomfortable sensation that everyone is familiar with—hunger.

   - Feeling hunger usually causes you to find something to eat, so you eat until you start to feel full, which causes you to stop eating. And then you generally don't eat again until sufficient time has passed for you to experience the hunger sensation again. ... And that begins the cycle all over again.

   - Ask youths if that sounds similar to or different from the kinds of *reinforcing feedback systems* they learned about in Design challenge 4. (If they need

further guidance, ask if there's anything "snowballing," or rapidly escalating and/or decreasing over time.)

- In general, the focus of the conversation should be on how the actions in the hunger/eating dynamic keep things *balanced and well functioning* over time, rather than causing a runaway effect.

2. Ask youths to name the elements of the hunger system, and explain how they work together. List the elements on the board, and use arrows to identify the relationships between them. You might want to use a connection circle diagram to reinforce its utility in helping to document systems. Emphasize that in the feedback they see about hunger and eating—in contrast to reinforcing feedback loops—when something increases, something else happens that eventually reduces that very thing.

3. Explain that this kind of situation is another example of a *balancing feedback loop*, because it describes a relationship between elements that keep the system in balance, rather than cause it to grow or shrink.

RESEARCH AND IMAGINE: FINDING BALANCE IN "THE SNEETCHES"—20 MINUTES

In this activity, we read and analyze the short story "The Sneetches," by Dr. Seuss, to explore a balancing feedback loop within a story.

1. Read "The Sneetches" aloud to the group. Ask the youths if they think what happened to the Sneetches seems to form a system. Once group members have had a chance to share their opinions, ask them to keep this question in mind, and in particular to look for interconnections—as you read aloud the story a second time.

2. Ask group members to describe what they think is happening in the story. Note the elements that youths mention on the board, and make sure that everyone seems to have a good sense of the elements and their relationships to one another. Ask the group if it seems like this system works the same as the system in *The Butter Battle Book*, or if it is different. Try to draw out the youths' focus on the interconnections that are at play between the Star-Belly and Plain-Belly Sneetches, and the role that Sylvester McMonkey McBean plays in the story.

3. Break up into groups of two or three youths and distribute the "Connection Circle" handout to help them model the story.

4. Explain that each group has a goal: to try to model the relationship between the elements in the story. **Note:** At this point, it is not important that youths have a term to describe the relationship, but rather that they are starting to look at the ways in which what happens to one kind of Sneetch impacts what happens to another kind of Sneetch.

5. Encourage youths to think about the multiple characters who contribute to the central action. **Note:** For your own reference only, examine a connection circle diagram created for "The Sneetches," on the next page.

6. If possible, have enough copies of "The Sneetches" on hand so that each group has a copy. Otherwise, make a couple of copies and let the youths know they are available for reference during this activity.

A BALANCING LOOP IN "THE SNEETCHES"

There is one significant balancing loop in "The Sneetches": the loop between the Star-Belly and Plain-Belly Sneetches. The mechanism that propels the loop is Sylvester McMonkey McBean, but the *cause* of the loop is the attitudes of the opposing groups. We might call these two groups the "trend-setting" Sneetches and the "trend-following" Sneetches. The balancing loop works as follows: As the trend-following Sneetches attempt to look like the trend-setting Sneetches, the trend-setting Sneetches respond by changing their look. Specifically, the trend-setting Sneetches have stars, the trend-following Sneetches *get* stars, and the trend-setting Sneetches respond by *removing* stars. The trend-following Sneetches then also remove *their* stars, and the trend-setting Sneetches respond by *getting their stars back*. The cycle continues practically indefinitely ... or at least until they all run out of money.

RESEARCH AND SHARE: BALANCING FEEDBACK — 20 MINUTES

Youths come together to discuss and share their diagrams.

1. Bring the groups together and ask some of them to share the relationships that they have observed. Make sure to focus attention on the connections between the elements and how those connections cause what happens next.

2. Distribute the "Balancing Feedback Loops Examples" handout and review the definition and examples with the group.

    •   Contrast balancing feedback with reinforcing feedback. Ask if anyone can see immediate differences between the two types of feedback:

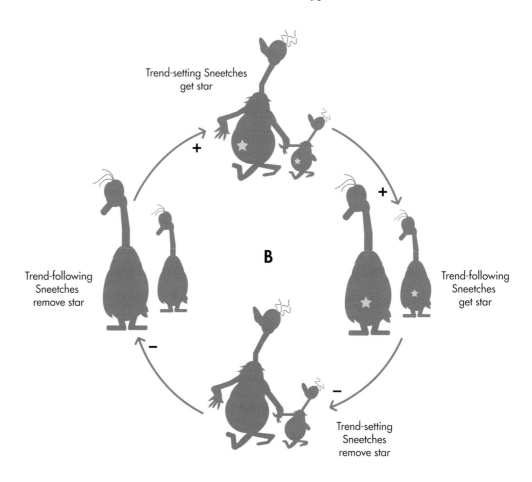

- *Reinforcing feedback* is "self-reinforcing" and tends to get out of control, to "snowball" in a way that can be hard to stop. (Remind youths of the escalation in *The Butter Battle Book*, which they explored in part 2 of Design Challenge 4.)

- *Balancing feedback*, on the other hand, is "self-limiting," and by nature aims to establish control and balance in a system. In many ways, balancing and reinforcing feedback loops are opposites, and sometimes people even put into place balancing mechanisms in order to *prevent* reinforcing feedback loops from happening. (As when the FDIC insured bank deposits to prevent bank runs, a situation group members discussed in part 1 of Design Challenge 4.)

WHAT TO EXPECT

At this point, youths should be able to easily identify elements and interconnections within a story. They should also be able to use the connection circle diagram to analyze the interconnections within a story and discuss balance and potential leverage points within a system.

	Novice	Expert
Systems thinking concepts	• Struggles to identify examples in the story of mechanisms that kept the system in balance. • In modeling the system on the connection circle does not include arrows that demonstrate relationships among elements, or includes arrows but uses them incorrectly. • Thinks causally (rather than interactively) about the system (one element causes another, rather than one element interacts with numerous others to produce system dynamics). • Understands the idea of interconnections between multiple elements, but struggles to understand how those interconnections balance each other.	• Clearly identifies the examples of balancing mechanisms in "The Sneetches." • Is able to demonstrate both the elements and their relationships (via arrows, used accurately), on the connection circle. • Sees the overall outcome of the system as the result of interactions among multiple elements. • Can describe how those elements interact in a way as to balance one another. • Has a sense of how elements of the system interact and impact one another, and can predict these changes.

DESIGN CHALLENGE 5, PART 2

BALANCING FEEDBACK LOOPS

Balancing feedback loops generate actions aimed at creating or preserving a desired state. Generally speaking, balancing feedback processes keep systems stable. They can be referred to as "self-limiting," which makes them the opposite of reinforcing feedback loops).

Balancing Feedback Loops

Definition

Goal-seeking processes that generate actions aimed at moving a system toward, or keeping a system at, a desired state. Generally speaking, balancing feedback processes stabilize systems.

Examples

Hunger

Shannon is hungry so she eats. When Shannon eats her feeling of hunger decreases, which causes her to stop eating. Eventually, Shannon's body uses up the energy from her food intake and will require more, causing her to be hungry again.

A Flushing Toilet

When you flush a toilet the water level drops, which activates the mechanism in the back reservoir to fill up with water. The back reservoir stops filling up with water once the level returns to normal.

Itching and Scratching

When your skin itches, you scratch it to relieve the itchy feeling. Once the itchy feeling subsides you stop scratching, until the itch returns.

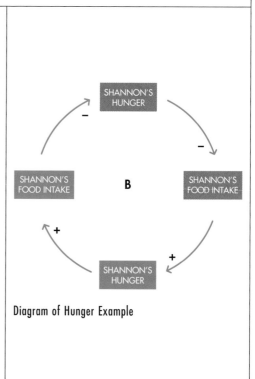

Diagram of Hunger Example

PART 3: WHERE TO DIRECT CHANGE: EXPLORING LEVERAGE

Revisiting the *New Yorker* article, "Million Dollar Murray," introduced in part 1, youths consider how to determine effective places in which to intervene in a system in order to effect maximal change. This opens discussions of the idea of *leverage points* and their related potential problem, *fixes that fail.* An optional activity asks youths to consider local community issues they might want to focus on for their final project in Design Challenge 6.

Time: 45 minutes

STUFF TO HAVE HANDY

• Copies of the magazine article "Million Dollar Murray," used in part 1 (one for each youth)

HANDOUTS

• "Finding Balance in Our Community" (optional)

RESEARCH: PRODUCTIVE POINTS TO INTERVENE—40 MINUTES

Youths return to "Million Dollar Murray," the story that began this challenge, using their systems thinking lens to consider how to identify the best place in a system to try to make changes.

1. Pass out copies of "Million Dollar Murray" and read the entire article, either in a guided reading or independently. Instruct youths to be on the lookout for the solution that was proposed to help deal with the chronically homeless like Murray. **Note:** Remember, the reading level in this article is quite high, and it contains some concepts that might be challenging for your group. Try giving youths a focus before reading—such as "Look for places where people are fighting the problem of homelessness."

2. Debrief with the whole group the solution that the cities of St. Louis and Denver proposed to deal with the problem of chronic homelessness (beginning on page 102 of the article). Make sure that everyone understands the solution they implemented.

3. Return to the connection circle diagram constructed in part 1. Ask youths to think about how they see the proposed solution as *interrupting* or changing the balancing feedback loop that kept Murray moving back and forth between stability and homelessness. As a group, create a new representation of the system with the solution in place.

4. Introduce the idea of *leverage points*, defined as particular places within a system where a small shift in one thing can produce big changes in everything. But not every place in a system is a leverage point; sometimes changing one thing in a system will produce such small effects that the system doesn't change.

5. Ask youths to think about whether the St. Louis and Denver solution described in the article targeted a leverage point. If so, why was that leverage point such an important place in the system of homelessness to intervene?

- It is important for youths to understand that the most effective leverage point is not always obvious. In the Murray example, it does not seem obvious that the place to intervene is with the people who seem most hopeless—it seems much more obvious to start with the people who require the least assistance to stop being homeless.

- However, such a solution does not take into consideration all of the factors of the system (cost, health care, etc.) and so would not result in such significant (economic) effects.

6. Next, introduce the idea of *fixes that fail*: any kind of solution to a problem that fixes a problem temporarily but fails to fix it permanently—and might even make it worse over time. Fixes that fail are often put in place quickly, sometimes without much reflection on the possible consequences.

7. Return to the story of "The Sneetches." Ask youths to think about whether there was a good leverage point in that balancing feedback loop where someone could have intervened to stop the cycle. What would a productive leverage point have been, and how would they have known?

IMAGINE: SELECTING AND RESEARCHING AN ISSUE FOR THE FINAL CHALLENGE—5 MINUTES (OPTIONAL)

Throughout the unit, youths have become more and more attuned to issues that are present in their communities. In Design Challenge 6 youths will engage in an extensive design process to create a Scratch project that suggests a way to address one issue that they've identified.

1. You might wish to have youths spend a short time discussing in pairs which issue they think they might want to focus on for the Design Challenge 6 project, drawing both from group discussions as well as the community interviews they conducted earlier.

2. A sample handout has been provided to help facilitate this conversation; see the optional "Finding Balance in Our Community" handout.

3. Anyone who has already identified a topic can begin research in their own time.

Note This activity should be optional; youths can decide to wait to select and begin research until Design Challenge 6 is underway. The advantage to including it here is that youths will spend more time thinking about and researching their issue and be more likely to have well-thought-out solutions to the problem they're interested in.

DESIGN CHALLENGE 5, PART 3

FINDING BALANCE IN OUR COMMUNITY

This handout will help you identify balancing feedback loops within your community.

Think of two examples of successful balancing loops that you see in your own community that help it meet a goal.

What are the elements of the balancing loop in those examples, and how do they work together?

Think of two examples of fixes that have failed in your community.

Using what you know about systems and feedback loops, can you explain why those fixes might have failed?

Total time: ~500 minutes

OVERVIEW

Understanding the idea of *leverage points*—places where a small change can make a big impact—is critical in order to make effective changes to systems. In this challenge youths explore this concept, as well as the related idea of *unintended consequences*, by reading one more children's novel, *The Lorax,* and identifying possible leverage points in the system of that story. This prepares youths for the final design activity, a Scratch project that depicts using leverage points to make a positive change to a systemic issue in their community.

PRODUCT

Youths design and create a Scratch project that depicts how they could use leverage points to make a positive change to a systemic issue in their community.

TARGETED SYSTEMS THINKING CONCEPTS

When attempting to make a change in a system, systems thinkers consider where best to intervene in the system so that the greatest change can come from a small effort. In short, it's important to think about a system's *leverage points*. At the same time, whenever we want to intervene in a system and change it, we have to be careful of *unintended consequences*—unplanned effects that change the way a system operates.

PARTS

PART 1: INTRODUCTION TO LEVERAGE POINTS

Leverage points are places in systems where small shifts in one thing can produce big changes in everything. Youths will be introduced to this concept through a number of short videos related to systemic social issues. They will then further explore this concept, as well as the related idea of unintended consequences, as they read the book *The Lorax* and identify leverage points in that story.

Time: 125 minutes

PART 2: LEVERAGE POINTS DESIGN CHALLENGE: PRELIMINARY RESEARCH AND DESIGN

Youths research one issue and its accompanying leverage points in their community, and then create a storyboard representing how these leverage points might bring a big change to the system to help it achieve goals they identify as important.

Time: 170 minutes

PART 3: FINAL DESIGN PERIOD

Youths create, iterate, and share their final Scratch projects.

Time: ~200 minutes

KEY DEFINITIONS

Leverage points. Particular places within a system where a small shift in one thing can produce big changes in everything, called *leverage points*, are difficult to find because they often lie far away from either the problem or its obvious solution. Because of the multitude of cause-and-effect relationships, feedback loops, and system structures, a seemingly small change can be amplified, often in unexpected ways. Not every place in a system is a leverage point—sometimes changing one thing in a system will produce only small effects that aren't felt throughout the system.

Unintended consequences. The unexpected and unwanted result of an action that occurs even though the person taking the original action did not want it to happen. *Unintended consequences* are often the result of *fixes that fail* or an attempt to find a leverage point in a system without considering long-term implications to those actions (i.e., someone failed to keep *time horizons* in mind).

Time delay. The time lag between an action in a system and the evidence of its effects.

Time horizon. The overall period of time that a person looks at something in order to understand it.

COMMON CORE STATE STANDARDS COVERED—ENGLISH LANGUAGE ARTS

- R.6–12.3 (anchor standard)
- R.6–12.7 (anchor standard)
- RI.7.3
- W.6–12.2 (anchor standard)
- W.8.6
- W.8.7
- W.6–12.7 (anchor standard)
- W.6–12.9 (anchor standard)
- RST.6–8.3
- RST.6–8.7
- RST.11–12.9
- SL.7.2
- SL.6–12.4 (anchor standard)
- SL.7.5
- WHST.6–8.4
- WHST.6–8.5
- WHST.6–8.6
- WHST.6–8.7

NEXT GENERATION SCIENCE STANDARDS

- 3–5-ETS1–1
- 3–5-ETS1–2
- 3–5-ETS1–3
- MS-ETS1–1
- MS-ETS1–2
- MS-ETS1–3
- MS-ETS1–4
- MS-ESS3–3

MATERIALS OVERVIEW

STUFF TO HAVE HANDY

- A computer for each youth with Internet access and Scratch pre-loaded
- Digital projector
- Computer speakers
- Chart paper and markers
- Copies of *The Lorax* (one for each group member)
- Video: *The Meatrix*: themeatrix.com
- The Girl Effect videos
    - *The Girl Effect: The Clock Is Ticking*: girleffect.org/why-girls/#&panel1-1
    - *The Girl Effect*: girleffect.org/why-girls/#&panel1-2

HANDOUTS

- "Finding Leverage in *The Lorax*"
- "Scratch Project Storyboard"
- "Connection Circle"
- "Telling Stories About Systems: Key Questions"

OVERALL CHALLENGE PREPARATION

- Watch *The Meatrix* and The Girl Effect videos to become familiar with the leverage points in these videos.
- Read *The Lorax* and familiarize yourself with the possible leverage points and unintended consequences in the story.

PART 1: INTRODUCTION TO LEVERAGE POINTS

Leverage points are places in systems where small shifts in one thing can produce big changes in everything. Youths will be introduced to this concept through a number of short videos related to systemic social issues. They will then explore this concept, as well as the related idea of unintended consequences, further as they read the book *The Lorax* and identify leverage points in that story.

Time: 125 minutes

STUFF TO HAVE HANDY

- Digital projector

- Copies of *The Lorax* (one for each group member)

- Computer pre-loaded with *The Meatrix* and two Girl Effect videos

HANDOUTS

- "Finding Leverage in *The Lorax*"

- "Connection Circle"

RESEARCH: INTRO TO FINAL PROJECT: LEVERAGE POINTS IN OUR COMMUNITY—5 MINUTES

Youths are introduced to the final challenge.

1. Explain that for the final part of the group's work in Scratch, they are going to be focusing on how we can change the systems around us, and specifically how to use *leverage points* in order to do that.

2. Let youths know that each of them will be focusing on one systemic issue that they've identified in their community, either taken from their interview of a community member or one they identified during group brainstorming sessions. They will create a Scratch project that shows how leverage points can be used to positively change the system related to that issue.

RESEARCH: WATCHING AND DISCUSSING *THE MEATRIX* AND *THE GIRL EFFECT*—20 MINUTES

Youths are exposed to systemic social issues through three short videos, each of which suggests leverage points that could be used to make positive changes on those issues.

1. Use a digital projector to show the three short videos you prepared before this session:

    a. *The Meatrix* (themeatrix.com) shows the nature of contemporary "factory farms" and proposes one solution to the problem: sustainable family farms. (4 minutes)

    b. The Girl Effect (girleffect.com/why-girls) contains two videos proposing "the simple case for investing in girls":

        • *The Girl Effect: The Clock Is Ticking* (3 minutes) outlines the risks facing girls who grow up in poverty, including vulnerability to molesters, child marriage, teen pregnancy, HIV/AIDS, and continuing the intergenerational cycle of poverty. It ends with the flipside, showing what changes are possible when the cycle is stopped by age 12.

- *The Girl Effect* (2.5 minutes) is about leveraging the unique potential of adolescent girls to end poverty for themselves, their families, their communities, their countries, and the world. It's about making girls visible and changing their social and economic dynamics by providing them with specific, powerful, and relevant resources.

2. Between each video, facilitate brief discussions to highlight the most important systems ideas. The following questions can be helpful conversation starters:

- What were the main problems or issues discussed in the video?
- What are the main elements of the system?
- How do they interact with one another?
- Did you notice any common patterns within the issue?
- What solutions were proposed for the problems described in the video?
- How might those solutions disrupt, interrupt, or change the system?

Note: You might also wish to work together to sketch simple Behavior Over Time (BOT) graphs after each video to illustrate the key trends depicted.

3. Consider recording the responses to each of these debriefings on the board or chart paper to use as a reference in the discussion that follows. A chart with a column for each video in which you list responses to the questions might be especially useful.

4. Encourage the group not to take what was in the videos at face value: These may be good solutions to the problems, but youths should always learn more and think critically about any problem before accepting someone else's solutions. Going deeper into an issue is part of what they will be doing for the final project.

RESEARCH: LEVERAGE POINTS DISCUSSION—20 MINUTES

Youths compare the video and leverage point strategies.

1. Revisit solutions to each problem that the videos proposed. Ask youths if the solutions proposed in each were different in any way. Which solution seemed most powerful: eating from family farms to solve the problems of factory farming (in *The*

Meatrix) or early intervention for young girls to solve the problems of poverty (in The Girl Effect videos)? Explain your reasoning.

2. Finally, ask youths to explain the role of *leverage points* in each video. **Note:** Don't expect them to know what the term means or even to answer this question completely. The aim is to get an idea of the youths' initial conceptions about the concept.

3. Based on their responses and correcting any misconceptions that the youths might have, formally introduce the idea of leverage points:

    *   *Leverage points* are particular places within a system where a small shift in one thing can produce big changes in everything. Leverage points are difficult to find because they often lie far away from either the problem or its obvious solution.

    *   Because of the multitude of cause-and-effect relationships, feedback loops, and system structures, a seemingly small change can be amplified, often in unexpected ways. Not every place in a system is a leverage point—sometimes changing one thing in a system will produce only small effects that aren't felt throughout the system.

4. Explain that not all solutions to problems are equal—and that some solutions make use of leverage points and some do not. There are many possible solutions to every problem, but some only treat one of the symptoms, without solving the basic problems. Take the problem of poverty in The Girl Effect videos:

    *   Imagine that the producers of the video proposed a different solution, such as to provide free medicine to women who contract HIV as a result of having been poor when they were young. Now, that sounds like a good thing to do, right?

    *   *But,* would that solution help to end poverty?

    *   On the other hand, the solution the video producers do propose—of making sure that girls of age 12 get health care and stay in school—leads to a "snowball effect" in which those girls' lives may turn out differently, benefiting generations.

    *   You could show this solution in a *causal loop diagram* (for more information on such diagrams, see the section Tools for Making Systems Visible in the Advanced Design Challenges).

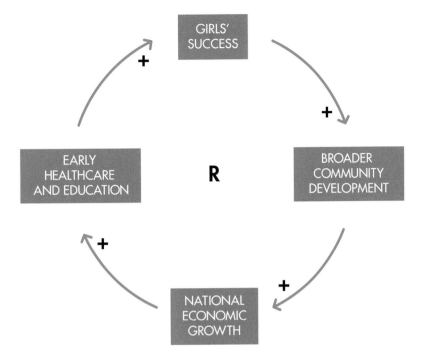

5. Emphasize that leverage points have very distinct characteristics that make them different from "any old solution":

    •   A leverage point allows the greatest change with the smallest shifts.

    •   They rarely try to put a Band-Aid on an existing problem (you can reference *fixes that fail* here, like the one in "The Sneetches") but rather aim to do something that will *prevent the problem from arising in the first place.*

    •   Leverage points often lie "far away" from the problem you're trying to solve, and are usually not the first thing that comes to mind when you think of what will help you solve the problem.

VOICES FROM THE FIELD

It's important that the concept of thinking in systems be constantly reinforced, especially when it comes to delving into the concept of leverage points. Though youths were introduced early on to this concept, it must be made clear that leverage points are solutions, true enough, but not just any solution. It is the smallest shift to create the greatest amount of change.

—JANIE BROWN, GREAT BEAR WRITING PROJECT

6. Introduce the idea of *unintended consequences*, and remind them about the importance of keeping in mind *time horizons* and *time delays*:

- *Unintended consequences* are one or more unexpected and unwanted results of an action taken in a system. Unintended consequences are often the result of *fixes that fail* or an attempt to find a leverage point in a system without considering long-term implications to those actions—someone failed to keep *time horizons* in mind.

- *Time delay* is the time lag between an action in a system and the evidence of its effects.

- *Time horizon* is the overall period of time it takes for a person to look at something in order to understand it.

7. Emphasize that when finding a leverage point and trying to make big changes by altering an important part of a system, it's possible that your action may have unintended consequences that can lead to unexpected results. You can relate the idea of unintended consequences to the idea of *fixes that fail*. Some fixes fail and the system just reverts to the way it was. Other times, you might apply a fix that

fails and then results in the system becoming worse than it originally was in terms of meeting its goals. When this happens, it's an example of unintended consequences.

8. *Optional:* If the youths in your group seem to have a good grasp of systems thinking at this point, you might explore the relationship among *balancing feedback loops*, *reinforcing feedback loops*, *leverage points*, *fixes that fail*, and *unintended consequences*, because these concepts are all interconnected. For example:

    • Many leverage points use balancing feedback loops as mechanisms for changing a system, though others can utilize reinforcing feedback loops (virtuous cycles), and still others seek to change the *mental models and behaviors* of the actors in the system.

    • On a similar note, unintended consequences can result from fixes that fail, though not all fixes that fail produce unintended consequences.

9. In the next activity youths will identify leverage points for change in another system.

RESEARCH AND CREATE: READING AND MODELING *THE LORAX*—35 MINUTES

Youths read the book *The Lorax* to hone their skill at identifying leverage points.

1. Distribute copies of *The Lorax* and have the youths read the book on their own or as part of a group read-aloud.

2. Review the events of the story to attune youths to the big picture, using prompts like these to develop a good list of elements from the Lorax system:

    • What was the main trend that you saw happening in the story?

    • Name specific elements in the story that changed over time. (For example, the happiness of the animals, number of Thneeds, number of trees, amount of money the Once-ler made, etc.).

3. Break up into small groups of 2–3 youths to create connection circles that explain the big trends and changes that the group as a whole just described. Give each group a "Connection Circle" handout to work on. Allow about 10 minutes for this activity. (For a full description of the connection circle diagramming technique, see the section Tools for Making Systems Visible in the Advanced Design Challenges).

4. Next, ask for groups to volunteer to share their circles and explain how they reasoned the interconnections in *The Lorax*.

5. Point out different ways that groups illustrated the elements and connections. **Note:** Remind the group that there is no one "correct" way to create a connection circle for a given system, but that similar connections should show up somewhere—the act of finding the connections and any loops that result is the important thing in this exercise.

6. Use the diagrams to transition into a broader discussion about the book in the next activity.

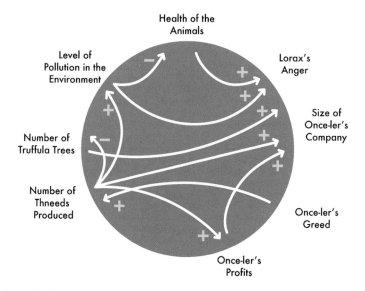

Sample Connection Circle Diagram for *The Lorax.*

SHARE: LET'S TALK: *THE LORAX* DISCUSSION—15 MINUTES

A whole-group analysis and discussion about *The Lorax* creates two important learning opportunities for the youths and an important assessment opportunity for the instructor. First, such a discussion provides a nice review of the ideas and terms that have been covered in previous challenges. Second, it transitions youths from simply *describing* systems to understanding how to most effectively *engage* (and *change*) those systems. The following prompts can help you facilitate this discussion. Remind youths to refer to their connection circles from the previous activity as a reference.

• What patterns do you see in how the system in the story operates?

• Are any feedback loops present in the system? What sort (balancing or reinforcing)? How do these feedback loops operate? (For example, the sale of Thneeds creates a reinforcing feedback loop that drives the Once-ler to invest in his factories and look for more ways to harvest Truffala trees.)

- What are some problems and/or unintended consequences within the system? (Degradation of the environment [in other words, extinction of the Truffala trees, loss of habitat], wildlife stress [like the Bar-ba-loots, Swomee-Swams and Humming-Fish leaving the forest], unsustainability of the Thneed business.)

VOICES FROM THE FIELD

Using *The Lorax* created a great opportunity for discussing potential leverage points in the community, as well as the ones identified in the story. Using a concept map to lead the group discussion of *The Lorax* is a great idea. Within the map, a focus can be made on the elements, interconnections, feedback loops as well as the leverage point.

—JANIE BROWN, GREAT BEAR WRITING PROJECT

IMAGINE: FINDING LEVERAGE IN *THE LORAX*—15 MINUTES

Youths work in small groups to identify potential leverage points in the story.

1. Have youths return to their same small groups and distribute the "Finding Leverage in *The Lorax*" handout, along with a set of markers, to each group.

2. Instruct groups to develop two solutions to the Lorax problem that rely on leverage points (changing one thing to cause the whole system to change in some way). For each solution ask them to identify at least one *potential* unintended consequence of that solution (what might go wrong if that solution is implemented?).

SHARE: LEVERAGE POINT PRESENTATIONS—15 MINUTES

Youths share their findings with the larger group.

1. Ask for a volunteer from as many of the breakout groups as time allows to present what they identified as solutions, as well as any potential unintended consequences.

2. Debrief each presentation as a whole-group exercise. Ask youths what they think of the solutions proposed. Do they think they would work? Why or why not? Were the identified unintended consequences bad enough to make the solution unworkable? Are there any other unintended consequences that weren't considered?

WHAT TO EXPECT

At this point, youths should have a good understanding of systems and should be able to identify some new systems thinking concepts, including potential leverage points in the system. *The key here is to connect leverage points to prior concepts and to identify leverage points, contrasting them with other points in the system that might be changed but would produce only minor effects on the system.*

	Novice	Expert
Systems thinking concepts	• Struggles to identify how elements in the story interact. • Struggles to identify the kinds of feedback loops that exist, or cannot explain how those feedback loops work. • Sees all of the systems thinking concepts learned to date as separate and not connected. Is unable to draw connections across the various stories and concepts encountered. • Has an emergent understanding of leverage points and perhaps generalizes to think that every or nearly every place in a system is a leverage point without deeper reflection on which of those points, if changed, will have rippling effects on the whole of the system. • Able to identify the intended consequences of a particular leverage point but struggles to identify other unintended consequences.	• Sees the overall outcome of the system as the result of interactions among multiple elements. • Can describe how those elements interact and identify the kind of feedback loop that is created. • Is able to relate leverage points to prior concepts, including the concepts of balancing feedback loops, reinforcing feedback loops, fixes that fail and unintended consequences, as they are all interconnected. • Can identify potential leverage points and those particular places within a system where a small shift in one thing can produce big changes in everything. • Understands that not every place in a system is a leverage point—sometimes changing one thing in a system will just have small effects that aren't felt throughout the system. • Is able to identify the intended and unintended consequences of a particular leverage point.

DESIGN CHALLENGE 6, PART 1

FINDING LEVERAGE IN *THE LORAX*

In your group, think of two solutions that you could offer to solve the problem in *The Lorax*. Explain how your solutions would change one thing but impact the entire system. Then think about a potential unintended outcome that could result from each change.

SOLUTION 1

What one thing would you recommend to change in the system described in *The Lorax*?

Why might that change impact the entire system?

What is a possible unintended consequence that could arise from this change?

SOLUTION 2

What one thing would you recommend to change in the system described in *The Lorax*?

Why might that change impact the entire system?

What is a possible unintended consequence that could arise from this change?

DESIGN CHALLENGE 6, PART 1

CONNECTION CIRCLE

Use the circle below to map connections within the system.

1. First, list the important elements of the system around the outside of the circle. Keep in mind that your elements should be things that increase or decrease over time in the system.

2. Use arrows to start mapping the connections between the elements in terms of one causing another to increase or decrease. Remember to:

   a. Use arrows to indicate the "direction" of the relationship (which element is causing, which element is being affected).

   b. Use plus (+) and minus (-) signs near the heads of the arrows to indicate whether the relationship is causing an increase or decrease in the affected element.

PART 2: LEVERAGE POINTS DESIGN CHALLENGE: PRELIMINARY RESEARCH AND DESIGN

Youths research one issue and its accompanying leverage points in their community, and then create a storyboard representing how these leverage points might bring a big change to the system to help it achieve important goals.

Time: 170 minutes

STUFF TO HAVE HANDY

- Digital projector
- Paper
- Chart paper and markers

HANDOUTS

- "Scratch Project Storyboard," several copies per youth
- "Telling Stories about Systems: Key Questions"

RESEARCH: INTRO TO THE LEVERAGE POINTS DESIGN CHALLENGE—5 MINUTES

In this activity you will introduce the culminating design challenge, which asks youths to put everything they've learned about feedback loops and leverage points toward the solution of a community problem.

1. Remind youths that they've identified a community problem in prior Design Challenges that they were interested in addressing.

2. Explain that in the final design project youths will create a Scratch project that describes and identifies some sort of leverage point/solution to a problem they have identified in the local community.

3. Let them know that in the coming days they'll undergo a more rigorous design cycle than for any other project so far, incorporating all of the following steps:

    a. In-depth research

    b. Creating a set of graphs and systems diagrams of their issue

    c. Storyboarding their Scratch project

    d. An initial drafting period in Scratch

  e. Peer feedback on preliminary designs

  f. A final design period

  g. Publishing the final project and group presentations

4. It's also useful to let youths know what the overall timeframe for this process will be (how many days/weeks it will occur over, how much time will likely be available for each part of the process, etc.). This will obviously be contingent on the specific context that you're working in.

RESEARCH: LEARNING MORE ABOUT YOUR ISSUE—70 MINUTES

To understand the full scope of a community problem and start thinking about possible solutions, youths will need to conduct research about their chosen issue.

Note While we outline just 70 minutes here, we recommend extending and adjusting this research period as appropriate for your context, possibly through having youths conduct research independently of the group meeting time. This might mean spending more research time in group or as homework.

Additionally, if there are particular research strategies you want to incorporate (e.g., understanding how to identify credible online sources, triangulating sources, etc.), this is a good time to do so.

> **VOICES FROM THE FIELD**
>
> During the research time, some youths needed to be assisted on how to research a community issue. When I was talking to the youths, their reason for skipping research is that they "know" the issue already. When they say they "know" it, really it meant that they knew what issue they were going to show. We had to guide them on what they should be looking for (solutions that people have proposed or tried, things that caused the issue, how it has affected the community, etc.).
>
> —JENILYNN REDILA, CHICAGO QUEST

1. At this point, everyone should have made a final decision on which community issue they want to be the focus of their final project. This will likely be an issue that emerged from their interviews with community members, though it can also be something that they've identified independently.

2. It's important that youths have enough clarity at this point to start researching, so you may need to work with some youths to help them make that final decision. For example, you could encourage them to explore the local news to find problems in the community.

3. Provide computer access for additional research. Direct youths to look for 3–5 solutions that have either been tried or proposed in relation to their topic and consider them as possible inspiration for their project. They may discover one solution uses a leverage point that would work for them.

4. Another potential way to guide their research is to post the following questions on the board (or create a handout):

   • Where did this issue come from? What caused it?

   • Why does this issue continue to be a problem? Why hasn't it been solved already? What patterns or structures are keeping the problem going?

   • Which of these patterns or structures would need to change in order to solve the problem?

   • What new patterns and structures could you introduce to solve the problem?

5. Consult with each youth during this period to see how they're coming along in their issue selection and research.

VOICES FROM THE FIELD

It seemed to work best for our youths to discuss community issues as a group because each one had different ideas/perspectives of issues within their community and it was easier for us (teachers) to record their thoughts on newsprint/board so that everyone could contribute.

—TRINA WILLIAMS, GREAT BEAR WRITING PROJECT

SHARE: GATHERING ISSUES IN A COLLECTIVE SPACE—5 MINUTES

Youths work to gather their issues and to make them public for later discussion.

1. As youths solidify their topic, ask each to post their chosen issue beside their name on the board or chart paper, creating an "issue cloud" of the group's planned projects.

2. The issue cloud should remain visible to everyone during all design phases. This makes it transparent to everyone what issues their peers are working on so that they can consult one another other if they're working on similar issues.

Note The remainder of the design process of this challenge will be fluid, because youths will be working independently and therefore moving through the stages at individual rates.

VOICES FROM THE FIELD

It was very helpful for youths to have a guiding question as a focal point of direction before they started working in Scratch.

—TRINA WILLIAMS, GREAT BEAR WRITING PROJECT

IMAGINE: ISSUE GRAPHING AND DIAGRAMMING—25 MINUTES (OPTIONAL)

Once they've selected an issue, ask youths to create a connections circle (and possibly a causal loop diagram) of their issue, drawing on the modeling techniques they've been using throughout the curriculum. Within their diagrams they should include how the leverage point/solution they've identified fits in and affects the system of their community.

IMAGINE: STORYBOARDING—35 MINUTES

Youths create a storyboard that helps to outline what their project will look like in Scratch.

1. The next step in the design process is the creation of the storyboard that will guide the Scratch project. Distribute the "Scratch Project Storyboard" handout. They can use the handout to sketch out the plans for different scenes in their project, including sprites, dialogue, and what Scratch commands they think they'll use. **Note:** Keep a lot of extra copies available.

2. An additional resource, the "Telling Stories about Systems: Key Questions" handout, contains guiding questions to help designers stay attuned to systemic aspects of their issue.

3. Check in with youths as they complete their storyboards, giving feedback when necessary.

4. Let youths know that when they've completed their storyboard, they should check in with you (or another facilitator/instructor) to get approval to begin designing in Scratch.

CREATE: LEVERAGE POINT PROJECT DRAFTING IN SCRATCH—30 MINUTES

Give students 30 minutes to work on their storyboards. In the next part, they will go through several iterations of the design process, based on these storyboards.

DESIGN CHALLENGE 6, PART 2

Name: _____ Date: _____ Topic: _____

Working Title:_____

SCRATCH PROJECT STORYBOARD

SCENE#

Scratch Code	Sketch
Description	Dialogue

Use as many copies of this storyboard as needed to plan your story.

DESIGN CHALLENGE 6, PART 2

TELLING STORIES ABOUT SYSTEMS: KEY QUESTIONS

As you draft and create your stories, keep these questions in mind to make sure that you're thinking about things from a systems perspective:

What's the problem or issue you're concerned with?

What are the "big trends" associated with the issue? How has the issue changed over time?

What are the key elements of the system? How are they connected to one another?

What would the community look like if the problem was solved?

What kinds of changes would make that solution possible?

PART 3: FINAL DESIGN PERIOD

Youths create, iterate, and share their final Scratch projects.

Time: 200 minutes

STUFF TO HAVE HANDY

- Digital projector
- Paper
- Chart paper and markers

RESEARCH: INTRODUCTION—2 MINUTES

Remind youths about the big goal for the remainder of the challenge: to create a story or project in Scratch that illustrates how leverage points can be used to solve a problem in their community.

SHARE: PAIR, SHARE, AND FEEDBACK ON STORYBOARDS OR DRAFTS—30 MINUTES

Youths engage in a peer feedback process on their storyboards or drafts.

VOICES FROM THE FIELD

The challenge of this activity was maintaining balance or structure during the exploration and development of Scratch projects. To resolve this particular issue, I suggest giving youths a sheet to record at least five new concepts or combinations they saw in others' projects that they would like to use in their own project. During iteration, these concepts should be put into action and youths should be encouraged to write at least one major change that they made to their project and how it helped to enhance their project. This could be used as an exit ticket.

—JANIE BROWN, GREAT BEAR WRITING PROJECT

---

1. As youths complete their storyboards or drafts, create feedback pairs to share what they've accomplished so far.

2. Ask each partner to give both warm and cool feedback (see the section called Tools for the Advanced Design Challenges and advice on the following):

- *General flow of the story*: Comment on how well the story holds together.

- *Illustrating systems concepts*: Comment on how well the story identifies a systemic problem and proposes a viable solution based on a leverage point.

- *Scratch technique* (if applicable): Comment on how the project uses Scratch blocks to help tell a story. Invite partners to offer any technical assistance, advice, or support.

3. Have pair groups switch after 10 minutes so that both partners receive feedback on their projects.

VOICES FROM THE FIELD

What I found useful during the pair, share, feedback activity was to model how to have a constructive and meaningful conversation in pairs. We gave them sentence starters to help them find direction on how to give useful feedback. Saying that it's "good" didn't cut it. What was good about it and why was it good? Did it help with the flow of the story? Here are some sample starters:

- Is there a community issue? Does the story make sense?

- When they split up into partners, the sentence starters we offered to them were:

  - "I suggest that …"

  - "I wanted to know how …"

  - "Why did you …"

  - "I can see that you …"

While a youth was giving feedback, we had the other write it down. This way, both are actively involved in the process. After a few minutes, they would switch and look at the other's project.

—JENILYNN REDILA, CHICAGO QUEST

CREATE, ITERATE, AND PUBLISH: SCRATCH DESIGN TIME—130 MINUTES

Youths engage in their primary design period in Scratch, integrating feedback they got on their draft.

1. Youths should begin creating, revising, and iterating directly after the feedback session, basing their work on that feedback. Let them know that they'll have two hours to complete their projects.

2. Emphasize that while this sounds like a lot of time, it will go by quickly, so make sure to stay focused on the big picture *first*, and adding special touches only after the full story has been created. Have them continually ask themselves:

    • Am I effectively communicating my issue?

    • Have I made it clear what leverage point I'm using in my solution?

    • Am I managing my time well so that I can complete the project on time?

3. During this period, monitor progress and assist where necessary.

4. When projects are done, ask youths to share their project at the Scratch website, using whichever sharing process you've set up.

VOICES FROM THE FIELD

Walking around, I found that some youths were still caught up with playing with Scratch and finding out how it works. To balance that out, I asked youths to verbally tell me about the issue that they were focusing on just to make sure they were aware of what the task was. While they were talking, I started to draw out a mini diagram on a post-it. Once they saw what I was doing, it helped provide a jumping point for them, and they started to continue the diagramming on their own.

— JENILYNN REDILA, CHICAGO QUEST

SHARE: FINAL GROUP PRESENTATIONS — 40 MINUTES

Youths gather to share their work and elicit feedback.

1. Once the design period is complete, ask for volunteers who are willing to share their Scratch projects with the group. Project individual projects so the whole group can watch as the designer presents his or her story.

2. As youths are sharing, encourage them to explain (if it's not evident in the project), how the project illustrates how a leverage point could effect change on the issue from their community.

3. Invite feedback and encouragement from the broader group as youths present.

VOICES FROM THE FIELD

For youths who feel the pressure of presenting incomplete projects, it will be important to encourage them to display regardless because their fellow Scratchers can and will offer suggestions for them and inform them of missing elements, chains/loops, or leverage points. This is also a good time to make Scratch Cards available for reiteration of their Scratch projects.

— JANIE BROWN, GREAT BEAR WRITING PROJECT

SAMPLE PROJECTS: LEVERAGE POINTS

Community members band together to solve a local problem in a youth's Scratch project. (Credit: by Luis)

A youth's Scratch project depicts community members taking collective action to solve a problem in their neighborhood. (Credit: Antonio)

A youth uses alternating scenes and constant narration to help raise awareness of domestic abuse. (Credit: Simone)

A youth simulates a televised interview format in a Scratch project to present a way to handle neighborhood graffiti. (Credit: Tené)

While most of the prior examples propose solutions to community problems, they don't necessarily illustrate particularly compelling examples of *leverage points* (i.e., the idea of leveraging existing dynamics in the system to make a big change). This sample project draws on the Perry Preschool research project (http://en.wikipedia.org/wiki/ HighScope) to illustrate a leverage point. The basic premise: This famous study found that a group of toddlers from at-risk backgrounds who were given free preschool had dramatically improved longitudinal outcomes than toddlers in a control group. In other words, by making a small tweak to the existing system (i.e., the offering of free preschool services), the project was able to leverage existing dynamics in the system to have dramatic outcomes, as illustrated in this Scratch project.

(continued)

DELVING DEEPER INTO SYSTEMS THINKING

The significant problems we face cannot be solved at the same level of thinking we were at when we created them.

—Albert Einstein

We are caught in an inescapable network of mutuality, tied in a single garment of destiny. Whatever affects one directly affects all indirectly.

—Dr. Martin Luther King Jr.

So what is systems thinking, and why is it important? With so little time to cover what seems like so much, why should systems thinking get a seat at the educational table? We find the answer in part by looking at the vast problems in the world around us, which range from environmental degradation to global financial meltdowns, growing inequality to ballooning costs of health care, and so many more issues. At their core, these difficulties are about systems, and all can be linked fundamentally to perspective: people have a tendency to look at things in terms of isolated parts instead of interdependent wholes. In short, to solve these complex problems, we need to view the world as a set of complex systems.

We believe that teaching systems thinking holds promise for supporting the development of a generation of young people who look at things differently, through "new lenses" that will allow them to effectively meet the challenges of a world that is more connected than ever. These lenses involve looking before leaping, an orientation toward understanding the big picture, and the approach of *interpreting* things differently rather than *doing* them differently. After all, change in the ways we *do* things naturally follows from a change in the way we *see* things. Rather than focusing on a narrow analysis of phenomena that we too often assume are standing still, a systems thinking approach always assumes that the world is in constant motion, and that in that world, nothing exists in isolation. So the systems thinker learns to focus on the dynamics that surround, shape, and are shaped by whatever it is that we want to understand, whether it be in the realm of science, sociology, economics, or English literature. Systems thinkers seek to understand the impact of their actions on the often tightly interconnected system of which they are a part.

WHAT MAKES A SYSTEMS THINKER DIFFERENT? IT'S ALL ABOUT PERSPECTIVE!

As mentioned previously, much of systems thinking deals with changing our perspectives on situations and adopting the kinds of perspectives that people aren't often taught. Specifically, several practices are engaged in regularly by someone acting from a systems thinking perspective:

- Looking at the world in terms of integrated and interdependent wholes, as opposed to isolated parts

- Knowing that most complex problems involve dynamic systems that are in motion, rather than static parts that stand still

- Viewing situations from multiple levels of perspective, focusing on the connections between events and the underlying patterns, systemic structures, and assumptions from which those events emerge

- Considering how a particular stakeholder's position within a system will affect his or her ideas and assumptions about a system's function and how it should operate

- Adjusting the sense of time—by expanding the range of time considered when looking at a problem, you can gain insights into how certain actions in a system might have delayed effects

- Identifying the various dynamics, especially circular ones in the form of feedback loops, which lead a system to function in a particular way and move in a particular direction

- Focusing on finding leverage points that can be used to make lasting changes, as opposed to falling back on short-term fixes

- Considering the unintended consequences of intervening in a system

Think about the difference between a person who is able to do the things on that list and one who cannot. In an interconnected world, young people who are trained as systems thinkers have a powerful way of understanding, participating in, and changing the structures that affect their lives and those of people they care about.

THINKING BELOW THE WATERLINE: MULTIPLE LEVELS OF PERSPECTIVE

One of the most important things to keep in mind when it comes to looking at systems is that much of what happens can't be seen at first glance. The most obvious and visible parts of systems are big events—they scream for our attention, and often much of the work done in systems is in *reaction* to these events. Staying on the level of events keeps us in a response frame of mind—the term "putting out fires" best expresses what it means to think about systems only on the level of events. To counter this, a powerful metaphor emerged in the systems thinking world: the idea of a system as an iceberg, with events as the visible tip "above the surface," but the real action happening "below the waterline," where *patterns* of behaviors are driven by *systemic structures* emerging from *mental models*.

Let's take an example inspired by the story *A River Ran Wild*, by Lynne Cherry, a book we use as a mentor text in Design Challenge 3 of *Script Changers*. The story documents the history of the Nashua River and the way that it went from being a pristine source of life for Native American tribes in the 1400s to a polluted dumping ground for factory waste beginning with the British colonies, reaching its height as the industrial revolution occurred, only to be cleaned up and restored as a result of citizen organizing in the 1970s.

Say a child went swimming in Nashua while it was still polluted and became sick. Just focusing on the level of *events*, the response might be simply to get the child medical treatment. Problem solved, right? Of course not. Moving down to the level of *patterns*, one could see that this sort of sickness wasn't a one-time deal, and could then start thinking proactively. This might involve starting processes that could clean the river by adding filtration mechanisms, an acceptable stop-gap measure, but if more factories get built and increase dumping in the river, then the filtration mechanisms might be overwhelmed. By working to change the *structure* that governed the system—in this case, the regulations around dumping hazardous chemicals into the river—environmental activists in the 1970s thought creatively to come up with a more sustainable solution. But most environmentalists acknowledge that long-term change in our environmental systems will involve moving down to the deepest and most influential level of systems— engaging with the *mental models* that drive systemic structures: challenging assumptions that lead to an exploitative view of nature and promoting those that assume interdependence between the natural world and human civilization.

But "thinking below the waterline" doesn't necessarily mean a person should always assume the only levels that matter are the ones below the surface. One big part of being a systems thinker means deciding where it's most important to act at a given

THE ICEBERG
Looking below the Waterline

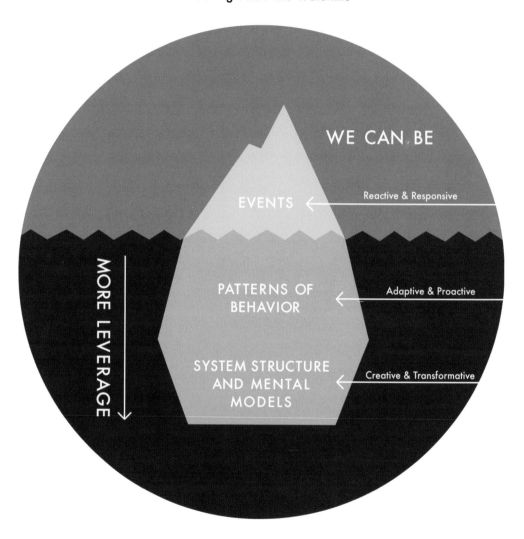

point. Sometimes the greatest need is on the level of events—certainly in the example above, the first thing to be done is to get the child to a doctor. But a systems thinker moves fluidly between looking at a system from different levels, with each perspective informing a broader understanding of how the system works and what it means to take action in it.

THINKING ACROSS THE TABLE: CONSIDERING MENTAL MODELS

Most systems in the world involve human beings one way or another. These might be designers of mechanical systems, or participants in social and "living" systems that are co-created through human interaction and intervention. And of course, the person looking at a system and trying to understand it is also a human being. All of these people hold *mental models*—evolving sets of ideas and assumptions about a system and how it works. Consciously or not, people use their mental models of how a system works when they decide how they're going to act in a system. When one's mental model changes, the ways that one relates to and acts within systems change with it. And so understanding the different actors involved in a system and how they're approaching a system is crucial to putting together a picture of what is happening in a system, to establishing a clearer mental model of our own.

From a systems perspective, mental models are important for two big reasons that we alluded to above. The first has to do with the fact that any "map" we create of a complex system is essentially a map of our mental models. The more clarified our mental models and the more we examine and test our own assumptions about how they work, the closer to reality (that is, the closer to representing a complex set of interconnections) the map will be. The second is that in a given system, the myriad actors involved are always bringing their mental models to the table. The ability to "think across the table" and understand and empathize with the people involved in a system is often the key to making sense of what's happening and to making changes that will actually be sustainable, because they are taking into account how stakeholders in the system think.

Let's take the example of the Nashua River in *A River Ran Wild* again—as we mentioned earlier, the mindset that led to the pollution of the river was one that assumed an extractive, exploitative view of nature—one that understood the role of human beings as one that is solely oriented toward taking what one needs from the natural world, as opposed to one based on mutual dependence and interconnection. Understanding that this was the mental model held by the settlers allows us to get to the heart of the how we might change these systems in a sustainable way, and also helps us make sense of the decisions that were made by the people who polluted the river.

RESETTING THE CLOCK: TIME HORIZONS AND DELAYS

A final key way that systems thinkers shift perspectives is by taking an expansive view of time. This, of course, is connected to ideas we already shared about moving from the level of events to the level of patterns. An event is one point in time, patterns always occur over time. And so systems thinkers, in order to get the "big picture," must often have expanded *time horizons*—the overall periods of time that you look at something in order to understand it. When we change our time horizons, we can start to see how actions taken at one point in time can have effects way down the line. A classic example is agricultural cycles. If we plant a seed for a tree and then only check in on it a couple of days later, we're of course missing the big picture. By expanding our time horizon, our general "grain size" of what's an important unit of time, we start to see how that single action of planting a seed results in a new life form. The same principle applies in many community issues. An increase in the number of public spaces like parks and gardens in a neighborhood might not immediately look like it's doing very much, but over time might yield great benefits in terms of the ties that develop among the community members that use the space. This principle is known as *time delays*—the time lag between an action in a system and the evidence of its effects. As a rule of thumb, systems thinkers try to have more expansive time horizons so that they can better ferret out delays that might otherwise be invisible.

WHAT MAKES A SYSTEM A SYSTEM?

One of the key things that makes systems thinkers different is that they "know a system when they see one," and can tell the difference between a system and well, a bunch of "stuff." So let's address the question of what a system is, and isn't. A system *isn't* just a whole bunch of stuff that happens to be lumped together geographically or topically. Systems have particular qualities, and knowing and being able to identify these is a key part of being able to look at things systemically.

Here's one definition of system that we like to use: A *system* is a collection of interacting *elements* that interact to *function* as a whole, where the whole is always greater than the sum of its parts. If you change one element the whole functions differently. All of these elements are set up in a particular way, interacting in relation to one another, which is called a system's *structure*. The structure of a system determines the specific *behaviors* of different parts and the specific *system dynamics* that result from the interactions among the elements.

In a designed system or, alternatively, one with intentional actors, these elements work together in order to accomplish an intentional *purpose* or *goal* that someone brings to the system. But regardless of that intentional goal, a system will always function in a certain way that is moving the system toward achieving a certain state. (Note that these terms are defined in great detail in Appendix A.)

Linda Booth Sweeney, a leader in the field of systems thinking, likes to talk about the difference between systems and heaps (Sweeney 2001). Both, she says, contain lots of "stuff," or parts. But a heap won't be changed much if you take away some of its parts. Think of a pile of laundry. Add or take away a couple of shirts or a towel, and you still have a pile of laundry—not really a substantive change. Now think of a washing machine. Try taking off the door handle, adding a slot for detergent that doesn't connect to the rest of the machine, or changing the amount of electricity that feeds the machine. Good luck getting socks clean! That pile of laundry is a heap, where adding and taking away things won't really affect the pile very much (if at all) in terms of how it functions in the world. But a washing machine is a system—we can't just add, take away, or change elements willy-nilly since these often are interconnected in specific ways, often feeding back on one another, and have specific roles or behaviors that allow the system to function in a particular way.

A SYSTEM'S GOAL, PURPOSE, AND FUNCTION: NOT ALL ARE CREATED EQUAL

One of the tricky elements of systems is the fact that there's often a difference between the way that a system is *actually* working (its *function*) and how we *want* it to work (its *goal*). This is why so many of us try to intervene in existing systems—because they're not working well (or maybe they're working well for *some*, but not for all).

There are many cases where a system is functioning exactly as it was intended to do by someone designing or intervening in it. Let's take the example of a game. A game can be considered a system because how the game is played and how the game play unfolds are the results of multiple interactions among different components. The *function* of the system (the experience of playing the game) might be really difficult—and a designer might have meant it to be so (her *goal* might have been to create a difficult game). On the other hand, sometimes the overall function of a system is *at odds* with the intended goal that someone has for the system. For instance, from one perspective, the *goal* or purpose of a car is to take someone from point A to point B; but when the car's transmission gives out, the car will not *function* as a system to meet that goal.

It's important to be able to reflect not only on how a system might be functioning currently, but also on how a designer might have intended it to operate (or intended to change it). A given system might have multiple goals that are at play simultaneously, but come into conflict. The person who designed the washing machine has a pretty straightforward goal: get clothing clean (without destroying it in the process). Many systems are more complex than a washing machine, however, and have a less straight-forward purpose. For example, the educational system has many elements (e.g., teach-ers, youths, school buildings, assessments, and educational standards), all of which, presumably, are meant to work together in order to ... do what? Well, that question is actually a matter of some dispute. Like many other systems, such as health care, social services, economies, businesses, and communities, the educational system has more than one person who acts as a "designer"—that is, there are multiple actors bringing varying goals and purposes to the design of a given system and contributing to the way that it is configured.

In the case of the educational system, some people believe that the purpose of being educated is to develop a population that is well prepared to engage in the project of democracy (this was Thomas Jefferson's view), while others see its purpose as preparing young people to compete in the global economy. These are only two possible goals, and while there might be some overlap of goals, we probably can agree that an educational system that aims at only one of the goals likely would look different from one that aims at the other. Knowing that any given system can have different stakeholders working toward different goals sometimes can help us understand why a system is not function-ing as well as it could be. After all, not all goals are compatible.

Often though, the way systems actually operate, the way they're functioning, is more organic and not actually intentional. Many environmental issues that result from the interaction of human behavior with natural ecosystems, for instance, can be described in terms of systems where the function is not one that anyone intended. Global warming results from interaction of many interrelated elements (human fossil fuel emissions, carbon dioxide's capacity to retain heat, the particular make-up of the earth's atmosphere that captures certain gases, etc.) all "working together" such that the system functions to increase global climate over time. Obviously, this was not anyone's intention, but it points to the fact that while many systems are designed and have intended goals or consequences (like that washing machine), others have their own logic and function that is driven by an emergent system structure (like economies and ecosystems).

FEEDBACK LOOPS AND THE NONLINEAR NATURE OF COMPLEX SYSTEMS

In general, when we think about the way things work we default to linear explanations that often hide the larger dynamics of systems that underlie interactions. In a linear view, one thing happens, and this causes something else to occur, and then something results from that, and on and on. Think of a Rube Goldberg machine: those crazy contraptions that might start with a ball going down a ramp, hitting and knocking over a bottle, which hits a spring-loaded spoon that launches another ball into the air, and so on until it fries your morning eggs. This view, of things interrelating through linear chains of events, does work some of the time to explain how things happen … but it doesn't work for everything. As Booth Sweeney notes: "[M]any things—both human-created and in nature—do not operate in a linear manner. The scale used to quantify an earthquake's power is one example. An earthquake of magnitude 5 is ten times more powerful than an earthquake of magnitude 4. Traffic jams, weather patterns, and epidemics are other examples of nonlinearities. In living systems, as in each of these examples, the puzzling behavior associated with nonlinear phenomena emerges not out of a series of straight lines of cause and effect but out of myriad interconnections, feedback loops, and networks. Within these twisty, curvy, loopy interconnections, even the slightest change can have enormous and disproportionate effects." (Sweeney 2001)

Thus, systems are more usefully understood by focusing on the patterns of circular interconnections in systems, and the ways that those interconnections impact the overall function of that system. One way of understanding nonlinear patterns of interconnections involves looking for *feedback loops,* which describe relationships among elements that are characterized by circular or mutual causality, which means that different parts of the system shape and change one another in a reciprocal way in which each is looping back on the other. A good example can be seen when people start to practice something

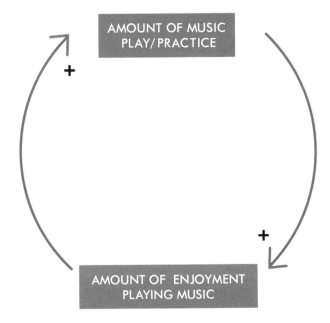

and develop a passion for it. I might begin to play the piano, which isn't gratifying at first because I'm not very good, but then as I practice I become better and enjoy playing more. Greater enjoyment of playing means that I end up practicing more, which results in getting better at the piano, which means that it's even *more* enjoyable to play and practice, which starts the whole cycle again, with the enjoyment and amount of practice escalating in each round. This particular kind of feedback is called a *positive* or *reinforcing* feedback loop.

Another example of nonlinear causality in everyday life is in the process of keeping the temperature of a home or an apartment constant. A thermostat detects when the temperature drops below a pre-set level, turning on the heat. It continues to monitor the temperature, and once it reaches its set level, the thermostat turns off the heat. Eventually heat escapes, maybe because the temperature outside drops, and the process starts itself over. This relationship is known as a *negative* or *balancing* feedback loop.

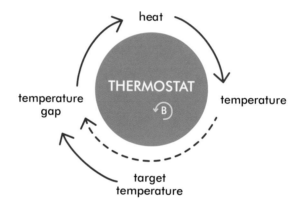

Overall, feedback loops involve two (and often more) elements within a system that continually affect one another in a circular or cyclical way. If you want to understand how change occurs or can occur, you want to understand feedback loops.

Reinforcing feedback loops are a bit more noticeable, mainly because they're characterized by things getting "out of control" or "snowballing" in some way. Think of microphone feedback. Sound produced by a speaker system is caught by a microphone and then reproduced by the speakers, amplified so that it is louder (and more unpleasant!). The amplified sound then gets caught by the microphone, starting the cycle again. This type of reinforcing feedback loop causes some kind of *escalation*. Of course, nothing can escalate forever, and so all reinforcing feedback loops can only go for so long before maxing out. This points to a core truth of most systems—that of *limited resources*.

Reinforcing feedback loops can go in the other direction as well, with a dynamic that results in things *decreasing* or *diminishing*. Take a bank run: people fear that their money isn't safe in a bank, which causes them to remove the money they have. This weakens the bank because it has less capital to operate with and is less able to make loans that keep it solvent. Other customers see this weakness, fear for their money, go and withdraw it, and start the whole cycle again until the bank collapses.

The key feature of both the microphone feedback and bank run examples is that they are *self-reinforcing* loops, in which the results of each cycle feed back into the start of a new, and more robust, version of the previous cycle.

Of course, not all reinforcing feedback loops produce "bad" behavior. We can probably agree that microphone feedback and bank runs aren't good things, but sometimes reinforcing feedback loops can result in positive outcomes. Think about agricultural cycles. Planting an apple tree and cultivating it can result in having many apples, both to eat and harvest seeds from. More seeds can then be planted which means more trees and more apples, and so on. Likewise, leaving your money in the bank and accruing interest is another good example of "positive" reinforcing feedback. The more money you put in, the more interest that accrues; the more interest you earn the more money you have, and so on. Reinforcing feedback loops such as these are referred to as *virtuous cycles*. In contrast, reinforcing feedback loops that are perceived as negative are called *vicious cycles*. Of course, whether the outcome of a reinforcing feedback loop is a good or a bad thing depends in large part on where someone stands within a system, and thus the ideas of vicious versus virtuous are, in part, a matter of opinion.

So there's a lot going on with reinforcing feedback loops: they can involve escalation or diminishment, can be seen as virtuous or vicious depending on where we stand, and occur in all sorts of ways and places. But one thing that's common to them is that they're usually, as mentioned, a bit easier to spot because of the ways they spiral out of control and often "flame out" once they exhaust themselves.

The other type of feedback loop, referenced in the thermostat example, is called a *balancing feedback loop*. These loops are generally a bit harder to notice because they are quietly self-correcting and self-regulating, hard at work keeping systems in a state of equilibrium (which is not necessarily good or bad) to prevent them from getting out of control. People often try to create new balancing loops after things have gone very wrong. Think back to that bank run example. Generally if a bank is declared insolvent these days, there isn't a bank run because after the Great Depression, the US government put the Federal Deposit Insurance Corporation (FDIC) into place. If a bank is a member of the FDIC, all deposits are insured by the government for up to $250,000. This check on the system disrupts the possibility of bank runs, since people don't need to fear that their money will be lost (as long as people have faith in the government's financial standing!). The FDIC is part of a balancing feedback structure, preventing the runaway situation (or vicious cycle!) of bank runs.

The sort of balancing feedback described above is everywhere. Coolant in a car engine serves a similar "balancing" function—by preventing the engine from overheating, it allows the system to keep functioning. Bathtubs have drains, which create balancing loops that prevent the tub from overflowing. Households full of knickknacks that accumulate over the years can have yard sales (or maybe sell things on the Internet these days) to create more space. A body gets low on energy, so it sends hunger signals to the brain, which prompts a person to eat, which satisfies the hunger and replaces nutrients and energy so that the body can continue to function. In general, balancing feedback loops aim to keep or move a system toward some state of equilibrium that allow it to continue to meet its goals.

Many systems that are well established (or entrenched, depending on your perspective) have numerous balancing feedback loops that allow them to continue to function and keep the system at equilibrium. In one sense this can be good, if the systems are doing what we want them to do, but this feature of systems can also be a challenge—it makes systems that we're trying to change resilient to our tinkering. So, balancing feedback loops can cut both ways depending on our goals in relation to a system, just like reinforcing ones.

The tricky thing about our various types of feedback loops (balancing and reinforcing) is that they rarely occur in isolation. A lot of the time, multiple balancing and reinforcing feedback loops co-occur and even intersect within a system to create what can be somewhat mind-bending configurations. A simple example can be found in the story *Anno's Magic Seeds*—a reinforcing feedback loop causes an abundance of food as each seed planted creates two more. Anno creates a balancing loop to deal with this overflow by starting to sell the excess produce in the market. The reinforcing loop creates the excess; the balancing loop keeps it in check. The two loops work together. When we get to much larger-scale systems with many more elements, these kinds of intersections become common, and understanding them becomes key to figuring out how to improve a system that is out of balance.

Now that we have a sense of what systems are and the kinds of structures found in them that drive their behavior, we can look to ideas central to the process of enacting change in systems—after all, we're not just interested in having kids observe and understand systems, we want to have them become empowered designers of and change agents within them!

LEVERAGE POINTS: INTERVENING AND CHANGING SYSTEMS

Understanding how systems work is all well and good, but if that insight isn't used to actually do something in the world, then it's just an academic exercise. Our vision of teaching systems thinking is rooted in the idea that young people eventually will become designers of new systems and redesigners of the systems that they inherit from us, and so some of the core ideas that we focus on are those related to how to change and intervene in systems.

When we think about changing systems, we think about *leverage points*. What makes a leverage point unique and powerful is that it's a place within a system where "a small change in one thing can produce big changes in everything," as activist and systems theorist Donella Meadows says. In a now-foundational book in the systems thinking world called *Leverage Points: Places to Intervene in a System* (1999) Meadows outlines different ways we can think about possible leverage points that range from less effective (e.g., changing the amount of "stuff" associated with certain parts of a system or changes to the structures that handle the movement of this "stuff") to more effective (e.g., changing the rules that govern a system, or better yet, the mindset that leads to things like rules, goals, and structure). While we won't go through all of the leverage points Meadows outlined, we want to stress that focusing on leverage points isn't like generating any old solution to a problem; they are designed not only to keep in mind the structures of a system, but also to take advantage of these structures so that a little change can go a long way.

In a wonderful example of leverage points at work, Meadows shares the story of the Toxic Release Inventory, which required every factory that released air pollutants to document and report data on these pollutants publicly. When the inventory was instituted in 1986 by the US government, toxic emissions were reduced dramatically. The inventory didn't levy fines or make the process of releasing these chemicals into the air illegal—it simply made the information public. By 1990, toxic emissions in the United States dropped by 40 percent. Factory owners did not want to be known publicly as polluters, so they changed their practices. The availability of information to different stakeholders within a system (in this case, citizens) changed the way that this system operated. The Toxic Release Inventory targeted a leverage point: it didn't aim to remake the whole system to prevent pollution; rather, it just added one small part that wasn't there before. It was a minor change, but it had a big effect.

Part of the challenge of making change in a system is that systems are complex, and we often don't know how they'll respond when we introduce new factors into them. Often, people go for stock solutions to problems not amenable to quick fixes and play into one of the common challenges associated with trying to change systems: inadvertently creating *fixes that fail*.

Unfortunately, we're all too familiar with these "solutions." Someone who racks up a high credit card balance and interest pays the card off by opening up a new credit card account, only to find himself in the same situation (or worse). A company tries to save money by cutting down on maintenance costs, but the machinery malfunctions that result lead to more costs than they would have had in the first place. Road congestion leads people to demand more roads, but when these new roads are built they create more incentives to use cars and so congestion stays the same or even increases. Most of these involve a mode of thinking that's both short term (in the time scale it envisions) and narrow (in how it frames the problem).

Related to fixes that fail are *unintended consequences*, in which one problem might be fixed, but it causes something else to happen in another part of a system that no one intended or guessed would happen. For instance, in an effort to control cane field pests in Australia, cane toads were introduced; but not only did they fail to fix the pest problem, they became a serious problem in and of themselves. In another instance of unintended consequences "down under," a law making bicycle helmets mandatory resulted in fewer young people cycling overall because they found it unfashionable, with counterproductive effects for the overall health of that demographic. In international politics, counterterrorism analysts note the phenomenon of "blowback," in which covert military operations meant to fight terrorism result in increased terrorist activity.

The idea of leverage points empowers us to think about the ways we can make big changes, while fixes that fail and unintended consequences point to how careful we need to be when we intervene in systems. Ideally, a systems thinker keeps both these sides of the coin in mind, understanding how important it is to be deliberate and conscientious when interacting with systems while not shying away from acting within them when intervention is needed.

Appendix A

GLOSSARY OF KEY TERMS

Identifying a system. Conceptual understanding that a system is a collection of parts, or *elements*, which *interconnect* to *function* as a whole. The "whole" of the system is always more than simply "the sum of its parts," because the way that the elements are set up, called a *system's structure*, determines the interactions among the elements. These interactions actually change the ways particular elements *behave* in a system. Systems are characterized by circular (rather than linear) patterns of cause and effect.

Identify the way a system is functioning. The function of a system describes the overall behavior of the system—what it is doing or where it's going over time. A system's function might emerge naturally based on interconnections among elements, or it might be the result of an intentional design (in which case, we might also call refer to the function of a system as its goal). Regardless, the function of a system is the result of the dynamics that occur among elements' interconnected behaviors. *For example, the respiratory system in the body, when it's working correctly, functions to keep a balance of the necessary gases inside the body and unnecessary gases in the environment surrounding it.*

Distinguishing the goal of a system. The goal of the system is what a system that was intentionally designed to do. Sometimes this might be the same as the *functioning* of the system ... other times the goal and the function are not aligned. A given system might have multiple goals or purposes that are at play simultaneously, and come into conflict. Being able to understand system purpose or goal gives a sense of the ideal state of a system from a particular perspective.

Identifying elements. Identifying the parts of a system that contribute to its functioning. *Elements* have certain qualities and/or *behaviors* that determine how they *interconnect* with other elements, as well as define their role in the system. Without being able to effectively identify the parts of a system, it's hard to understand how a system is actually *functioning* and how it might be changed. *For example, a neighborhood is made up of available housing, number of people, amount of local business, levels of employment, availability of public spaces, etc.*

Identifying behaviors. Identifying the specific ways that *elements* act within a system, or the role that they're playing. These behaviors are the basis of a *system's dynamics* or *interconnections*—the ways its elements interact with other elements (like through various types of feedback loops). Being able to identify behaviors becomes important when we change systems, as often an element will look the same after the change, but its behavior will be different. *In a neighborhood, the behavior of a store is to sell goods or services, as well as employ people. In a story, each character will behave in ways created by the author. A character might be angry and will therefore act aggressively toward other characters in the story.*

Identifying interconnections. Identifying the different ways that a system's parts, or *elements*, interact with each other through their *behaviors*, and through those interactions, change the behaviors of other elements.

Perceiving dynamics. Perceiving a system's dynamics involves looking at a higher level at how the system works. Dynamics in a system are often characterized by circles—patterns that "feed back" on one another. These are called *feedback loops*.

Make systems visible. When we learn to "make the system visible"—whether modeling a system on the back of a napkin, through a computer simulation, a game, a picture, a diagram, a set of mathematical computations, or a story—we can use these representations to communicate about how things work. At their best, good pictures of systems help both the creator and the "reader" or "audience" to understand not only the parts of the system (the elements), but also, how those elements work together to produce a whole. *For example, a map is a visual model of a certain area. Different maps will include or leave out different details about that area, depending on their purpose. A map of New York City that's used to navigate its subway system looks very different from a map of New York City that's used to navigate its streets by car.*

Systems diagram. This diagram is used to visualize the dynamics that occur between elements in a system, intended to capture how the variables interrelate. One way of diagramming a feedback loop uses an "R" with a clockwise arrow around it to indicate a reinforcing feedback loop (see below). A "B" with a counterclockwise arrow around it would indicate a balancing feedback loop, which "counters" something in a system. The plus sign indicates an increase in that amount of an element in a system, and a minus sign indicates a decrease in the amount of an element in a system. There are other ways to create systems diagrams, but the most important thing about a good systems diagram is that it not only shows the elements in a system, but is able to show the relationships between the elements through the arrows, symbols, and text. *Example of a system diagram showing the reinforcing feedback relationship between a character's angry thoughts and feelings:*

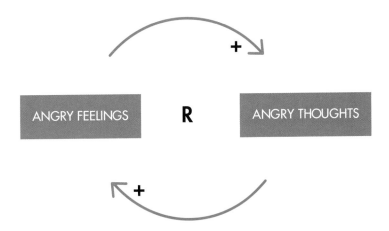

Feedback loops. Relationships between two or more elements of a system, where actions by these elements interact in a circular fashion—something that element A does affects element B, which then circles back and affects element A. There are two types of feedback loops, *balancing* and *reinforcing*.

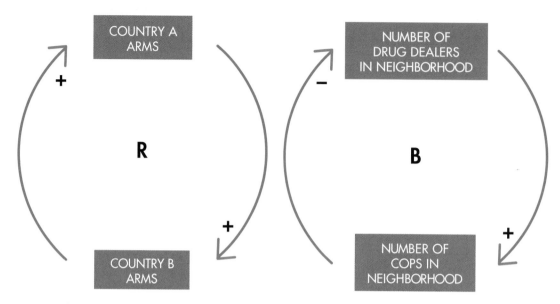

Examples of reinforcing feedback loop (on the left) and balancing feedback loop (on the right).

Reinforcing feedback loops.   Relationships where two or more elements of a system cause each other to increase, such as in escalation cycles, or decrease, such in resource drain cycles, in a way that's "out of control" or creates a "snowball effect." Reinforcing loops encourage a system to reproduce certain behaviors, though these behaviors always "exhaust" themselves after the resources fueling the growth or diminishment run out. This is also called "limits to growth." *For example, a reinforcing loop that escalates might be a new hot shoe style—more people wear the style, which then makes more people aware of the new style and its popularity, which causes it to become even more popular.*

A reinforcing feedback loop that drains or diminishes resources is a bank run—people hear that a bank won't be able to return deposited money, and so people keeping their money at that bank withdraw it. This weakens the bank, which makes more people concerned that the bank will fail and their money will be lost, causing more withdrawals and keeping the cycle going.

There are two types of reinforcing feedback loops: *vicious cycles* and *virtuous cycles.*

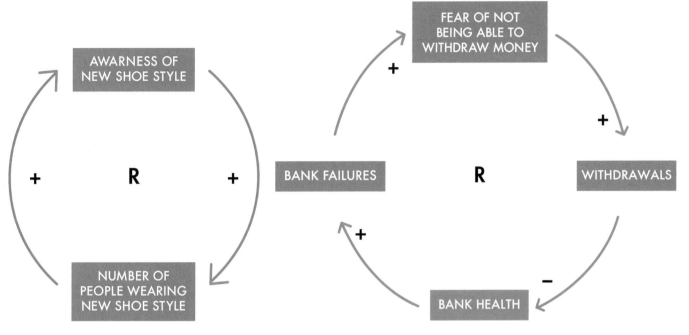

Diagrams of a reinforcing feedback loop that results in escalation (on the left) and resource drain (on the right).

Vicious cycle. Reinforcing feedback loop that causes a negative outcome in terms of the goal of the system. One thing to keep in mind is that the same thing might be a vicious cycle to one person, but a virtuous cycle for another person who has different goals. *For example: Two kids get into a disagreement while on the playground. One of them calls the other one a name, the other responds by pushing the first kid. The situation continues to escalate until they're having a full-on fight.*

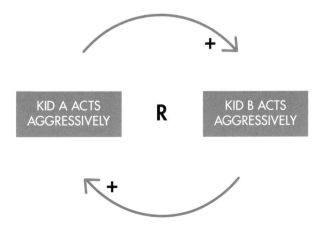

Virtuous cycle.   Reinforcing feedback loop that causes a positive outcome in terms the goal of the system. One thing to keep in mind is that the same thing might be a virtuous cycle to one person, but a vicious cycle for another person who has different goals. *For example, a farmer plants a seed that over time becomes a plant that provides fruit that have many seeds. He then plants many of those seeds, which produces more fruit, now with many more seeds. Each round of planting produces more fruit with more seeds, creating a snowball effect.*

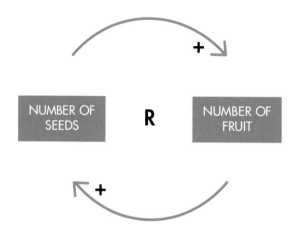

Balancing feedback loops. Relationships where two or more elements of a system keep each other in balance, with one (or more) elements leading to increase, and one (or more) elements leading to decrease. These processes keep a system at the desired state of equilibrium, the system goal. Usually, balancing feedback processes stabilize systems by limiting or preventing certain processes from happening. Having a sense of how balancing feedback loops operate can give a person a sense of what will make a system stable. *For example, when gas prices go up, this causes more people to carpool, which decreases gasoline consumption. Since there's less demand, gasoline prices eventually go down again, causing fewer people to carpool, starting the cycle over again.*

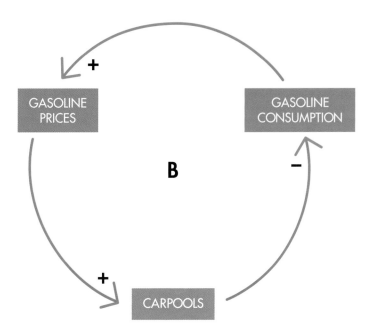

Nested systems. Systems that are a smaller part of other systems. Almost all systems are nested within larger systems. With nested systems, a larger system will affect the way that a subsystem behaves, and the subsystem will affect the way that the larger system behaves. The nature of systems as nested within one another means that it's usually possible to zoom in or out of systems in order to see systems that are either around them (if those systems are bigger) or within them (if those systems are smaller).

Designing a system. Creating a system through engaging in an iterative design process, one that entails cycles of feedback, troubleshooting, and testing. One of the most effective means of developing systems thinking is to regularly create and iterate on the design of systems.

Fixes that fail. Any kind of solution to a problem that fixes the problem temporarily but fails fix it in the long term, and might even make it worse over time. Fixes that fail are often put in place quickly, usually without much reflection on what consequences they'll have for the system. *For example, a city's roads are congested, so the government decides to build more roads to make more room for all the cars. But people who didn't have cars see that it's now easier to drive around the city, so go and buy cars—with the roads remaining as congested as they were before.*

Leverage points. Particular places within a system where a small shift in one thing can produce big changes in everything. Leverage points are difficult to find because they often lie far away from either the problem or its obvious solution. It is because of the multitude of cause-and-effect relationships, feedback loops, and system structures that a seemingly small change can be amplified, often in unexpected ways. Not every place in a system is a leverage point—sometimes changing one thing in a system will produce only small effects that aren't felt throughout the system. *For example, making sure that young women in developing countries get education and health services when they are very young helps to make issues like poverty less of a problem in the long run for all people in a developing country. In a mystery story a detective might look for one key piece of information that will allow him to solve the case.*

Unintended consequences. The unexpected result of an action taken in a system that the actor taking that original action did not want to happen. Unintended consequences are often the result of *fixes that fail* or someone aiming to find a *leverage point* in a system but not considering long-term implications to those actions. For example, a company starts to cut down trees in order to manufacture products. As a result, many of the animals that lived in that forest have to leave to find new habitats, something that wasn't envisioned or expected when the logging started.

Mental model. An evolving set of ideas and assumptions about a system and how it works. Consciously or not, people use their mental models of how a system works when they decide how they're going to act in a system. When someone's mental model changes, the ways that they relate to and act within systems change with them. From a systems perspective, mental models are important because any "map" we create of a complex system is essentially a map of our mental models. The more clarified our mental models, the closer to reality (that is, the closer to representing a complex set of interconnections) the map will be.

Considering how mental models shape action in a system. The ability to consider the assumptions, ideas, and intentions that a given actor might have in relation to a system, and how these affect that actor's behavior within the system. Mental models are often correct about what elements are included in a system, but frequently draw wrong conclusions about a system's overall behavior. *For example, throughout most of human history, people thought that disease came about spontaneously. The introduction of the germ theory of disease, the idea that many diseases are caused by microorganisms, changed people's ideas and opened the door for most of modern medicine and the importance of hygiene. When we tell a story, we are sharing a mental model of how we understand a situation, a set of events, or characters.*

Looking at a system from multiple perspectives. The ability to understand that different actors in a system will have different mental models of the system and consider each of these perspectives when engaging in action within a system. This is also called "thinking across the table."

Considering multiple levels of perspective. The ability to move fluidly between different levels of perspective within a system, from events, to patterns to system structures, to mental models. The most visible level of a system is an *event,* that is to say, visible instances of elements interacting in a system. Using the metaphor of a system as an iceberg, events are "above the waterline"—they're easy to see. When we start to think "below the waterline," we start to see three other levels of perspective: patterns (recurring sets of events), structures (ways the elements are set up in a system which give rise to regular patterns) and mental models (which shape systems structures.) Switching between different levels of perspective when looking at a system deepens understanding of how a system operates.

Time delays. The time lag between an action in a system and the evidence of its effects. *For example, there's a long delay between the point when you plant a seed in the ground and the appearance of a fruit-bearing tree.*

Time horizons. The overall period of time that you look at something in order to understand it. *For example, if we only look a complex system like an economy for a short period of time, we might misunderstand how it's behaving and miss the effects of actions taken far into the past.*

ADDITIONAL RESOURCES

SCRATCH AND THE SCRATCH COMMUNITY

SCRATCH: PROGRAMMING FOR ALL

By Mitchel Resnick, John Maloney, Andrés Monroy Hernández, Natalie Rusk, Evelyn Eastmond, Karen Brennan, Amon Millner, Eric Rosenbaum, Jay Silver, Brian Silverman, and Yasmin Kafai

web.media.mit.edu/~mres/papers/Scratch-CACM-final.pdf

SCRATCH

scratch.mit.edu/

Scratch is a programming language that makes it easy to create your own interactive stories, animations, games, music, and art—and share your creations on the web.

SCRATCHED

scratched.media.mit.edu

A wide variety of educators have been supporting Scratch creators, in both formal and informal learning environments. In response to this growing community of educators working with Scratch, we developed ScratchEd. Launched in July 2009, ScratchEd is a new online community where Scratch educators share stories, exchange resources, ask questions, and find people.

SCRATCH INTRO FACILITORIAL VIDEO

techtv.mit.edu/videos/379-scratch-intro-facilitorial

CLASSROOM 2.0 SCRATCH WIKI

wiki.classroom20.com/Scratch

YOUTH VOICES MISSION: INTERACTIVE ETHICAL STORY USING SCRATCH

www.youthvoices.net/node/34288

SUPER SCRATCH PROGRAMMING ADVENTURE!

By the LEAD Project
Go on an adventure in this new book about Scratch. With colorful comics and step-by-step instructions, Super Scratch Programming Adventure! teaches kids to program fun, playable video games with Scratch. Find out more about the book, plus download a sample at nostarch.com/scratch.

SYSTEMS AND SYSTEMS THINKING

WATERS FOUNDATION: SYSTEMS THINKING IN SCHOOLS

www.watersfoundation.org

CLOUD INSTITUTE FOR SUSTAINABILITY EDUCATION

www.cloudinstitute.org

CREATIVE LEARNING EXCHANGE

clexchange.org

CENTER FOR CONNECTED LEARNING AND COMPUTER-BASED MODELING

ccl.northwestern.edu

STORYTELLING (DIGITAL AND OTHERWISE)

DIGITALES: THE ART OF TELLING DIGITAL STORIES

www.digitales.us

JASON OHLER: ART, STORYTELLING, TECHNOLOGY AND EDUCATION

www.jasonohler.com/storytelling/index.cfm

IRA GLASS ON STORYTELLING (PART 1 OF 4)

www.youtube.com/watch?v=loxJ3FtCJJA&feature=player
_embedded

AARON SHEPARD'S STORYTELLING PAGE

www.aaronshep.com/storytelling

SCRIPTFRENZY: WRITER'S RESOURCES

www.scriptfrenzy.org/howtoguides

50+ WEB 2.0 WAYS TO TELL A STORY

50ways.wikispaces.com

PIXAR'S 22 RULES TO PHENOMENAL STORYTELLING [INFOGRAPHIC]

pbjpublishing.com/blog/2012/07/09/pixars-22-rules-to
-phenomenal-storytelling-infographic

DIGITAL STORYTELLING EXAMPLES IN SCRATCH

scratch.mit.edu/studios/138297

SCRIPT CHANGERS ASSESSMENT

Name: _____   Date: _____

1. What is the relationship between the following three things? You can explain your answer in words or pictures.

    (a) studying, (b) grades, and (c) interest in the subject matter.

    Based on your answer, what do you think would happen to studying and grades if your interest in the subject matter went *down*?

2. Think of an example of a system you are a part of or have observed in your community that is an example of either reinforcing or balancing feedback (or both). Briefly draw a picture or a model of the elements in that community, and explain how those elements interconnect.

    What would happen to the system if one of the elements was removed?

3.   *Marla was reading a book called* The River Ran Wild. *The story tells about the Nashua River, which was bright and clean, and had many fish and wildlife living on it. But as a community settled around the river, things began to change. The abundant fish in the river caused more people to come and join the community. As time passed, towns were built, which attracted more people. Mills were built on the river, using the water to power the millwheels, and to take advantage of the fact that there was an existing community that could provide the mill with workers. The rivers were also used as a place to dump mill waste. Eventually these towns grew into cities, which attracted people more quickly than ever, and the increase in people (and thus mills) caused more pollution than ever.*

(a) What kind of relationship can we see in this story? What are the elements of the system, how are they interacting, and what are the consequences?

A woman named Marion Stoddard organized her neighbors and her community to try to clean up the Nashua River, even though it seemed like an impossible task. Children brought jars of dirty river water to show to politicians. They told their parents, "We just want this river the way it was when you were kids. You could swim in it. You could fish in it." Eventually people listened, so laws were passed to stop the paper mills from dumping chemicals and dyes into the river. The people also worked to get the first Clean Water Act passed—in Massachusetts.

(b) What did Marion Stoddard do to change the system? What did she identify as the leverage point? From the perspective of a system, how could you explain how her change impacted the way the system that you described in part A was working?

4. What is the relationship between the amount of grass that is growing in a field, the number of rabbits who live in the area (rabbits eat grass), and the number of wolves in the area (wolves eat rabbits). Explain your answer in either words or pictures.

(a) If someone decided to kill all the wolves, what would happen to the rabbits and the grass?

(b) Is this an example of *balancing feedback* or *reinforcing feedback?* (circle the one that is correct)

SYSTEMS THINKING CONCEPT CARDS: SCRIPT CHANGERS

The following cards have been included for you to use any way that works well in your setting, such as printing a set for each youth, creating a classroom deck to store in a resource center, or even using them as game cards for a whole-group games or activities (like *Jeopardy!*, Flyswatter, Baseball, and so on).

01.
IDENTIFYING A SYSTEM

Identifying a system and distinguishing it from other kinds of things that aren't systems. Specifically, a system is a collection of two or more elements and processes that interconnect to function as a whole. Speed and comfort in a car, for example, are created by the interactions of the car's parts and thus are "greater than the sum" of all separate parts of the car. The way a system works is not the result of a single part but is produced by the interaction among the elements and/or individual agents within it. A key way to differentiate things that are systems from things that aren't is to consider whether the overall way something works in the world will change if you remove one part of it.

02.
IDENTIFY THE WAY A SYSTEM IS FUNCTIONING

The function of a system describes the overall behavior of the system—what it is doing or where it's going over time. A system's function might emerge naturally based on interconnections among elements, or it might be the result of an intentional design (in which case, we might also refer to the function of a system as its goal). Regardless, the function of a system is the result of the dynamics that occur among elements' interconnected behaviors.

03.
DISTINGUISHING THE GOAL OF A SYSTEM

The goal of the system is what it was intentionally designed to do. Sometimes this might be the same as the functioning of the system, other times the goal and the function are not aligned. A given system might have multiple goals or purposes that are at play simultaneously and sometimes come into conflict. Being able to understand a system's purpose or goal gives a sense of its ideal state from a particular perspective.

04.
IDENTIFYING ELEMENTS

Identifying the parts of a system that contribute to its functioning. Elements have certain qualities and/or behaviors that determine how they interconnect with other elements, as well as define their role in the system. Without being able to effectively identify the parts of a system, it's hard to understand how a system is actually functioning and how it might be changed.

05.
IDENTIFYING BEHAVIORS

Identifying the specific actions, roles, or behaviors that a component of a system displays under various conditions. Being able to identify behaviors becomes important when we change systems, as often a component will look the same after the change, but its behavior will be different.

SYSTEMS THINKING CONCEPT CARDS:
SCRIPT CHANGERS

06.

IDENTIFYING INTERCONNECTIONS

Identifying the different ways that a system's parts, or elements, interact with each other through their behaviors, and through those interactions, change the behaviors of other elements.

SYSTEMS THINKING CONCEPT CARDS:
SCRIPT CHANGERS

07.

PERCEIVING DYNAMICS

Perceiving a system's dynamics involves looking at a higher level at how the system works. Dynamics in a system are often characterized by circles—patterns that "feed back" on another. These are called feedback loops.

SYSTEMS THINKING CONCEPT CARDS:
SCRIPT CHANGERS

08.

CONSIDERING THE ROLE
OF SYSTEM STRUCTURE

Understanding how a system's elements are set up in relation to one another gives insight into the behavior of a component. A system's structure affects the behaviors of its elements and the overall dynamics and functioning of a system. For instance, how a city's highway system is structured affects overall traffic patterns and car movement within it. Being able to see a system's structure gives insights into the mechanisms and relationships that are at the core of a system, which can be leveraged to create systemic changes.

SYSTEMS THINKING CONCEPT CARDS:
SCRIPT CHANGERS

09.

MAKING SYSTEMS VISIBLE

When we learn to "make the system visible"—whether modeling a system on the back of a napkin, through a computer simulation, a game, a picture, a diagram, a set of mathematical computations, or a story—we can use these representations to communicate about how things work. At their best, good pictures of systems help both the creator and the "reader" or "audience" to understand not only the parts of the system (the elements), but also how those elements work together to produce a whole.

SYSTEMS THINKING CONCEPT CARDS:
SCRIPT CHANGERS

10.

SYSTEMS DIAGRAM

This diagram is used to visualize the dynamics that occur between elements in a system, intended to capture how the variables interrelate. One way of diagramming a feedback loop uses an "R" with a clockwise arrow around it to indicate a reinforcing feedback loop. A "B" with a counterclockwise arrow around it would indicate a balancing feedback loop, which "counters" something in a system. The plus sign indicates an increase in that amount of a component in a system, and a minus sign indicates a decrease in the amount of a component in a system. There are other ways to create systems diagrams, but the most important thing about a good systems diagram is that it not only shows the elements in a system, but is able to show the relationships between the elements through the arrows, symbols, and text.

SYSTEMS THINKING CONCEPT CARDS:
SCRIPT CHANGERS

11.

FEEDBACK LOOPS

Relationships between two or more elements of a system, where actions by these elements interact in a circular fashion: something that element A does affects element B, which then circles back and affects element A. There are two types of feedback loops, balancing and reinforcing.

SYSTEMS THINKING CONCEPT CARDS:
SCRIPT CHANGERS

12.
REINFORCING FEEDBACK LOOPS

Relationships where two or more elements of a system cause each other to increase, such as in escalation cycles, or decrease, such in resource drain cycles, in a way that's "out of control" or creates a "snowball effect." Reinforcing loops encourage a system to reproduce certain behaviors, though these behaviors always "exhaust" themselves after the resources fueling the growth or diminishment run out. This is also called "limits to growth." There are two types of reinforcing feedback loops: "vicious" cycles and "virtuous" cycles.

SYSTEMS THINKING CONCEPT CARDS:
SCRIPT CHANGERS

13.
VICIOUS CYCLE

Reinforcing feedback loops that cause a negative outcome in terms of the perceived goal of the system. One thing to keep in mind is that the same thing might be a vicious cycle to one person, but a virtuous cycle for another person who has different goals.

SYSTEMS THINKING CONCEPT CARDS:
SCRIPT CHANGERS

14.
VIRTUOUS CYCLES

Reinforcing feedback loops that cause a positive outcome in terms the perceived goal of the system. One thing to keep in mind is that the same thing might be a virtuous cycle to one person, but a vicious cycle for another person who has different goals.

SYSTEMS THINKING CONCEPT CARDS:
SCRIPT CHANGERS

15.
BALANCING FEEDBACK LOOPS

Relationships where two or more elements of a system keep each other in balance, with one (or more) elements leading to increase, and one (or more) elements leading to decrease. These processes keep a system at the desired state of equilibrium, the system goal. Usually, balancing feedback processes stabilize systems by limiting or preventing certain processes from happening. Having a sense of how balancing feedback loops operate can give a person a sense of what will make a system stable.

SYSTEMS THINKING CONCEPT CARDS:
SCRIPT CHANGERS

16.
STOCKS & FLOWS

Stocks are an accumulated amount of something within a system (like money in a bank account, fish in a pond, trees in a forest, or jobs in an economy), and flows are the rate at which stocks in a system change either through increasing or decreasing (money comes in and out of a bank account due to wages paid, interest, and purchases. Fish come in and out of a pond due to birth rates, death rates, and fishing rates, etc.). Stocks are always nouns; they're the "stuff" of systems, while flows are always verbs; they're the "movement" of systems. Understanding stocks and flows gives someone an insight into how different parts of the system change over time.

SYSTEMS THINKING CONCEPT CARDS:
SCRIPT CHANGERS

17.
LIMITED RESOURCES

In any system, it is important to understand which resources are finite, ones that will run out at a certain point. Keeping in mind which resources are limited helps people make decisions about how best to maximize resources.

SYSTEMS THINKING CONCEPT CARDS:
SCRIPT CHANGERS

18.
NESTED SYSTEMS

Systems that are a smaller part of other systems. Almost all systems are nested within larger systems. With nested systems, a larger system will affect the way that a subsystem behaves, and the subsystem will affect the way that the larger system behaves. Having a sense of nested systems helps people keep an eye on how systems interconnect and are always part of bigger pictures.

SYSTEMS THINKING CONCEPT CARDS:
SCRIPT CHANGERS

19.
DYNAMIC EQUILIBRIUM

A state in which stocks and flows are balanced so the system is not varying widely, but still has internal dynamic processes that are continually in flux even though the system is stable overall. For example: in economics dynamic equilibrium might be used to talk about the constant flux of money movement in otherwise stable markets; in ecology, a population of organisms stabilizes when birth rate and death rate are in balance.

SYSTEMS THINKING CONCEPT CARDS:
SCRIPT CHANGERS

20.
DESIGNING A SYSTEM

Creating a system through engaging in an iterative design process, one that entails iterative cycles of feedback, troubleshooting, and testing. One of the most effective means of developing systems thinking is to regularly create and iterate on the design of systems, and doing so in a way that creates opportunities for students to think about generic systems models that apply across multiple domains and settings.

SYSTEMS THINKING CONCEPT CARDS:
SCRIPT CHANGERS

21.
FIXES THAT FAIL

Any kind of solution to a problem that fixes the problem temporarily but fails to fix it in the long term, and might even make it worse over time. Fixes that Fail are often put in place quickly, usually without much reflection on what consequences they'll have for the system. They're important to see since they're often the ways that people respond to problems in a system.

SYSTEMS THINKING CONCEPT CARDS:
SCRIPT CHANGERS

22.
LEVERAGE POINTS

Particular places within a system where a small shift in one thing can produce big changes in everything. Leverage points are difficult to find because they often lie far away from either the problem or the obvious solution. It is because of the multitude of cause and effect relationships, feedback loops, and system structures that a seemingly small change can be amplified, often in unexpected ways. Not every place in a system is a leverage point—sometimes changing one thing in a system will produce only small effects not felt throughout the system. Leverage points are important since they let us know where to focus our energies when we try to change systems.

SYSTEMS THINKING CONCEPT CARDS:
SCRIPT CHANGERS

22.
UNINTENDED CONSEQUENCES

The unexpected result of an action taken in a system that the actor taking that original action did not want to happen. Unintended Consequences are often the result of fixes that fail or someone aiming to find a leverage point in a system but not considering long-term implications to those actions—someone failed to keep in mind time horizons. Having a good sense of potential unintended consequences means that someone will carefully consider before too hastily intervening in a system.

SYSTEMS THINKING CONCEPT CARDS:
SCRIPT CHANGERS

23.

CONSIDERING HOW MENTAL
MODELS SHAPE ACTION IN A SYSTEM

The ability to consider the assumptions, ideas, and intentions that a given actor might have in relation to a system, and how these affect that actor's behavior within the system. Mental models are often correct about what elements are included in a system, but frequently draw wrong conclusions about a system's overall behavior.

SYSTEMS THINKING CONCEPT CARDS:
SCRIPT CHANGERS

24.

LOOKING AT A SYSTEM FROM
MULTIPLE PERSPECTIVES

The ability to understand that different actors in a system will have different mental models of the system and consider each of these perspectives when engaging in action within a system. This is also called "thinking across the table."

SYSTEMS THINKING CONCEPT CARDS:
SCRIPT CHANGERS

25.

CONSIDERING MULTIPLE LEVELS
OF PERSPECTIVE

The ability to move fluidly between different levels of perspective within a system, from events, to patterns to system structures, to mental models. The most visible level of systems are events, visible instances of elements interacting in a system. Using the metaphor of a system as an iceberg, events are "above the waterline" – they're easy to see. When we start to think "below the waterline," we start to see three other levels of perspective: patterns (recurring sets of events), structures (ways the elements are set up in a system which give rise to regular patterns), and mental models (which shape systems structures). Switching between different levels of perspective when looking at a system deepens understanding of how a system operates.

SYSTEMS THINKING CONCEPT CARDS:
SCRIPT CHANGERS

26.

TIME DELAYS

The time lag between an action in a system and the evidence of its effects. For example, there's a long delay between the point when you plant a seed in the ground and the appearance of a fruit-bearing tree.

SYSTEMS THINKING CONCEPT CARDS:
SCRIPT CHANGERS

27.

TIME HORIZONS

The overall period of time that you look at something in order to understand it. For example, if we only look a complex system like an economy for a short period of time, we might misunderstand how it's behaving and miss the effects of actions taken far into the past.

SYSTEMS THINKING CONCEPT CARDS: SCRIPT CHANGERS

UNDERSTANDING SYSTEMS:
DIGITAL DESIGN FOR A COMPLEX WORLD

SCRIPT CHANGERS CHALLENGE CARDS

Script Changers Challenge Cards make your students take their Scratching to the next level! Each of the challenges offers inspiration for open-ended projects and offers hints that will help them dive right in. Challenges are rated from easy to hardcore and come with some hints to help get things started. Use with youth that come early to meetings or classes, have an extra lunch break and want to go deeper, or for youth that finish early during group projects.

LEVELS
- ⬤ EASY
- ✦ MEDIUM
- ✿ HARD
- ✺ HARDCORE

OVERVIEW
This deck contains 4 different categories of challenges from which to pick:

CATEGORIES

GOING DEEP IN SCRATCH
All of these challenges aim to extend and deepen skills and areas of Scratch that youth might not explore through the storytelling activities included in the book.

BE A FAN!
All of these challenges aim to have youth bring in their existing interests in pop culture to create fan-based projects in Scratch that make them think about existing stories and characters in new ways.

REMIXING SCRATCH PROJECTS
All of these challenges aim to have young people learn to remix and appropriate parts of existing Scratch projects that they find in the Scratch online community.

A NEW CHAPTER
All of these challenges aim to have young people create new kinds of stories. They can be used with Scratch, but also with other storytelling platforms including film, audio/podcasting, comics and other multimedia storytelling tools.

01 DANCE PARTY

LEVEL

EASY

CATEGORY

GOING DEEP IN SCRATCH

Create a project that has characters dancing to music.

EXPLANATION

Scratch can be great for bringing together character movement with music. Using certain blocks, it's possible to create a Scratch "dance party."

HINTS

Write your own music using the SOUNDS blocks. You can also import music files under the "Sounds" tab on a sprite or on the stage. Use combinations of costumes, LOOKS and/or MOTION blocks to make your sprites dance.

---

02 FRIENDLY STORY

LEVEL

MEDIUM

CATEGORY

GOING DEEP IN SCRATCH

Write a short story that involves two characters. Ask a friend or two to help you record the dialogue.

EXPLANATION

You can collaboratively create stories in Scratch by getting your friends involved. You can act as a director, asking them to do multiple recordings until you get the dialogue to sound just the way you want.

HINTS

Find a nice quiet place to record so that your friends' voices will come through. A good approach is to create a separate sound file for each line of the dialogue so that you can easily manipulate the timing of specific parts of the dialogue with the "play sound until done" block.

---

03 DRAW SOMETHING

LEVEL

EASY

CATEGORY

GOING DEEP IN SCRATCH

Create a project using Sprites that you only draw yourself.

EXPLANATION

It's pretty easy to create a project in Scratch using things from the Scratch library, but can you do it by drawing the sprites yourself?

HINTS

You can use the "Paint new sprite" button for this challenge, but if drawing on the computer isn't your thing, you can draw on paper and then scan or take a digital picture of your drawing to import it into Scratch. This is actually what professional animators do!

SCRIPT CHANGERS
CHALLENGE CARDS

CLASSIC ARCADE

LEVEL

HARD

CATEGORY

GOING DEEP IN SCRATCH

Re-create a classic arcade game like PacMan, Pong, or Space Invaders in Scratch.

EXPLANATION

See if you're able to think through the rules and design of a classic arcade game, and make a version of it in Scratch. If you've never played one or it's been a long time, search the web or look at example projects in the Scratch community.

HINTS

The CONTROL and EVENTS blocks are really helpful when making games. Use the "when _____ key pressed" blocks in conjunction with MOTION blocks to create a Sprite that you can move around with your arrow keys. The SENSING blocks are also useful in games, particularly the "touching color ___ " blocks.

SCRIPT CHANGERS
CHALLENGE CARDS

AMAZING MAZES

LEVEL

HARD

CATEGORY

GOING DEEP IN SCRATCH

Create a maze game in Scratch.

EXPLANATION

Scratch let's you create games, see if you're able to think up an idea for a game that involves making your way through mazes.

HINTS

The CONTROL, EVENTS and SENSING blocks are really helpful when making games. Use the "when___key pressed" blocks in conjunction with MOTION blocks to create a character that you can move around, and the "touching color ___" and "forever if" blocks to create the conditions so that your character can't move across walls.

SCRIPT CHANGERS
CHALLENGE CARDS

NEVER ENDING STORY

LEVEL

MEDIUM

CATEGORY

GOING DEEP IN SCRATCH

Make a story in Scratch that never ends.

EXPLANATION

First, come up with a story whose ending could cause the whole story to start again. Then figure out a way to make that actually happen in Scratch, so that when the last scene in the story happens, it loops back to the beginning, and the whole thing keeps repeating itself.

HINTS

Use the "broadcast" and "receive" EVENTS blocks to create a sequence of steps. Then have the last step link to the first to create a loop. You can also use a combination of change costume blocks, like "next costume," with a "forever" block to get the same effect.

07
RANDOMNESS

LEVEL

MEDIUM

CATEGORY

GOING DEEP IN SCRATCH

Make a Scratch project that involves the "pick random __ to __" block in some way.

EXPLANATION

Most Scratch projects play out exactly as you program them. But what if you added in some randomness? See if you can find a creative way to integrate the "pick random" block into a Scratch project.

HINTS

Think about how randomness can be applied in a Scratch project (e.g., a Magic 8-Ball). What sorts of things might be able to change randomly? Costumes? Movements? The appearance of sprites? The "pick random" block found in the OPERATORS palette can be inserted anytime you see an oval shape. Try using it in one of your existing projects inside one of your MOTION or CONTROL blocks. Also try adding it to your LOOKS and SOUND blocks too to see what happens!

08
ETCH-A-SKETCH

LEVEL

HARD

CATEGORY

GOING DEEP IN SCRATCH

Making a Scratch project that acts like an "etch-a-sketch" allows a user to draw things using the arrow keys.

EXPLANATION

The old etch-a-sketch was fun because it gave its user a very limited tool that actually made it a little difficult to draw, but when you did draw something it was that much more exciting when it turned out well. Can you recreate this sort of tool and experience in Scratch?

HINTS

Try PEN blocks in combination with MOVEMENT blocks as the basis for a project like this. "Pen down" will need to be used every time you want to start drawing. Use the "clear" block to clear your screen and the other blocks to control the look of your pen marks.

09
MOVE YOUR BODY

LEVEL

HARD

CATEGORY

GOING DEEP IN SCRATCH

Create a Scratch project that makes a user move their body to interact with it.

EXPLANATION

Scratch's "video" SENSING block allows you to use a webcam to sense a user's movements. Use this block to make a whole new type of creative Scratch project.

HINTS

Head onto the Scratch community to see how others have incorporated this sort of functionality into their projects. Draw inspiration, and get started on your own!

SCRIPT CHANGERS
CHALLENGE CARDS

10 KALEIDOSCOPE

LEVEL

HARDCORE

CATEGORY

GOING DEEP IN SCRATCH

Make a Scratch project that acts like a kaleidoscope to make new patterns depending on what the user does.

EXPLANATION

Kaleidoscopes combine many overlapping colors and movement in order to create a dazzling visual experience. Can you create an experience like this in Scratch?

HINTS

Use multiple sprites that have PEN blocks in them in combination with MOTION blocks as the basis for a project like this. "Forever if" blocks are helpful to create smooth drawings. Alternatively, try using your "Duplicate" button at the top of the screen to create multiple sprites that act the same way when keys are pressed or the mouse is moved.

SCRIPT CHANGERS
CHALLENGE CARDS

11 TYPEWRITER

LEVEL

HARDCORE

CATEGORY

GOING DEEP IN SCRATCH

Make a Scratch project that reproduces the function of a typewriter by using the keyboard to input and edit text.

EXPLANATION

You might be used to using word processing programs to create text on a screen, but can you make a Scratch project that does this?

HINTS

Think about how the "stamp," "costume switch," and MOTION blocks might be used together in this kind of project.

SCRIPT CHANGERS
CHALLENGE CARDS

12 SWEET MUSIC

LEVEL

HARDCORE

CATEGORY

GOING DEEP IN SCRATCH

Create a musical instrument in Scratch

EXPLANATION

Scratch's SOUND blocks offer a lot of options that can let someone make a musical instrument.

HINTS

Create existing instruments (e.g., a piano or trumpet) or come up with entirely new ones!

SCRIPT CHANGERS
CHALLENGE CARDS

13
BLOG IT!

LEVEL

MEDIUM

CATEGORY

GOING DEEP IN SCRATCH

Share your project in the Scratch online community and then embed, email, or link to your project on your blog or other social network.

EXPLANATION

Being able to repost your projects to communities outside of the Scratch website is one of the great parts of the Scratch online community. Give it a try to see if you can get some cross-traffic to view your project!

HINTS

Check out the "Link to the Project" on your project's webpage in Scratch. The code is provided to embed your project as an image or an applet. You can also bookmark your project here too.

SCRIPT CHANGERS
CHALLENGE CARDS

14
THAT SCENE...

LEVEL

MEDIUM

CATEGORY

BE A FAN!

Are you a fan? Recreate your favorite scene and even add yourself!

EXPLANATION

Create a project that recreates one of your favorite scenes or interactions from a book, comic, video game, TV show, graphic novel, or movie that you like.

HINTS

Consider what it is about that scene or interaction that makes you like it so much. Is there a way to get those aspects into Scratch, even if it's not possible to totally recreate the whole thing? Take a picture of yourself in Scratch or import one from your computer's hard drive to add yourself to the scene.

SCRIPT CHANGERS
CHALLENGE CARDS

15
FANFIC IN SCRATCH

LEVEL

MEDIUM

CATEGORY

BE A FAN!

Create a project that involves a character that you like and tells a story about a new situation they find themselves in.

EXPLANATION

Characters that you love don't have to stay in the books, movies, or games where you found them. In this project you can be a super fan by extending the storyline and imagining new situations. This is commonly called "fanfiction" and there are many different Internet sites devoted to fanfiction writers.

HINTS

Think about how that character has acted in the past and use that to imagine what sorts of ways he or she (or it!) would act in a new situation.

16 CROSSOVER

LEVEL

MEDIUM

CATEGORY

BE A FAN!

Create a project that involves characters from two different books, comics, video games, TV shows, graphic novels or movies.

EXPLANATION

Find two characters from separate television shows, video games, books, comics, graphic novels or movies that you're a fan of and make a story where they interact.

HINTS

Think about how those characters have acted in the past and use that to imagine what sorts of ways they might act if they encountered each other in a new situation.

---

17 IMAGE MASHUP

LEVEL

MEDIUM

CATEGORY

BE A FAN!

Create a project that has sprites whose costumes only come from images on the web.

EXPLANATION

Don't use sprites from Scratch for this one; instead, mash up images that you find on the Internet to create unique characters.

HINTS

If it's available, using image-editing software like Adobe Photoshop or Aviary.com can make it easier to combine different images from the web.

---

18 A GAMER'S TALE

LEVEL

MEDIUM

CATEGORY

BE A FAN!

Create a project that tells part of the story of a video game that you play.

EXPLANATION

Think about a game that you like and what kind of storyline it has around it. Can you take a part of that story and bring it into Scratch?

HINTS

Do a search on the web (try Google Images) to see if you can import characters (look for sprite sheets) and backgrounds from the actual game into your project. To delete a solid area in Scratch, click the color area that looks like a white and gray checkered pattern and then choose the fill tool.

SCRIPT CHANGERS
CHALLENGE CARDS

19
COSTUME SWAP

LEVEL

EASY

CATEGORY

REMIXING SCRATCH PROJECTS

Take an existing Scratch project and modify its sprites in an interesting way to create an entirely new project.

EXPLANATION

Head to the Scratch example project library or to the online community and find a project that catches your eye. Swap out the sprites and replace them with ones that change the original project in an interesting or funny way.

HINTS

Think about how the meaning and experience of the original project changes when you change visual elements. Does any part of the project stop working or making sense? In what way? How could you fix it? Remember to give your project a new title when you save it.

SCRIPT CHANGERS
CHALLENGE CARDS

20
FRANKENSTEIN

LEVEL

HARDCORE

CATEGORY

REMIXING SCRATCH PROJECTS

"Mash up" or combine two existing Scratch projects to create a third.

EXPLANATION

Head to the Scratch example projects library or to the online community and find two projects that you think could be interesting if they were combined in some way. Use the "import project" and/or the "export sprite" functions to bring the content into Scratch and make these two existing projects into something entirely new.

HINTS

There are lots of different things you can reuse from different projects — combinations of scripts, sounds, sprites, specific costumes, backgrounds, and even types of interactions between sprites. Remember to give your project a new title when you save it.

SCRIPT CHANGERS
CHALLENGE CARDS

21
BACKWARDS ENGINEERING

LEVEL

MEDIUM TO HARDCORE

CATEGORY

REMIXING SCRATCH PROJECTS

Find an existing Scratch project and "backwards engineer" it — recreate it without looking at its code.

EXPLANATION

Head to the Scratch online community and find a project that catches your eye. Without looking "under the hood" at the project's code, try to re-create it from the ground up, sprites, sounds, scratch blocks and all.

HINTS

Pay attention to both the look and feel of the project, but also the interactions between sprites that are determined by the blocks. Are you able to make the project look and act the same?

SCRIPT CHANGERS CHALLENGE CARDS

22
I DON'T LIKE YOUR RULES

LEVEL

HARD

CATEGORY

REMIXING SCRATCH PROJECTS

Take an existing game made in Scratch and change the rules.

EXPLANATION

Either by going to the "Games" folder in the Scratch library or through finding one in the Scratch online community, load a game and change the rules of an existing game.

HINTS

Start with something simple, like Pong or Pacman, and make your way up to more complex games!

SCRIPT CHANGERS CHALLENGE CARDS

23
CHOOSE YOUR OWN ADVENTURE

LEVEL

HARDCORE

CATEGORY

A NEW CHAPTER

Create a "Choose Your Own Adventure" Story

EXPLANATION

Choose your own adventure stories create multiple pathways that a "reader" can take as they experience the story, with divergent storylines and even different endings.

HINTS

Before you get started, write out the different pathways and storylines on a draft. Start simple and try to create just one choice in your first story. The different "if" blocks found under the CONTROL palette are helpful for creating choices for your reader. The SENSING block, "ask _____ and wait" combined with the "if __ else___" and "=" block found under the OPERATORS palette can also be helpful for more advanced stories.

SCRIPT CHANGERS CHALLENGE CARDS

24
NEWSCAST

LEVEL

MEDIUM

CATEGORY

A NEW CHAPTER

Create a story in the form of a newscast.

EXPLANATION

Newscasts are particular types of stories. You can create one about something happening in your neighborhood or in the world, or even something you made up.

HINTS

Think about what kind of things make a newscast look and sound like a newscast. Can you recreate those in your story? What are you doing to make sure the person that experiences it knows that it's a newscast?

SCRIPT CHANGERS CHALLENGE CARDS	SCRIPT CHANGERS CHALLENGE CARDS	SCRIPT CHANGERS CHALLENGE CARDS

25 ALL ABOUT PERSPECTIVE

LEVEL

MEDIUM

CATEGORY

A NEW CHAPTER

Create a story about one event told from multiple perspectives.

EXPLANATION

Every story can be seen from many different perspectives. Create a story that shows how one event can be seen totally differently depending on who you are, where you're from, or your experience of a certain event.

HINTS

Think about situations where people don't agree about what happened, and how they might have come to see a situation differently. Can you create a story that gives various sides of a situation?

26 WHODUNNIT?

LEVEL

MEDIUM

CATEGORY

A NEW CHAPTER

Create a story about a mystery that eventually gets solved.

EXPLANATION

Make the experience of the story one that has some suspense, and gets the person who sees it to want to know the ending!

HINTS

Take inspiration from mystery stories you've read — what do the authors do to build suspense?

27 SUPPLY & DEMAND

LEVEL

HARD

CATEGORY

A NEW CHAPTER

Create a story about something in your local economy that shows how it's a system.

EXPLANATION

All economies are complex systems. Create a story that shows how things like feedback loops, unexpected consequences or leverage points might play out in a local economy, like your neighborhood.

HINTS

Think about what kinds of components make up a local economy, like consumers, stores, manufacturers, workers in factories, etc., and what kind of interactions they have with one another. If there is a problem, how would you propose to solve it?

SCRIPT CHANGERS
CHALLENGE CARDS

28
GOING GREEN

LEVEL

HARD

CATEGORY

A NEW CHAPTER

Create a story about something in the environment that shows how it's a system.

EXPLANATION

The earth's environment is a complex system. Think up a story that shows how things like feedback loops, unexpected consequences, or leverage points might play out in the environment.

HINTS

Think about what kinds of components make up the environment, like animals, plants, water sources, and, of course, human beings, and what kind of interactions they have with one another. Need to know more about different parts of the environment? Do an Internet search to find out more.

SCRIPT CHANGERS
CHALLENGE CARDS

29
MR. SMITH GOES TO WASHINGTON

LEVEL

HARDCORE

CATEGORY

A NEW CHAPTER

Create a story about democracy that shows how it's a system.

EXPLANATION

Governments are complex systems. Think up a story that shows how things like feedback loops, unexpected consequences, or leverage points might play out in a democratically-governed country.

HINTS

Think about what kinds of components make up a democracy, like voters, elected officials, laws, different branches of government, and what kind of interactions they have with one another. Need to know more about the government? Do an Internet search to find out more about your local or federal government or the government in another part of the world.

SCRIPT CHANGERS
CHALLENGE CARDS

30
YOU NEVER STEP IN THE SAME RIVER TWICE

LEVEL

HARDCORE

CATEGORY

A NEW CHAPTER

Create a story in Scratch that plays out differently every time someone reads it.

EXPLANATION

Interactive stories don't always have to play out in the same way — make a project that has multiple ways that it unfolds.

HINTS

Figure out how to use the "pick random" block in order to work on this challenge.

31
THROUGH YOUR LENS

LEVEL

MEDIUM

CATEGORY

A NEW CHAPTER

Create a story that integrates pictures you took around your neighborhood.

EXPLANATION

Sometimes having real life pictures can show someone something that might be hard to convey just in words. Take pictures from where you live, and think about how they can help you tell a story.

HINTS

Think about the relationship between an image and the words that you're layering on top of it, and how this might create something that neither could achieve on their own. You might also want to try to take pictures at various distances from the object you're photographing and experiment with them in Scratch.

32
PSA

LEVEL

MEDIUM

CATEGORY

A NEW CHAPTER

Create a story that's in the style of a "Public Service Announcement," or PSA.

EXPLANATION

A PSA is a message on TV, billboards, or other media (e.g., "Say No to Drugs!") to help raise awareness and change public attitudes or behavior. Think of some kind of issue that you think the public should be better informed about and create a PSA around it. Aim to inform and empower; avoid scaring your viewers.

HINTS

Be sure to research your issue so that you're giving people accurate information!

REFERENCES

Brown, A. L. (1992). Design experiments: Theoretical and methodological challenges in creating complex interventions in classroom settings. *Journal of the Learning Sciences* 2 (2): 141–178.

Buechley, L. (2006). A construction kit for electronic textiles. In *Wearable Computers, 2006 10th IEEE International Symposium on Wearable Computers*, 83-90.

Colella, V. (2000). Participatory simulations: Building collaborative understanding through immersive dynamic modeling. *Journal of the Learning Sciences* 9 (4): 471–500.

Colella, V. S., E. Klopfer, and M. Resnick. (2001). *Adventures in modeling: Exploring complex, dynamic systems with StarLogo.* Williston, VT: Teachers College Press.

Danish, J. A., K. Peppler, D. Phelps, and D. Washington. (2011). Life in the Hive: Supporting inquiry into complexity within the zone of proximal development. *Journal of Science Education and Technology* 20 (5): 454–467.

Draper, F. (1989). Letter to Jay Forrester. Personal communication, Orange Grove Junior High School, 1911 E. Orange Grove Rd., Tucson, AZ 85718. May 2, 1989.

Goldstone, R. L., and U. Wilensky. (2008). Promoting transfer by grounding complex systems principles. *Journal of the Learning Sciences* 17 (4): 465–516.

Hmelo-Silver, C. E., and M. G. Pfeffer. (2004). Comparing expert and novice understanding of a complex system from the perspective of structures, behaviors, and functions. *Cognitive Science* 28 (1): 127–138.

Hmelo-Silver, C. E., R. Jordan, L. Liu, and E. Chernobilsky. (2011). Representational tools for understanding complex computer-supported collaborative learning environments. In *Analyzing Interactions in CSCL* (83–106). Springer. http://link.springer.com/chapter/10.1007%2F978-1-4419-7710-6_4#page-1.

Iyenger, S. (2001). *Is anyone responsible? How television frames political issues.* Chicago, IL: University of Chicago Press.

Kafai, Y. B. Constructionism. (2006). In *Cambridge Handbook of the Learning Sciences*, ed. K. Sawyer, 35–46. New York: Cambridge University Press.

Lenhart, A., and M. Madden. (2007). *Social networking websites and teens: An overview*. Washington, DC: Pew Internet and American Life Project.

Lyneis, D. (2000). Bringing system dynamics to a school near you: Suggestions for introducing and sustaining system dynamics in K-12 education. International System Dynamics Society Conference. Bergen, Norway.

Maloney, J. H., K. Peppler, Y. Kafai, M. Resnick, and N. Rusk. (2008). Programming by choice: urban youth learning programming with scratch. *ACM SIGCSE Bulletin* 40 (1): 367–371.

Meadows, D. (1997). Places to intervene in a system. *Whole Earth* 91:78–84.

Papert, S. (1980). *Mindstorms: Children, computers, and powerful ideas*. New York: Basic Books, Inc.

Peppler, K. (2010). The New Fundamentals: Introducing Computation into Arts Education. In *20under40: Reinventing the Arts and Arts Education for the 21st Century*, ed. E. P. Clapp and M. J. Bellino. AuthorHouse: Bloomington, IN.

Peppler, K., and M. Warschauer. (2010). Uncovering literacies, disrupting stereotypes: Examining the (dis) abilities of a child learning to computer program and read. Paper presentation at the 2010 American Educational Research Association (AERA) Conference, Denver, CO.

Resnick, M. (2007). All I really need to know (about creative thinking) I learned (by studying how children learn) in kindergarten. Proceedings of the 6th ACM SIGCHI Conference on Creativity & Cognition, June 13–15, 2007, Washington, DC. doi:10.1145/1254960.1254961.

Resnick, M., J. Maloney, A. Monroy-Hernandez, N. Rusk, E. Eastmond, K. Brennan, et al. (2009). Scratch: Programming for all. *Communications of the ACM* 52 (11): 60–67. New York: Basic Books, Inc.

Rusk, N., M. Resnick, and S. Cooke. (2009). Origins and guiding principles of the Computer Clubhouse. In *The Computer Clubhouse: Constructionism and creativity in youth communities*, ed. Y. Kafai, K. Peppler, and R. Chapman. New York: Teachers College Press.

Salen, K. (2007). Gaming literacies: A game design study in action. *Journal of Educational Multimedia and Hypermedia* 16 (3): 301–322.

Salen, K., R. Torres, R. Rufo-Tepper, A. Shapiro, and L. Wolozin. (2010). *Quest to learn: Growing a school for digital kids*. Cambridge: MIT Press.

Sweeney, L. (2001). *When a butterfly sneezes: A guide for helping kids explore interconnections in our world through favorite stories*. Waltham, MA: Pegasus Communications.

Wilensky, U. (1999). NetLogo [Computer Program]: Center for Connected Learning and Computer-Based Modeling. Northwestern University, Evanston, IL.

Wilensky, U., and M. Resnick. (1999). Thinking in levels: A dynamic systems perspective to making sense of the world. *Journal of Science Education and Technology* 8 (1): 3–19.

INDEX

INTERCONNECTIONS CURRICULA SUMMARY SHEET:
SCRIPT CHANGERS

WHAT IS THE INTERCONNECTIONS CURRICULA?

Interconnections: Understanding Systems through Digital Design is a collection of curricula that support students to develop critical 21st century skills—systems thinking and digital design—by engaging in rich project-based learning using the latest technologies.

WHAT'S SYSTEMS THINKING, AND WHY IS IT IMPORTANT FOR MY STUDENTS?

As the world gets more complex and interconnected, we need to help our kids to understand and positively impact the dizzying number of systems around them. Systems thinking is a set of ideas and practices that allow kids to see through the "lens" of systems: how to take a "big picture" view of complex social structures and technologies, how to see the patterns and dynamics that drive systems, how to understand that the whole is usually greater than the sum of its parts.

HOW IS DIGITAL DESIGN DIFFERENT FROM OTHER USES OF EDUCATIONAL TECHNOLOGY?

Digital design is all about getting students the skills they need in order to be innovative, creative, and entrepreneurial thinkers. Rather than educational technologies that replicate a consumer mentality around learning, dumping information into students' brains, digital design activities put them in the driver's seat, having them come up with the ways technology can look in the world and preparing them for a world that increasingly expects them to engage in creative processes.

DIGITAL STORYTELLING AND COMPUTER PROGRAMMING, REALLY?

There are lots of great reasons we've found in our work to use digital storytelling and computer programming as the foundation for a classroom curriculum. Coding and creation of digital content are incredibly engaging, are an integral part of youth culture, and can be leveraged to get students excited about entering into some pretty important academic practices: giving and getting feedback, revising drafts, making arguments, problem solving, and more.

DOES THIS ALIGN TO STANDARDS?

Yes! All the Interconnections curricula have been aligned to the Common Core State Standards in areas including language arts, history and science, as well as the Next Generation Science Standards.

HOW MUCH TIME DOES THIS TAKE?

The *Script Changers* curriculum is designed to take about 20–30 hours overall, but of course can and will be adapted to fit your students' needs and abilities as well as your school culture. This means that we fully expect that you might take certain parts and extend them, cut other parts, or repurpose them to fit existing units of study.